SPORTS IN AMERICA

RECREATION, BUSINESS, EDUCATION, AND CONTROVERSY

ISSN 1557-5535

SPORTS IN AMERICA

RECREATION, BUSINESS, EDUCATION, AND CONTROVERSY

Robert Jacobson

INFORMATION PLUS® REFERENCE SERIES
Formerly Published by Information Plus, Wylie, Texas

Detroit • New York • San Francisco • San Diego • New Haven, Conn. • Waterville, Maine • London • Munich

THOMSON
★
GALE
™

Sports in America: Recreation, Business, Education, and Controversy
Robert Jacobson
Paula Kepos, Series Editor

Project Editor
John McCoy

Permissions
Margaret Abendroth, Edna Hedblad,
Emma Hull

Composition and Electronic Prepress
Evi Seoud

Manufacturing
Drew Kalasky

ISBN 0-7876-5103-6 (set)
ISBN 1-4144-0769-6
ISSN 1557-5535

This title is also available as an e-book.
ISBN 1-4144-1043-3 (set)
Contact your Thomson Gale sales representative for ordering information.

Printed in the United States of America
10 9 8 7 6 5 4 3 2 1

TABLE OF CONTENTS

PREFACE vii

CHAPTER 1

America's Sports Obsession 1

This chapter defines sports and explores the depth of Americans' passion for both professional and amateur sports. It summarizes sports participation, attendance, and viewership statistics. The chapter also briefly explores the major team and individual sports in the United States, as well as the Olympics, and examines the relationship between these sports and the media. Finally, it touches on the connection between sports and health and discusses the sports gambling phenomenon.

CHAPTER 2

Sports Participation and Attendance 11

What sports do people like to play, and what sports do they like to watch? Using data from a variety of sources, this chapter summarizes statistics for sports participation and attendance at sporting events, covering the major team sports and such emerging sports as snowboarding. It also examines the money Americans spend on sports equipment and which sports they spend it on.

CHAPTER 3

Sports and the Media 33

The sports and media industries are so intimately connected that it is sometimes difficult to determine where one ends and the other begins. This chapter explores the financial relationship between professional and college sports and television, from its roots in the early days of TV to the present. It also covers viewership numbers, viewing habits and gender, advertising issues, and public image concerns.

CHAPTER 4

Professional Team Sports 47

This chapter focuses on the major professional sports in America: baseball, football, basketball, hockey, and, more recently, soccer. How did these sports rise to their current status, and where are they headed? These questions are touched on in this chapter, along with the structure of the leagues and the often combative relationship between players and team owners.

CHAPTER 5

Other Professional Sports 61

Not every sports enthusiast is interested primarily in the major team sports. Many prefer, for example, the head-to-head competition of golf, tennis, auto racing, or boxing. This chapter covers these sports and a few others, discussing the organizing structures under which these sports operate and how much money is awarded in professional competitions.

CHAPTER 6

College and High School Sports 69

The role of school sports is a complicated one. College and high school athletics are at once both an element of a well-rounded education and a training ground for professional competition. These dual roles often come into conflict as college sports have become big business, and the lure of money and fame has begun to influence high school athletes. This chapter examines participation in school sports, the influence money has on the academic institutions that sponsor them, and other issues such as gender equity and the benefits of participation.

CHAPTER 7

The Olympics 95

The Olympics are an idealistic attempt to bring the world together to celebrate athletic achievement. While the movement often seems to have fallen short of that goal, the Olympics are wildly popular across the planet. This chapter explores the history and business aspects of the Olympic Games, including both the Summer and Winter Olympics and associated competitions for people with disabilities.

CHAPTER 8

Sports and Health 103

Physical activity is an important part of a healthy lifestyle. This chapter investigates some of the specific physical and mental health benefits of sports participation. It also covers the risks involved in athletic pursuits, from physical ailments like bruises and broken bones to emotional injuries and the effects of highly competitive environments on children.

CHAPTER 9

Performance-Enhancing Drugs 115

What are steroids? What are dietary supplements, and why are many of them banned in most sports? How are the governing bodies of sports attempting to stop athletes from using performance-enhancing substances? This chapter looks at the variety of substances athletes use in the belief that they will become stronger and faster and discusses the history of performance-enhancing substances from herbal concoctions used in the ancient Olympics to recent scandals in professional baseball, cycling, and other prominent sports.

C H A P T E R 1 0
Sports and Gambling 123
Americans like to bet on sports almost as much as they like to play them. Sports gambling in the United States is a lucrative business, much of it operating outside the law. This chapter surveys the scope of sports gambling in America, from pari- mutuel betting on horse races and sports bookmaking in Nevada to the office Super Bowl pool and offshore Internet betting opera- tions. It also considers point-shaving scandals and other problems associated with sports gambling.

IMPORTANT NAMES AND ADDRESSES 131

RESOURCES 133

INDEX 135

PREFACE

Sports in America: Recreation, Business, Education, and Controversy is part of the *Information Plus Reference Series*. The purpose of each volume of the series is to present the latest facts on a topic of pressing concern in modern American life. These topics include today's most controversial and most studied social issues: abortion, capital punishment, care for the elderly, crime, the environment, health care, immigration, minorities, national security, social welfare, women, youth, and many more. Although written especially for the high school and undergraduate student, this series is an excellent resource for anyone in need of factual information on current affairs.

By presenting the facts, it is Thomson Gale's intention to provide its readers with everything they need to reach an informed opinion on current issues. To that end, there is a particular emphasis in this series on the presentation of scientific studies, surveys, and statistics. These data are generally presented in the form of tables, charts, and other graphics placed within the text of each book. Every graphic is directly referred to and carefully explained in the text. The source of each graphic is presented within the graphic itself. The data used in these graphics are drawn from the most reputable and reliable sources, in particular from the various branches of the U.S. government and from major independent polling organizations. Every effort has been made to secure the most recent information available. The reader should bear in mind that many major studies take years to conduct, and that additional years often pass before the data from these studies are made available to the public. Therefore, in many cases the most recent information available in 2006 dated from 2003 or 2004. Older statistics are sometimes presented as well if they are of particular interest and no more recent information exists.

Although statistics are a major focus of the *Information Plus Reference Series*, they are by no means its only content. Each book also presents the widely held positions and important ideas that shape how the book's subject is discussed in the United States. These positions are explained in detail and, where possible, in the words of their proponents. Some of the other material to be found in these books includes: historical background; descriptions of major events related to the subject; relevant laws and court cases; and examples of how these issues play out in American life. Some books also feature primary documents or have pro and con debate sections giving the words and opinions of prominent Americans on both sides of a controversial topic. All material is presented in an even-handed and unbiased manner; the reader will never be encouraged to accept one view of an issue over another.

HOW TO USE THIS BOOK

Sports have an enormous presence in American life. Most Americans engage in sporting activities of one type or another and enjoy watching sports in person or on TV. Americans' passion for sports has made it a major industry worth billions of dollars. It has also brought with it a host of problems. Illegal sports gambling is commonplace. Athletes at all levels have been caught using performance-enhancing drugs. Professional athletes and their teams squabble over their shares of the profits to the dismay of fans. The lure of money has also had a corrupting influence on major college sports and encouraged student athletes to quit school and go pro at an increasingly young age. Meanwhile, less popular sports, including many women's sports, struggle for attention and funds.

Sports in America: Recreation, Business, Education, and Controversy consists of ten chapters and three appendices. Each of the chapters examines a particular aspect of sports and American society. For a summary of the information covered in each chapter, please see the synopses provided in the Table of Contents at the front of the book. Chapters generally begin with an overview of the basic facts and background information on the chapter's topic, then proceed to examine subtopics of particular interest. For example, Chapter 9, Performance-Enhancing Drugs, begins with a history of the use of drugs to increase strength, stamina, and other athletic traits. Particular attention is paid to recent scandals in American sports. This is followed by a description of the major types of performance-enhancing drugs and their effects. The serious, long-term health consequences of the drugs are also examined. Next, the chapter gives an overview of what is known about drug use within youth, college, and professional sports. The final section of the chapter outlines the efforts undertaken by the U.S. government and the World Anti-Doping Agency to combat performance-enhancing drug use. Readers can find their way through a chapter by looking for the section and subsection headings, which are clearly set off from the text. They can also refer to the book's extensive Index if they already know what they are looking for.

Statistical Information

The tables and figures featured throughout *Sports in America: Recreation, Business, Education, and Controversy* will be of particular use to the reader in learning about this issue. These tables and figures represent an extensive collection of the most recent and important statistics on sports and their role in American society—for example, graphics in the book cover the earnings of professional sports leagues, the percentage of college students who gamble on sports, the number of Americans who participate in various sports, spending on athletic scholarships by gender, and racial and ethnic differences in TV audiences for sports. Thomson Gale believes that making this information available to the reader is the most important way in which we fulfill the goal of this book: to help readers understand the issues and controversies surrounding sports in the United States and to reach their own conclusions.

Each table or figure has a unique identifier appearing above it for ease of identification and reference. Titles for the tables and figures explain their purpose. At the end of each table or figure, the original source of the data is provided.

In order to help readers understand these often complicated statistics, all tables and figures are explained in the text. References in the text direct the reader to the relevant statistics. Furthermore, the contents of all tables and figures are fully indexed. Please see the opening section of the index at the back of this volume for a description of how to find tables and figures within it.

Appendices

In addition to the main body text and images, *Sports in America: Recreation, Business, Education, and Controversy* has three appendices. The first is the Important Names and Addresses directory. Here the reader will find contact information for a number of government and private organizations that can provide further information on sports and related issues. The second appendix is the Resources section, which can also assist the reader in conducting his or her own research. In this section, the author and editors of *Sports in America: Recreation, Business, Education, and Controversy* describe some of the sources that were most useful during the compilation of this book. The final appendix is the detailed Index, which facilitates reader access to specific topics in this book.

ADVISORY BOARD CONTRIBUTIONS

The staff of Information Plus would like to extend its heartfelt appreciation to the Information Plus Advisory Board. This dedicated group of media professionals provides feedback on the series on an ongoing basis. Their comments allow the editorial staff who work on the project to make the series better and more user-friendly. Our top priority is to produce the highest-quality and most useful books possible, and the Advisory Board's contributions to this process are invaluable.

The members of the Information Plus Advisory Board are:

- Kathleen R. Bonn, Librarian, Newbury Park High School, Newbury Park, California

- Madelyn Garner, Librarian, San Jacinto College—North Campus, Houston, Texas

- Anne Oxenrider, Media Specialist, Dundee High School, Dundee, Michigan

- Charles R. Rodgers, Director of Libraries, Pasco–Hernando Community College, Dade City, Florida

- James N. Zitzelsberger, Library Media Department Chairman, Oshkosh West High School, Oshkosh, Wisconsin

COMMENTS AND SUGGESTIONS

The editors of the *Information Plus Reference Series* welcome your feedback on *Sports in America: Recreation, Business, Education, and Controversy*. Please direct all correspondence to:

Editors
Information Plus Reference Series
27500 Drake Rd.
Farmington Hills, MI 48331-3535

CHAPTER 1
AMERICA'S SPORTS OBSESSION

WHAT ARE SPORTS?

A sport is a physical activity that people engage in for recreation, usually according to a set of rules, and often in competition with each other. However, such a simple definition does not capture the passion many Americans feel for their favorite sports. Sports are the recreational activity of choice for a huge portion of the American population, both as spectators and as participants in sporting competitions. When enthusiasts are not participating in sports, they are flocking to the nation's arenas and stadiums to watch their favorite athletes play or tuning in to see games and matches broadcast on television. Table 1.1 gives a sport-by-sport view of spectator interest in the United States, based on polling data from the Gallup Organization.

There are two broad categories of sports: professional and amateur. A professional athlete is paid to participate; an amateur athlete is one who participates merely as a pastime, not for pay. The word "amateur" comes from the Latin word for "love," suggesting that an amateur athlete plays simply because he or she loves the game.

SPORTS PARTICIPATION

Sports participation is difficult to measure because there are many different levels of participation, from backyard games to organized leagues, but analysts continue to refine research methods. The most direct approach is through surveys. One of the most extensive regular surveys is the *Superstudy of Sports Participation* conducted annually by a company called American Sports Data, Inc. (ASD) (http://www.americansportsdata. com/ss_participation2.asp). The information collected by ASD is analyzed by such organizations as SGMA International, the trade association for sporting goods manufacturers. Chapter 2 contains detailed information from the *Superstudy* as well as other surveys of sports participation.

Table 1.2 ranks sports by total participation. According to the National Sporting Goods Association (NSGA), the trade association for sporting goods retailers, more Americans play basketball than play any other team sport (http://www.nsga.org/public/pages/index.cfm?pageid=1). The NSGA estimated that about 27.8 million people age seven and over played basketball in 2004. Another organization, the SGMA, estimated the number of basketball players even higher that year, at about 34.2 million people age six and over (http://www.sgma.com/). The NSGA reported that other popular team sports include softball (12.5 million participants), volleyball (10.8 million), and touch football (9.6 million). Participation in some team sports, including tackle football, softball, and basketball, showed a decline from 2003 to 2004, but other team sports gained participants. Baseball, soccer, and volleyball all experienced modest increases in participation, and ice hockey experienced a dramatic 24.9% expansion in participation from 2003 to 2004. (See Table 1.2.)

Americans love to participate in individual sports as well. The NSGA estimated that about 43.8 million Americans went bowling in 2004, making it the most popular of all competitive sports nationally. (See Table 1.2.) The SGMA also identified bowling as the most popular competitive sport, and estimated the number of participants even higher, at about 53.6 million Americans in 2004. Billiards is also exceedingly popular as a recreational sport. About 34.2 million people shot pool in the United States in 2004, according to the NSGA, which was a 3.7% increase over 2003. Proprietors of bowling and billiards facilities are attempting to overcome a seedy reputation in order to draw in a new generation of enthusiasts.

About 25.7 million Americans went golfing in 2004, according to the SGMA (http://www.sgma.com/). This was significantly fewer than the 30.4 million people who participated at golf's peak in 2000. The vast majority of golf rounds (91%) were played by a core of about 12.8

TABLE 1.1

Fans by sport, 2004

Sport	Percentage of Americans who are fans
Professional football	64
College football	54
Professional baseball	52
Figure skating	41
College basketball	41
Professional basketball	38
Auto racing	30
Professional golf	30
Professional tennis	24
Professional ice hockey	23
Professional wrestling	10

SOURCE: Jeffrey M. Jones, "Fans of Major Sports, All Americans," in *Six in 10 Americans Are Pro Football Fans*, The Gallup Organization, February 4, 2005, http://www.gallup.com/poll/content/?ci=14812&pg=1 (accessed September 22, 2005). Copyright © 2005 by The Gallup Organization. Reproduced by permission of The Gallup Organization.

TABLE 1.2

Sports participation, by total participation, 2004

[Participated more than once (in millions). Seven (7) years of age and older.]

Sport	Total	Percent change*
Exercise walking	84.7	3.8%
Camping (vacation/overnight)	55.3	3.5%
Swimming	53.4	2.2%
Exercising with equipment	52.2	3.9%
Bowling	43.8	4.6%
Fishing	41.2	−3.6%
Bicycle riding	40.3	5.3%
Billiards/pool	34.2	3.7%
Workout at club	31.8	8.0%
Aerobic exercising	29.5	5.1%
Hiking	28.3	6.1%
Basketball	27.8	−0.1%
Weight lifting	26.2	1.4%
Running/jogging	24.7	3.2%
Golf	24.5	−4.6%
Boating, motor/power	22.8	−5.9%
Target shooting	19.2	7.0%
Hunting with firearms	17.7	−1.1%
Backpack/wilderness camp	17.3	14.4%
Baseball	15.9	2.9%
Soccer	13.3	2.2%
Scooter riding	12.9	8.5%
Softball	12.5	−0.8%
In-line roller skating	11.7	−26.9%
Volleyball	10.8	3.3%
Skateboarding	10.3	15.1%
Tennis	9.6	0.5%
Football (touch)	9.6	2.6%
Paintball games	9.4	28.0%
Football (tackle)	8.2	−5.3%
Mountain biking (off road)	8.0	−2.3%
Canoeing	7.5	na
T'ai Chi/yoga	6.7	2.5%
Snowboarding	6.6	4.2%
Skiing (alpine)	5.9	−12.8%
Hunting with bow & arrow	5.8	17.5%
Archery (target)	5.3	36.6%
Water skiing	4.7	−13.2%
Martial arts	4.7	−3.4%
Cheerleading	4.1	na
Muzzleloading	3.8	12.1%
Kick Boxing	2.8	−8.1%
Sailing	2.6	na
Hockey (ice)	2.4	24.9%
Skiing (cross country)	2.4	21.6%

Note: 31.8 million people indicated they 'worked out at club' in 2004, an 8.0% increase over 2003. na=not available
*Percent change is from 2003

SOURCE: "2004 Participation—Ranked by Total Participation," National Sporting Goods Association, 2005, http://www.nsga.org/public/pages/index.cfm?pageid=150 (accessed September 22, 2005)

million adults who golfed at least eight times a year. Tennis, while less popular now than at its peak in the late 1980s, has been enjoying a comeback in the 2000s. In 2004 about 18.3 million people hit U.S. tennis courts, according to the SGMA's analysis of *Superstudy* data.

An interesting transition is taking place in youth sports participation. Generally, participation among youth in traditional team sports has been declining for several years. One exception is soccer, which is becoming a major sport in the United States. Instead of tossing a football, an increasing number of young Americans are also opting for "extreme" sports like snowboarding. Golf has also enjoyed an increase in participation among youth since the mid-1990s, as has lacrosse, a modern game derived from a Native American competition that became popular among French pioneers in Canada. U.S. Lacrosse reported in its *Participation Survey: A Review of National Lacrosse Participation in 2004* that 351,852 people played lacrosse in 2004, compared with 253,931 in 2001, and that over the previous decade the number of people playing lacrosse nationally had increased more than 10% per year (http://www.uslacrosse.org/pdf/usl_participationsurvey04.pdf).

Another way to gauge interest in sports is by examining how much money people spend on equipment. According to the NSGA, American consumers spent nearly $23 billion on sporting goods in 2004. Table 1.3 shows consumer purchases of sporting goods broken down by sport.

SPORTS ATTENDANCE

In addition to participation, another measure of interest in sports is the number of people who attend games in person. Sports attendance in the United States is dominated by the four major team sports: baseball, football,

basketball, and hockey. In professional team sports, attendance is affected by two main factors: the size of the market in which the team plays and the team's current success. Big-city teams and winning teams typically draw bigger crowds than small-town teams and losing teams.

Major League Baseball (MLB) reported in a press release (October 3, 2005) that close to seventy-five million people attended MLB games during the 2005 regular season, an all-time high and a 2.6% increase over 2004. Average attendance at an MLB game was nearly 31,000. The National Basketball Association (NBA) also set a

TABLE 1.3

Consumer sports equipment purchases, by sport, 2004

[In millions]

	2004	2003
Archery	$331.6	$320.3
Baseball & softball	$346.0	$340.4
Basketball	$310.7	$306.3
Billiards & indoor games	$627.2	$624.8
Bowling	$181.7	$176.9
Camping	$1,531.4	$1,486.7
Exercise	$5,011.8	$4,957.2
Fishing tackle	$2,014.8	$1,981.4
Football	$83.4	$83.2
Golf	$3,148.1	$3,046.0
Hockey & ice skates	$142.0	$147.6
Hunting & firearms	$2,870.2	$2,653.7
Optics	$858.8	$846.6
Racquetball	$29.6	$29.4
Skin diving & scuba gear	$351.3	$337.8
Skiing, downhill	$457.5	$462.1
Skiing, cross-country	$40.7	$43.8
Skiing, snowboards	$269.9	$272.6
Soccer balls	$63.5	$62.4
Tennis	$361.7	$343.1
Volleyball & badminton sets	$33.7	$32.9
Water skis	$48.9	$51.0
Wheel sports & pogo sticks	$580.1	$603.8
Team goods sales	$2,517.2	$2467.8
Total equipment	**$22,934.3**	**$22,393.8**

SOURCE: "2004 Consumer Equipment Purchases by Sport (in millions)," National Sporting Goods Association, 2005, http://www.nsga.org/public/pages/index.cfm?pageid=162 (accessed September 22, 2005).

new season attendance record during the 2004–05 regular season, according to a press release dated April 21, 2005, drawing over twenty-one million spectators to its arenas (http://www.nba.com/hawks/news/200405_NBA_Attendance.html). Football set a new record for the 2004 regular season as well. Total paid attendance across the National Football League (NFL) was about seventeen million, according to the NFL Web site (http://www.nfl.com/history/chronology/2001-#2004). The 2004–05 National Hockey League season was cancelled due to a labor dispute. The previous year, NHL attendance was a little over twenty million according to data available on ESPN.com. In contrast to the other major team sports, which have set attendance records in the last couple of years, NHL attendance has been shrinking steadily for the last several years.

The other big sports draw in the United States is auto racing. NASCAR, the nation's major stock car racing circuit, attracted about 4.4 million spectators in 2004 according to ESPN.com. Chapter 2 presents more detailed discussion of major sports attendance in the United States.

PROFESSIONAL SPORTS
Team Sports

Throughout most of the twentieth century, professional team sports in the United States meant baseball, football, basketball, and hockey. However, since the

1990s soccer has been gaining popularity and is often included in discussions of professional sports in America. Detailed information on professional team sports is provided in Chapter 4.

Major League Baseball has long been considered America's "national pastime." MLB currently consists of thirty teams, divided into the sixteen-team National League and the fourteen-team American League. Each league is in turn divided into three divisions. The MLB season consists of 162 games, running from early April through late September, followed by playoffs and finally the championship series known as the World Series. MLB was a $4.1 billion industry in 2005, according to data published online by Plunkett Research, Ltd. (http://www.plunkettresearch.com/sports/sports_statistics_1.htm).

The premier professional football league in the United States is the National Football League. The NFL generated league-wide revenue of $4.8 billion in 2004–05 according to Plunkett Research, making it the richest of the major sports. There are thirty-two teams in the NFL, divided into two conferences, the National Football Conference (NFC) and the American Football Conference (AFC). The NFC and AFC are each divided into four divisions. NFL teams play a sixteen-game season, which begins around Labor Day. It ends with a single-elimination playoff series, culminating in the Super Bowl in early February. The Super Bowl is the biggest sporting event in the country in terms of viewing audience. About 133.7 million viewers tuned in to the 2005 Super Bowl according to NFL.com, making it the fifth most watched television show of all time.

The National Basketball Association (NBA), the top professional basketball league in the country, consists of thirty teams split into the Eastern and Western Conferences. Each conference has three divisions within it. The NBA season, which lasts for eighty-two regular season games, begins in early November. The regular season is followed by the NBA playoffs, which begin in April. According to data from Plunkett Research (http://www.plunkettresearch.com/sports/sports_statistics_1.htm), the NBA generates $3.1 billion in revenue, placing it behind both football and baseball. Unlike football and baseball, basketball has a women's professional league, the Women's National Basketball Association (WNBA). There are fourteen teams in the WNBA. They play a thirty-four–game regular season, after which the top four teams compete for the championship. Unlike any of the major men's professional sports, the WNBA loses money.

The top professional hockey league in North America is the National Hockey League (NHL), which actually encompasses two countries, the United States and Canada, and is arguably more popular in the latter. The NHL consists of thirty teams, divided into Eastern and

Western Conferences. These conferences are in turn broken into three divisions each. The NHL season, like that of the NBA, is eighty-two games long. It is followed by the Stanley Cup playoffs, which ultimately determine the NHL champion. The NHL has struggled for more than a decade. Even before the entire 2004–05 season was cancelled due to labor strife, the league's popularity was in decline. League-wide revenue, according to Plunkett Research, is about $2 billion, considerably less than any of the other major team sports.

While only hockey has experienced a labor dispute that resulted in cancellation of an entire season, each of these sports is occasionally subject to disputes that threaten their continuity, and sometimes result in cancellation of part of a season. Labor disagreements in professional sports often pit the league, which represents the interests of the team owners, against the players, who are represented by a labor union.

Individual Sports

Team sports get most of the media attention in the United States, but professional sports that feature individual competitors are also of considerable interest.

The premier golf tour in the United States and in the world is the PGA Tour, which in 2005 consisted of forty-eight official events offering over $250 million in total prize money (http://www.pgatour.com/info/company/about_us). The PGA Tour organization also runs a developmental tour called the Nationwide Tour and a tour for senior players called the Champions Tour. There are several other prominent regional professional golf tours based in other countries. Women's professional golf has a similar structure. The most prominent women's tour is the LPGA Tour, which is operated by the Ladies Professional Golf Association, and there are several other regional women's tours around the world.

Men's professional tennis is coordinated primarily by two organizations: the Association of Tennis Professionals, which operates the worldwide ATP Tour; and the International Tennis Federation, which coordinates the four international events that make up the Grand Slam of tennis. The 2005 ATP Tour included sixty-four tournaments in thirty-one countries (http://www.atptennis.com/en/). Women's professional tennis is organized by the Women's Tennis Association (WTA), which runs the premier women's tour, currently sponsored by Sony Ericsson. According to the tour's official Web site (http://www.wtatour.com/thewtatour/), the 2005 Sony Ericsson Tour included sixty-three events in thirty-three countries, in which one thousand players representing seventy-one nations competed for $57.8 million in total prize money.

Auto racing has enjoyed a huge surge in popularity in the United States since the mid-1990s. The most important racing circuit for stock cars—which resemble ordinary cars externally—is the National Association for Stock Car Auto Racing, or NASCAR. NASCAR sanctions over 1,500 races a year at over one hundred tracks in thirty-eight states, plus Canada and Mexico.

The other major type of racecar is the open-wheeled racer. There are two main open-wheeled racing circuits in the United States: the Indy Racing League (IRL, or IndyCar) and the Champ Car Series. The 2006 Champ Car Series includes fifteen races in the United States, Australia, Canada, Mexico, and South Korea between April and November; the 2006 IndyCar Series features fourteen races between March and September, most in the United States with one in Japan.

Boxing is unique among professional sports in that it has no single commission that regulates or monitors it nationwide. A number of organizations sanction professional boxing matches, including the World Boxing Association (WBA), the World Boxing Council (WBC), the World Boxing Organization (WBO), and the International Boxing Federation (IBF). Each follows its own set of regulations, employs its own officials, and acknowledges its own champions. A fighter can be recognized as champion by more than one organization simultaneously. Professional boxing in the United States has been plagued by corruption over the years, including tainted judging and fixed fights. Nevertheless, devoted fans tune in regularly to watch boxing on pay cable networks, and gamblers wager millions on the outcomes of boxing contests, injecting huge sums of money into the industry.

SPORTS AND THE MEDIA

For American sports enthusiasts, it is hard to separate the sports from the media industry that surrounds all aspects of professional and elite amateur sports. Leagues, teams, promoters, organizations, and schools make money through lucrative media contracts that give television networks the rights to broadcast sporting events over the public airwaves. For a full discussion of the intersection of sports and media, see Chapter 3.

History of Sports on TV

The history of sports on television began with the 1939 broadcast of a college baseball game between Columbia and Princeton universities. Five years later, NBC's *Gillette Cavalcade of Sports* became the first network-wide television sports show. When single-company sponsorship became too expensive during the mid-1960s, sports programming developed a new model in which different companies bought advertising spots throughout the program.

The amount of sports programming and the amount of money in televised sports has continued to grow quickly since then. According to the Museum of Broadcast Communications publication *Sports and Television*, in 1970 the networks paid $50 million for the rights to broadcast NFL games, $2 million for NBA broadcast rights, and $18 million for MLB. By 1985 those totals had grown to $450 million, $45 million, and $160 million respectively (http://www.museum.tv/archives/etv/S/htmlS/sportsandte/sportsandte.htm). In the 1980s the addition of cable television outlets extended the reach of televised sports even further. However, TV ratings for the four major team sports generally declined during the 1990s as competition for the same audience arose from other viewing options.

Major Sports on TV

In the 1950s baseball was the most popular televised sport. Since then, however, it has lost a large share of its audience to other sports, particularly football. While television ratings for World Series broadcasts declined for several years, they rebounded after 2002. According to data from Nielsen Media Research, 15.8% of American households tuned in to the 2004 World Series, and 25% of households that were using their televisions had them tuned in to the World Series. MLB has a $2.5 billion broadcast contract with Fox that runs through the 2006 season, and in September 2005 signed an eight-year, $2.37 billion deal with ESPN to air a series of Monday night games (http://www.mlb4u.com/leagueinfo.html).

Football has supplanted baseball as the reigning king of televised sports. Five of the ten top-rated television shows of all time have been sports programs, and four of those were Super Bowls. Super Bowl XXXIX in February of 2005 drew a Nielsen rating (percentage of households tuned in) of 43.4. The NFL signed a new round of television deals in April 2005, the most lucrative being the $1.1 billion contract resulting in the move of *Monday Night Football* from ABC to ESPN beginning in 2006. The NFL gets hundreds of millions of additional dollars from Fox, CBS, and NBC for various subsets of the NFL schedule. Table 1.4 shows the latest round of NFL television agreements.

Regular season NBA basketball has never drawn as big a viewing audience as the NFL has—probably because there are so many more games—but viewership expands significantly during the playoffs. Of the major sports, the NHL is struggling the most to maintain its television audience. Even at its peak, hockey drew far fewer viewers than the other major sports, and the cancellation of the 2004–05 season hurt the NHL further. At the other extreme, NASCAR has enjoyed a surge in its television audience in the 2000s, including an increased female audience and broader viewership in the Pacific Northwest and other regions of the country that have not traditionally favored auto racing.

TABLE 1.4

Latest NFL TV contracts, by network or satellite provider, April 2005

ESPN
Monday night
- 8 years, 2006–13
- $1.1 billion per year
- No Super Bowls

NBC
Sunday night
- 6 years, 2006–11
- $600 million per year
- Super Bowls in 2009 and 2012

Fox
Sunday afternoon NFC (National Football Conference)
- 6 years, 2006–11
- $712.5 million per year
- Super Bowls in 2008 and one other year during deal

CBS
Sunday afternoon AFC (American Football Conference)
- 6 years, 2006–11
- $622.5 million per year
- Super Bowls in 2007 and one other year during deal

DirecTV
Sunday Ticket satellite
- 5 years, 2006–10
- $700 million per year
- No Super Bowls

SOURCE: Created by Information Plus using information from various sources

AMATEUR SPORTS

College Sports

Most college sports take place under the auspices of the National Collegiate Athletic Association (NCAA). The NCAA is a voluntary association with a membership of about 1,250 colleges, college athletic conferences, and other organizations and individuals (http://www2.ncaa.org/about_ncaa/). The NCAA is divided into Divisions I, II, and III based on size, athletic budget, and related variables. Division I is further divided into three subdivisions, I-A, I-AA, and I-AAA. I-AAA includes schools that have substantial sports programs but do not field a football team. Within the NCAA, many major sports colleges are grouped into conferences, which function like divisions and leagues do in professional sports.

According to the NCAA's annual *Sports Sponsorship and Participation Report* (November 2004, http://www.ncaa.org/library/research/participation_rates/1982-2003/olympic_sports_supplement.pdf), over 375,000 student-athletes participated in championship sports at NCAA member schools in 2003–04. The average NCAA institution had about 366 athletes—209 men and 157 women. However, women's teams actually outnumber men's teams. Among men, the sport with the greatest number of Division I teams in 2003–04 was basketball, with 327. However, in terms of number of players, football was the leader, with over 25,000 participants. Among women, outdoor track and field had the most participants in 2003–04, with over 10,000 on the NCAA's 294 Division I teams. However, more colleges have women's basketball teams than have women's track and field teams.

For most of the twentieth century, men's college teams and athletes far outnumbered women's teams and athletes, and far more money went into men's sports. However, the gap has been closing, largely because of the passage in 1972 of Title IX, a law mandating gender equity in federally funded education programs. Under Title IX girls' sports were to be funded at the same rate as sports programs for boys. Since Title IX's mandatory compliance date of 1978, women's collegiate sports have experienced explosive growth.

Much to the discomfort of some in the academic world, college sports have become big business in the United States. Spending on sports programs has been rising at a faster rate than overall institutional spending across the NCAA. While college sports generate substantial revenue, that revenue does not cover the cost of running the entire athletic program at the vast majority of schools, largely because only a few sports—often only football and men's basketball programs—are actually profitable. According to the NCAA's annual *Revenues and Expenses of Divisions I and II Intercollegiate Athletics Programs Report* (February 2005, http://www.ncaa.org/), on revenues and expenses of college programs, the average Division I-A athletic program had total revenues of $29.4 million and expenses of $27.2 million in 2003. Football and basketball accounted for a huge share of both revenues and expenses.

High School Sports

The National Federation of State High School Associations (NFHS) conducts a detailed survey of high school sports participation each year. NFHS data show that over seven million students participated in high school sports in 2004–05 (http://www.nfhs.org/scriptcontent/VA_Custom/SurveyResources/2004-05_Participation_Survey.pdf). This total, a record high, represented nearly 53% of the national high school student body. Participation among boys was 4.1 million, while 2.9 million girls participated.

For years, football has been the most popular boys' high school sport. According to the *2004–05 NFHS High School Athletics Participation Survey*, a little over one million boys played high school football in 2004–05. Basketball was second, with about half as many participants. Among girls, basketball was the most popular high school sport, with 456,543 participants, followed by outdoor track and field with 428,198.

Analysis by the research group Child Trends of data from the *Monitoring the Future* study (National Institute on Drug Abuse) indicated that kids who participated in high school sports between 1991 and 2003 were less likely to engage in risky behavior, and more likely to do well in school. On the other hand, there is also evidence that the corrupting influence of money in big-time sports is beginning to trickle down to the high school level, including a series of reports in the *New York Times* in late 2005 of athletes buying diplomas and passing grades from bogus correspondence schools.

The Olympics

The idea behind the Olympic Movement is to bring the world together through sports, in the spirit of common understanding and noble competition. The Olympic Games are based on an athletic festival that took place in ancient Greece from about 776 BC until 393 AD. The Olympics were revived in their modern form in 1896. The Summer Olympics take place every four years, the same years in which February has twenty-nine days. The most recent Summer Olympics were held in Athens in August 2004. According to the Olympic Movement Web site, about 11,000 athletes from 202 countries competed in those games, and medals were awarded in 301 events covering twenty-eight sports (http://www.olympic.org/).

The Winter Olympics also take place every four years, halfway between the summer games. The Winter Olympics are much smaller than the Summer Olympics. According to the Web site of the Olympic Movement, the 2002 Winter Olympics in Salt Lake City, Utah, featured about 2,400 athletes from seventy-seven countries, competing in seventy-eight medal events in seven sports. Table 1.5 lists the sports that currently make up the Summer and Winter Olympic Games.

The founder of the modern Olympics was the French historian and educator Pierre de Coubertin. Coubertin believed that war could be averted if nations participated together in friendly athletic competition. His ideas have not proved true, but the Olympic Movement has thrived anyway. The inaugural Olympic Games took place in 1896 in Athens, Greece, where 245 athletes from fifteen countries competed in what was the largest international sporting event in history at the time.

The Winter Olympics arose initially as an outgrowth of the summer games. A handful of winter sports were included in early versions of the Olympics. The Winter Olympics finally became their own event in 1924. Until 1992, the Winter Olympics took place the same year as the summer games. Since 1994 they have been held between Summer Olympics.

Politics have frequently disrupted, or even cancelled, the Olympics. The 1916 Games were cancelled because of World War I, and World War II caused the cancellation of the 1940 and 1944 Olympics. Boycotts have also diminished the scope of the Olympic Games. The U.S. team, along with sixty-four other Western nations,

TABLE 1.5

Olympic sports

Summer games		Winter games
Aquatics	Hockey	Biathlon
Archery	Judo	Bobsleigh
Athletics	Modern pentathlon	Curling
Badminton	Rowing	Ice hockey
Baseball	Sailing	Luge
Basketball	Shooting	Skating
Boxing	Softball	Skiing
Canoe/kayak	Table tennis	
Cycling	Taekwondo	
Equestrian	Tennis	
Fencing	Triathlon	
Soccer	Volleyball	
Gymnastics	Weightlifting	
Handball	Wrestling	

SOURCE: Created by Information Plus using data from the International Olympic Committee, http://www.olympic.org/uk/sports/index_uk.asp

boycotted the 1980 Moscow Olympics in protest of the Soviet invasion of Afghanistan. In 1984 the Soviet Union and fourteen of its allies boycotted the Los Angeles Olympics, ostensibly because of security concerns, but more realistically as a response to the Moscow boycott. Scandals related to doping—such as the BALCO affair described in detail in Chapter 9—and bribery—including the implication of the organizing committee for the 2002 Salt Lake City Winter Games—have also marred the idealistic image of international cooperation and amateur athleticism upon which the Olympics were founded.

The International Olympic Committee (IOC) is the worldwide governing body for the Olympics. Each participating country has its own National Olympic Committee (NOC), whose role is to support that nation's Olympic team and to coordinate bids by cities within their country to host the Olympics. The United States Olympic Committee (USOC), headquartered in Colorado Springs, Colorado, is the NOC in the United States.

Individual sports are governed worldwide by International Federations (IFs), which make the rules for the events within their portfolio. On the national level, there are corresponding organizations called national governing bodies (NGBs). Some of the NGBs in the United States include USA Gymnastics, USA Swimming, and USA Track and Field. These organizations are in charge of choosing which athletes will represent the United States in that sport. In the host country the Olympic Games are planned by an Organizing Committee for the Olympic Games (OCOG), which takes care of the logistical preparations for the Olympics.

The Olympics generates billions of dollars through a handful of marketing programs. The biggest source of money is television broadcast revenue. Other sources include corporate sponsorships, ticket sales, and sales of licensed merchandise. Chapter 7 contains detailed information about Olympic revenue. It also includes descriptions of other Olympic-style meets—the Special Olympics, Paralympics, and Deaflympics.

SPORTS AND HEALTH

Participation in sports yields great health benefits. Many health benefits of physical activity have been well documented. Physical activity builds and maintains bones and muscles, reduces fat, reduces blood pressure, and decreases the risk of obesity and heart attacks. There is also substantial evidence that physical activity improves mental health and may help fend off depression. A number of studies, including a massive 2001 survey conducted by researchers at the University of Florida (http://news.ufl.edu/2001/03/07/body-image/), have linked sports participation with a better self-image and healthier attitude toward one's own body. Sports participation by youth has been shown to reduce the likelihood of engaging in risky behavior, though some studies, notably one involving female African-American students living in rural areas, have been more ambiguous on this point (Matthew J. Taylor, "Sports Participation, Delinquency, and Substance Use among Rural African-American Girls," University of Wisconsin–LaCrosse, August 2001).

These benefits do not come without risk, however. Every year, millions of people injure themselves participating in sports. The most common sports injuries are muscle sprains and strains, ligament and tendon tears, dislocated joints, and bone fractures. The most common body part to injure is the knee. Soft tissue injuries, such as bruises, sprains, and tendonitis, account for 95% of all sports injuries, according to Health A to Z.com (http://www.healthatoz.com/healthatoz/Atoz/ency/sports_injuries.jsp). Injuries that happen suddenly during an activity, such as those resulting from a fall, are called "acute" injuries, while injuries that occur through repeated overuse are called "chronic" injuries.

According to American Sports Data, Inc. (ASD) in *Comprehensive Study of Sports Injuries in the U.S.*, there were about twenty million sports injuries in the United States in 2002 (http://www.americansportsdata.com/prsportsinjuries.asp). Less than half of them required medical treatment. About 3.4 million sports injuries were serious enough to require an emergency room visit. Basketball, running, and soccer were the sports responsible for the greatest number of sports injuries in 2002, according to ASD. When considered as a percentage of the number of participants, however, tackle football jumps to the top of the list, with 18.8 injuries per one hundred players.

Sports participation brings special hazards for children and youth. Children who are placed under severe pressure to succeed by parents, coaches, and other adults are at risk of psychological damage. The stress of ultra-competitive sports participation leads to high rates of burnout among young athletes. Pressure to perform also puts children and youth at elevated risk of physical injury, as demands are put on young bodies not yet developed enough to withstand the strain. Chapter 8 explores both the health benefits and health risks of athletic participation.

Doping

The use of prohibited substances to give an athlete an unfair advantage over other competitors is called *doping*. Doping has been around almost as long as sports have. Historical writings suggest that athletes were using concoctions made of herbs or psychoactive mushrooms to give themselves a competitive edge as early as the ancient Olympics.

The modern era of doping began in 1935, when injectable testosterone was first developed by scientists in Nazi Germany. Testosterone is a male hormone that occurs naturally in the body. Boosting its levels in the blood is thought to increase strength and aggressiveness.

A couple of decades later, anabolic steroids—chemical variants of testosterone—were developed. Dr. John Ziegler, a team physician for the U.S. weight-lifting squad, learned about steroids from his Russian counterparts, and soon steroids were in wide use in the United States. By the late 1960s, the IOC had compiled a list of officially banned substances, but they had no effective way to monitor steroid use.

Steroids soon spread to professional football, and other sports requiring extreme strength and bulk. Professional and Olympic sports eventually developed into a kind of cat-and-mouse game between developers of performance-enhancing drugs and the governing bodies of sports that prohibited their use. The latter would invent a way to detect the latest drugs, only to discover that the former had invented a new method for avoiding detection. The issue of doping in elite athletics continues today.

One of the biggest doping scandals to date, the BALCO scandal, has been unfolding since 2003. BALCO, the Bay Area Laboratory Co-Operative, was a California-based drug distributor. The scandal erupted in the summer of 2003, when a disgruntled track coach named Trevor Graham provided authorities with a syringe containing a previously unknown steroid called THG. Authorities raided BALCO facilities, and uncovered not only large amounts of steroids but also documents implicating a number of high-profile athletes and trainers in football, baseball, and track and field.

Steroid use has been linked to many potentially serious health problems. These include liver and kidney

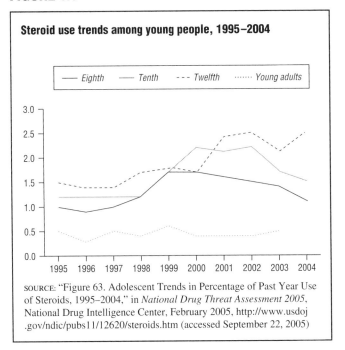

FIGURE 1.1

Steroid use trends among young people, 1995–2004

SOURCE: "Figure 63. Adolescent Trends in Percentage of Past Year Use of Steroids, 1995–2004," in *National Drug Threat Assessment 2005*, National Drug Intelligence Center, February 2005, http://www.usdoj .gov/ndic/pubs11/12620/steroids.htm (accessed September 22, 2005)

tumors, high blood pressure, elevated cholesterol, severe acne, and in men, shrunken testicles. Steroid use is also associated with emotional disturbances, including violent mood swings popularly known as "roid rage."

In addition to steroids, athletes turned to a number of other substances to gain an advantage before each was banned from sports. These include erythropoietin (EPO), a hormone that increases oxygen in the blood that was at the center of a 1998 doping scandal in cycling; andro-stenedione, which stimulates testosterone production and was made famous by the home-run leader Mark McGwire; and ephedra, an herbal stimulant that has been used in Chinese medicine for centuries.

Steroid use in youth sports has grown in recent years as young athletes emulate their idols. (See Figure 1.1.) According to the long-term study of youth attitudes and behavior *Monitoring the Future*, 2.5% of twelfth-graders in 2003 reported having used steroids in the previous year. Perhaps even more shocking is the fact that only 55.7% of high school seniors thought steroids were harmful.

Chapter 9 includes more detailed information on the variety of different anabolic steroids and other performance-enhancing substances that have been used over the years.

SPORTS AND GAMBLING

For millions of sports fans, the pleasure of watching a sporting event is enhanced by betting on the outcome. While gambling on sports (not including horse- and grey-hound racing) is technically legal only in the state of

Nevada, Americans nevertheless find ways to engage in sports wagering in huge numbers, whether through small-scale office pools or via offshore Internet gambling sites of questionable legality.

Legal Sports Betting

In Nevada legal sports betting is practiced through legitimate "bookmaking" operations, which are often affiliated with and located in a casino. Bookmakers set the "line," or margin of victory required to win the bet, for each game. Football is the biggest betting draw among the major team sports, accounting for about 40% of legal sports betting, according to the Nevada Gaming Commission. The Nevada Gaming Control Board reported in February 2005 (http://www.gaming.nv.gov/documents/pdf/pr_05superbowl.pdf) that more than $90.7 million was bet legally on the Super Bowl alone in 2005, a 12% increase from 2004 ($81.2 million) and nearly 27% more than was wagered in 2003 ($71.7 million).

While most sports gambling remains illegal, polls show that the majority of Americans are perfectly comfortable with sports gambling, even though a relatively small percentage actually participate. According to data from the Gallup Organization collected in December 2003, nearly two-thirds of adults approve of legalized gambling in general, though only 10% say they have bet on professional sports in the past year.

Gambling on horse racing, dog racing, and jai alai (a handball-like sport popular in Florida) uses what is called the pari-mutuel system. In this type of betting, all of the wagers go into a single pool, which is then split among the winners, with management taking a small share off the top. The American Gaming Association has estimated that total revenue from pari-mutuel gambling in the United States was about $3.8 billion in 2003, the vast majority ($3.4 billion) coming from horse racing.

Illegal Sports Betting

In spite of these impressive dollar amounts for both Nevada sports books and pari-mutuel gambling, these sums represent just the tip of the sports betting iceberg. Legal gambling in the United States is utterly dwarfed by illegal gambling. The American Gaming Association estimates that Nevada sports books account for only 1% to 3% of all sports gambling nationwide in a typical year. It is almost impossible to gauge how much money is bet on sports when illegal bets are included. The 1999 report of President Bill Clinton's Gambling Impact Study Commission estimated that illegal sports gambling in the United States amounted to between $80 billion and $380 billion a year (http://govinfo.library.unt.edu/ngisc/).

The newest frontier for sports gambling is the Internet. Christiansen Capital Advisors, LLC, a gaming and entertainment consulting firm, estimated that about $1 billion was bet on sports over the Internet in 2003, about one-quarter of it ($248 million) on professional football. Because most Internet gambling operations are based overseas, they fall outside the jurisdiction of U.S. gaming laws. While some authorities believe that these operations are nevertheless illegal based on current law, others disagree. Attempts by members of Congress to explicitly ban Internet gambling have made little progress as of late 2005.

CHAPTER 2
SPORTS PARTICIPATION AND ATTENDANCE

For when the One Great Scorer comes

to write against your name,

He marks—not that you won or lost

But how you played the game.

—Grantland Rice (1880–1954), sports writer

People have been playing games in one form or another ever since the first time a pair of humans decided to start grappling for fun rather than over food. The number and variety of sports in which people have participated through the ages is impossible to calculate. In North America, Native Americans were playing lacrosse and many other organized sports before Europeans settled permanently on the continent. In addition, one need only think of gladiators doing battle at the Colosseum in Ancient Rome to realize that people have been gathering to watch other people play sports for centuries as well. Following is a summary of sports participation and sports attendance in the United States, drawing information from government and industry publications.

SPORTS PARTICIPATION

There is no shortage of data available on sports participation in the United States. Participation is measured by market research firms, coordinating bodies of individual sports, and government agencies, among others. Sports participation is nevertheless a difficult thing to measure, and nobody has yet figured out how to measure it perfectly. Someone out for a casual walk or swim at the beach may not think of themselves as engaging in a sport, but those interested in selling walking shoes or studying the health benefits of physical activity might disagree. Then there is the matter of defining "participation"—does it mean a person plays the sport once a year, once a month, or only those who play almost every day? In addition to determining who qualifies as a

sports participant, the reliability of self-reported data presents additional problems. For example, can an individual accurately report that he played touch football with his friends twelve months ago rather than fifteen months ago? Distortion is inevitable, especially with regard to recreational activities that participants tend to engage in less frequently, like scuba diving. There is also a tendency when responding to this kind of survey to want to receive "credit" for having participated in a sport, especially a glamorous one like rock-climbing, even if the respondent has not undertaken the activity in several years. Another way to assess participation is through sales of sports equipment. However, this approach too has its perils. As Harvey Lauer, president of American Sports Data, Inc. (ASD), observed in "Sports Participation Research: Not Yet a Science" (http://www.americansportsdata.com/, 2005): "80% of all athletic/sports shoes are never sweated in."

Participation Superstudy

Each year, ASD, a leader in sports participation and fitness research, conducts a massive nationwide survey called the *Superstudy of Sports Participation*. SGMA International (http://www.sgma.com/), a trade association representing sporting goods manufacturers worldwide, analyzes data from the *Superstudy* and publishes reports on various aspects of sports participation in America. SGMA's annual *Sports Participation Topline Report* outlines major trends in every category of sports participation.

TEAM SPORTS. According to the *2005 Topline Report*, basketball was the most popular team sport in which to engage in 2004. About 34.2 million Americans age six and over reported that they played basketball at least once during the year. While basketball still enjoyed a comfortable lead over the next most popular team sport—volleyball at 22.2 million—about eight million fewer people played basketball in 2004 than had at its peak in 1993, when 42.2 million Americans hit the roundball courts. Football (16.4 million), softball (16.3 million), and soccer (15.9 million) were the other team sports with the most participants in 2004. Like basketball, participation in each of these sports has been trending downward in recent years. (See Table 2.1.) Table 2.2 ranks team sports based on participation data from 2003, which differ slightly from the 2004 data in the paragraph above.

SGMA's analysis of *Superstudy* data reveals that Americans appear to be losing their longstanding passion for team sports. According to SGMA, of the 35.4 million basketball players in 2003, eight million counted basketball as their favorite sport. Basketball also appears to have a greater share of adult players than most other sports. In contrast, court volleyball is thoroughly dominated by young people; 58% of all players in 2003 were under seventeen years old. SGMA also noted a gender gap in softball. About two-thirds of fast-pitch softball players were female in 2003, while over half (55%) of slow-pitch players were male.

Soccer, considered an exotic sport in the United States throughout much of the twentieth century in spite of its overwhelming global prominence, has gained ground on other team sports and can no longer be denied major sport status. It was voted the "hottest" sport in the country in SGMA's annual *State of the Industry Survey* in each year from 2001 through 2004. Between 1990–91 and 2003–04, participation on high school soccer teams grew by 88%. Memberships on U.S. Youth Soccer Association teams grew at a similar rate during that period, reaching 3.2 million in 2002–03 according to the SGMA's *State of the Industry* report released in early 2005. About 40% of all soccer players are girls, and among high school players the percentage is even higher, 47%. While *Topline Report* data suggest a leveling off in soccer participation in 2003–04, there is ample evidence that soccer's emergence as a major sport in America continues. Sales of soccer balls and equipment are increasing by 4% to 5% annually according to SGMA, with manufacturers' shipments totaling about $250 million in 2004. Soccer is clearly a youth movement, which bodes well for the future of the sport. The SGMA reported in *State of the Industry* that as of 2004, 70% of all soccer players were between the ages of six and seventeen, and another 25% were eighteen to forty-four; the remaining 5% included both those under six years old and those forty-five and older.

Just as the United States is catching up with the rest of the world in soccer participation, the rest of the world is catching up with the United States in basketball. Basketball, as noted above, remains the most popular team sport to play in the United States. According to the SGMA *State of the Industry Survey,* manufacturers' sales of basketballs and basketball equipment totaled about $380 million in 2004, a 1% increase over the previous year. Unlike soccer, basketball appeals to grown-ups almost as much as it does to children and teenagers. Nearly as many players (40% of the total) are ages twenty-four to forty-four as are six to seventeen (48%). Also unlike soccer, basketball remains a predominantly male sport. About 71% of all basketball players are boys or men according to *State of the Industry*. On the other hand, the gender tide may have turned with regard to organized basketball. The 2005 SGMA report noted that there are now more girls playing Amateur Athletic Union (AAU) youth basketball than there are boys.

INDIVIDUAL SPORTS. Bowling, golf, and tennis remain quite popular pastimes among the American public. According to the SGMA International in its *Sports Participation Topline Report 2005*, 53.6 million Americans bowled in 2004, making it the most popular of all competitive sports in the United States. Participation in bowling has essentially remained steady in recent years. While the popularity of bowling is stable, the sport has been undergoing a transformation in the form that participation takes. In the past, a large percentage of bowlers played on a team affiliated with a bowling league. The SGMA estimates that in the 1980s about two-thirds of all bowling was done by league bowlers; in the 2000s about one-third of all bowling takes place under the auspices of a league. The decline in the number of league bowlers has been compensated for by the addition of a great number of young, individual bowlers. However, these bowlers are less serious about the sport than league players—SGMA states that half of all bowlers hit the lanes three times or fewer in 2003—and as a result, sales of bowling equipment have stagnated in spite of strong numbers of people who can be counted as participants.

Another challenge facing bowling is that the number of places to bowl has been decreasing for the last several years, according to the United States Bowling Congress (http://www.bowl.com/). This trend is partly the result of consolidation, as older, smaller bowling centers are replaced by larger, state-of-the-art facilities, many of which feature upscale decor and good food service, in contrast to the stereotypical grimy, beer-splashed dens of the mid-twentieth century. Newer bowling centers usually offer modern, automated scoring, and better in-house balls and shoes. Some are megacenters offering other activities as well, including golf driving ranges, skating, or even basketball. Efforts to lure a younger crowd back to bowling alleys also include such special events as "Rock 'n' Bowl," or "Cosmic Bowling," which features glow-in-the-dark pins and discotheque or ultraviolet lighting.

As in the bowling industry, proprietors of billiards halls are attempting to shed the game's rough image in an

TABLE 2.1

Sports participation trends, 1987–2004

[In thousands of participants]

	1987 Benchmark	1990	1993	1998	2000	2002	2003	2004	1 year % change (2003–2004)	3 year % change (1998–2004)	17 year % change (1987–2004)
Team sports											
Baseball	15,098	15,454	15,586	12,318	10,881	10,402	10,885	9,694	−10.9%	−21.3%	−35.8%
Basketball	35,737	39,808	42,138	42,417	37,552	36,584	35,439	34,223	−3.4%	−19.3%	−4.2%
Cheerleading	n.a.	n.a.	3,257	3,266	3,574	3,596	3,574	4,131	+15.6%	+26.5%	+35.9%[a]
Ice hockey	2,393	2,762	3,204	2,915	2,761	2,612	2,789	1,998	−28.4%	−31.5%	−16.5%
Field hockey	n.a.	n.a.	n.a.	1,375	1,349	1,096	n.a.	n.a.	n.a.	n.a.	n.a.
Football (touch)	20,292	20,894	21,241	17,382	15,456	14,903	14,119	12,993	−8.0%	−25.2%	−35.9%
Football (tackle)	n.a.	n.a.	n.a.	n.a.	5,673	5,783	5,751	5,440	−5.4%	n.a.	−4.1%[d]
Football (net)	n.a.	n.a.	n.a.	n.a.	18,285	18,703	17,958	16,436	−8.5%	n.a.	−10.1%[d]
Lacrosse	n.a.	n.a.	n.a.	926	751	921	1,132	914	−19.3%	−1.3%	n.a.[c]
Rugby	n.a.	n.a.	n.a.	546	n.a.	n.a.	n.a.	n.a.	n.a.	n.a.	n.a.[c]
Soccer (indoor)	n.a.	n.a.	n.a.	n.a.	n.a.	n.a.	4,563	4,349	−4.7%	n.a.	n.a.
Soccer (outdoor)	n.a.	n.a.	n.a.	n.a.	n.a.	n.a.	16,133	14,608	−9.5%	n.a.	n.a.
Soccer (net)	15,388	15,945	16,365	18,176	17,734	17,641	17,679	15,900	−10.0%	−12.5%	+3.3%
Softball (regular)	n.a.	n.a.	n.a.	19,407	17,585	14,372	14,410	14,267	−1.0%	−26.5%	n.a.
Softball (fast-pitch)	n.a.	n.a.	n.a.	3,702	3,795	3,658	3,487	4,042	+15.9%	+9.2%	n.a.
Softball (net)	n.a.	n.a.	n.a.	21,352	19,668	16,587	16,020	16,324	+1.9%	−23.5%	n.a.
Volleyball (hard surface)	n.a.	n.a.	n.a.	n.a.	n.a.	11,748	11,008	11,762	+6.9%	n.a.	+0.1%[e]
Volleyball (grass)	n.a.	n.a.	n.a.	n.a.	n.a.	8,621	7,953	9,163	+15.2%	n.a.	+6.3%[e]
Volleyball (beach)	n.a.	n.a.	13,509	10,572	8,763	7,516	7,454	7,741	+3.9%	−26.8%	−33.0%[a]
Volleyball (net)	35,984	39,633	37,757	26,637	22,876	21,488	20,286	22,216	+9.5%	−16.6%	−38.2%[c]
Racquet sports											
Badminton	14,793	13,559	11,908	9,936	8,490	6,765	5,937	6,432	+8.3%	−35.3%	−56.5%
Racquetball	10,395	9,213	7,412	5,853	5,155	4,840	4,875	5,533	+13.5%	−5.5%	−46.8%
Squash	n.a.	n.a.	n.a.	289	364	302	473	290	−38.7%	0.0%	n.a
Tennis	21,147	21,742	19,346	16,937	16,598	16,353	17,325	18,346	+5.9%	+8.3%	−13.2%
Personal contact sports											
Boxing	n.a.	n.a.	n.a.	n.a.	1,085	908	945	1,140	+20.6%	n.a.	+5.1%[d]
Martial arts	n.a.	n.a.	n.a.	5,368	5,722	5,996	6,883	6,898	0.0%	+28.5%	n.a.
Wrestling	n.a.	n.a.	n.a.	n.a.	2,405	2,026	1,820	2,303	+26.5%	n.a.	−4.2%[d]
Indoor sport											
Billiards/pool	35,297	537	40,254	39,654	37,483	39,527	40,726	36,356	−10.7%	−8.3%	+3.0%
Bowling	47,823	53,537	49,022	50,593	53,844	53,160	55,035	53,603	−2.6%	+6.0%	+12.2%
Darts	n.a.	n.a.	n.a.	21,792	18,484	19,703	19,486	n.a.	n.a.	n.a.	n.a.
Table tennis	n.a.	20,089	17,689	14,999	13,797	12,796	13,511	14,286	+5.7%	−4.7%	−28.9%[a]
Wheel sport											
Roller hockey	n.a.	n.a.	2,323	3,876	3,287	2,875	2,718	1,788	−34.2%	−53.9%	−23.0%[b]
Roller skating (2×2 wheels)	n.a.	27,101	24,223	14,752	10,834	10,968	11,746	11,103	−5.5%	−24.7%	−59.0%[a]
Roller skating (inline wheels)	n.a.	4,695	13,689	32,010	29,024	21,572	19,233	17,348	−9.8%	−45.8%	+269.5%[a]
Scooter riding (non-motorized)	n.a.	n.a.	n.a.	n.a.	13,881	13,858	11,493	10,196	−11.3%	n.a.	−25.5%[d]
Skateboarding	10,888	9,267	5,388	7,190	11,649	12,997	11,090	10,592	−4.5%	+47.3%	−2.7%

TABLE 2.1

Sports participation trends, 1987–2004 [CONTINUED]

[In thousands of participants]

	1987 Benchmark	1990	1993	1998	2000	2002	2003	2004	1 year % change (2003–2004)	3 year % change (1998–2004)	17 year % change (1987–2004)
Other sports/activities											
Bicycling (BMX)	n.a.	n.a.	n.a.	n.a.	3,977	3,885	3,365	2,642	−21.5%	n.a.	−33.6%[d]
Bicycling (recreational)	n.a.	n.a.	n.a.	54,575	53,006	53,524	53,710	52,021	−3.1%	−4.7%	n.a.
Golf	26,261	28,945	28,610	29,961	30,365	27,812	27,314	25,723	−5.8%	−14.1%	−2.0%
Gymnastics	n.a.	n.a.	n.a.	6,224	5,268	5,149	5,189	5,273	+1.6%	−15.3%	n.a.
Swimming (recreational)	n.a.	n.a.	n.a.	94,371	95,268	92,667	96,429	95,268	−1.2%	+1.0%	n.a.
Walking (recreational)	n.a.	n.a.	n.a.	80,864	82,561	84,986	88,799	92,677	+4.4%	+14.6%	n.a.
Outdoors activities											
Camping (tent)	35,232	36,915	34,772	42,677	42,241	40,316	41,891	41,561	−0.8%	−2.6%	+18.0%
Camping (recreational vehicle)	22,655	20,764	22,187	18,188	19,035	18,747	19,022	17,424	−8.6%	−4.2%	−23.1%
Camping (net)	50,386	50,537	49,858	50,650	51,606	49,808	51,007	49,412	−3.1%	−2.4%	−1.9%
Hiking (day)	n.a.	n.a.	n.a.	38,629	39,015	36,778	39,096	39,334	+0.6%	+1.8%	n.a.
Hiking (overnight)	n.a.	n.a.	n.a.	6,821	6,750	5,839	6,213	6,396	+3.0%	−6.2%	n.a.
Hiking (net)	n.a.	n.a.	n.a.	40,117	40,133	37,888	40,409	40,713	+0.8%	+1.5%	n.a.
Horseback riding	n.a.	n.a.	n.a.	16,522	16,988	14,641	16,009	14,695	−8.2%	−11.1%	n.a.
Mountain biking	1,512	4,146	7,408	8,611	7,854	6,719	6,940	5,334	−23.1%	−38.1%	+252.8%
Mountain/rock climbing	n.a.	n.a.	n.a.	2,004	1,947	2,089	2,169	2,161	−0.4%	+7.8%	n.a.
Artificial wall climbing	n.a.	n.a.	n.a.	4,696	6,117	7,185	8,634	7,659	−11.3%	+63.1%	n.a.
Trail running	n.a.	n.a.	n.a.	5,249	5,232	5,625	6,109	6,486	+6.2%	+23.6%	n.a.
Shooting sports											
Archery	8,558	9,252	8,648	7,109	6,047	6,650	7,111	6,756	−5.0%	−5.0%	−21.0%
Hunting (shotgun/rifle)	25,241	23,220	23,189	16,684	16,481	16,471	15,232	15,196	−0.2%	−8.9%	−39.8%
Hunting (bow)	n.a.	n.a.	n.a.	4,719	4,120	4,752	4,155	3,661	−11.9%	−22.4%	n.a.
Paintball	n.a.	n.a.	n.a.	5,923	7,121	8,659	9,835	9,640	−2.0%	+62.8%	+9.9%[a]
Shooting (sport clays)	n.a.	n.a.	3,100	2,734	2,843	3,017	3,867	3,222	−16.7%	+17.8%	n.a.
Shooting (trap/skeet)	5,073	n.a.	n.a.	3,800	3,827	3,696	4,496	4,059	−9.7%	+6.8%	−20.0%
Target shooting (rifle)	n.a.	n.a.	n.a.	14,042	12,984	14,336	15,176	14,057	−7.4%	+0.1%	n.a.
Target shooting (handgun)[f]	n.a.	n.a.	n.a.	12,110	10,443	11,064	13,836	11,932	−13.8%	−1.5%	n.a.
Target shooting (net)[f]	18,947	21,840	23,498	18,330	16,293	17,558	19,788	18,037	−8.9%	−1.6%	−4.8%
Fishing											
Fishing (fly)	11,359	8,039	6,598	7,269	6,581	6,034	6,033	4,623	−23.4%	−36.4%	−59.3%
Fishing (freshwater-other)	50,500	53,097	50,198	45,807	44,050	42,605	43,819	39,433	−10.0%	−13.9%	−21.9%
Fishing (saltwater)	19,646	19,087	18,490	15,671	14,710	14,874	15,221	13,453	−11.6%	−14.2%	−31.5%
Fishing (net)	58,402	58,816	55,442	55,488	53,846	51,426	52,970	47,906	−9.6%	−13.7%	−18.0%
Winter sports											
Ice skating	n.a.	n.a.	n.a.	18,710	17,496	14,530	17,049	14,692	−13.8%	−21.5%	n.a.
Skiing (cross-country)	8,344	7,292	6,489	4,728	4,613	4,080	4,171	4,007	−4.0%	−15.2%	−52.0%
Skiing (downhill)	17,676	18,209	17,567	14,836	14,749	14,249	13,633	11,971	−12.2%	−19.3%	−32.3%
Snowboarding	n.a.	n.a.	2,567	5,461	7,151	7,691	7,818	7,110	−9.1%	+30.2%	+41.0%
Snowmobiling	n.a.	n.a.	n.a.	6,492	7,032	4,515	5,509	4,688	−14.9%	−27.8%	n.a.
Snowshoeing	n.a.	n.a.	n.a.	1,721	1,970	2,006	2,479	2,302	−7.1%	+33.8%	n.a.

TABLE 2.1

Sports participation trends, 1987–2004 [CONTINUED]

[In thousands of participants]

Water sports	1987 Benchmark	1990	1993	1998	2000	2002	2003	2004	1 year % change (2003–2004)	3 year % change (1998–2004)	17 year % change (1987–2004)
Boardsailing/windsurfing	1,145	1,025	835	1,075	655	496	779	418	−46.4%	−61.1%	−63.5%
Canoeing	n.a.	n.a.	n.a.	13,615	13,134	10,933	11,632	11,449	−1.6%	−16.0%	n.a.
Kayaking	n.a.	n.a.	n.a.	3,501	5,562	5,562	6,324	6,147	−2.8%	+75.6%	n.a.
Rafting	n.a.	n.a.	n.a.	5,570	4,431	4,431	4,553	4,209	−7.6%	−24.4%	n.a.
Jet skiing	n.a.	n.a.	n.a.	11,203	10,835	9,806	10,648	7,972	−25.1%	−28.9%	n.a.
Sailing	6,368	5,981	3,918	5,902	5,271	5,161	5,232	4,307	−17.7%	−27.0%	−32.4%
Scuba diving	2,433	2,615	2,306	3,448	2,901	3,328	3,215	3,430	+6.7%	−0.5%	+41.0%
Snorkeling	n.a.	n.a.	n.a.	10,575	10,526	9,865	10,179	11,112	+9.2%	+5.1%	n.a.
Surfing	1,459	1,224	n.a.	1,395	2,180	1,879	2,087	1,936	−7.2%	+38.8%	+32.7%
Wakeboarding	n.a.	n.a.	n.a.	2,253	3,581	3,142	3,356	2,843	−15.3%	+26.2%	n.a.
Water skiing	19,902	19,314	16,626	10,161	10,335	8,204	8,425	6,835	−18.9%	−32.7%	−65.7%

Notes: na=not available.
aFourteen-year change
bEleven-year change
cFive-year change
dFour-year change
eTwo-year change
f2003 figure is elevated due to change in category definition from "pistol" to "handgun."

SOURCE: Adapted from "SGMA Sports Participation Trends," in *The SGMA Report: Sports Participation Topline Report, 2005 Edition—Statistical Highlights from the Superstudy of Sports Participation,* SGMA International, 2005. http://www.sgma.com/reports/2005/report1113421275-27433.html (accessed September 22, 2005)

TABLE 2.2

Team sports participation, 2003

[In millions]

Rank	Sport	Number of participants (aged six and above)
1	Basketball	35.4
2	Soccer (outdoor)	16.1
3	Softball (regular)	14.4
4	Football (touch/flag)	14.1
5	Volleyball (hard surface)	11.0
6	Baseball	10.9
7	Volleyball (grass)	8.0
8	Volleyball (beach)	7.5
9	Football (tackle)	5.8
10	Soccer (indoor)	4.6
11	Cheerleading	3.6
12	Softball (fast-pitch)	3.5
13	Ice hockey	2.8
14	Lacrosse	1.1

Note: This information is based on participation numbers in 2003.

SOURCE: "Team Sports," in *Team Sports—An American Institution*, SGMA International, April 13, 2004, http://www.sgma.com/press/2004/press1081888640-15351.html (accessed September 22, 2005)

effort to attract to the sport new players who may have previously been put off by pool's unsavory reputation. According to the *Topline Report*, about 36.3 million people shot pool or billiards in 2004, down a bit from the previous few years but still slightly better than in the study baseline year of 1987. According to the SGMA, the profile of the typical billiards player has changed over the past few decades. American pool halls were once frequented primarily by older men, but in the twenty-first century pool is becoming a sport played increasingly by women and young people. Since the 1980s many facilities have upgraded their traditional low-budget style, and most no longer resemble the no-nonsense rooms immortalized in movies like *The Hustler*. New and refurbished billiards rooms, like contemporary bowling centers, are well-lighted, clean, and frequently part of multi-activity facilities offering numerous recreation options.

Golf peaked in popularity in 2000, when 30.4 million people hit the links. In 2004 the sport had 25.7 million participants, just below its level during the baseline year of 1987. The National Golf Foundation estimates that of that total, about 12.8 million adults were what they call "core golfers" in 2004, meaning they played at least eight times that year (averaging thirty-seven times) and are responsible for 91% of rounds played and 87% of golf-related spending. There are another 2.9 million junior golfers between the ages of twelve and seventeen who play that frequently (http://www.ngf.org/cgi/whofaqa.asp?).

While the *Topline Report* indicates that fewer people played tennis in 2004 than had in 1987, it appeared to be enjoying a resurgence in popularity. In 1987, 21.1 million

people played tennis at least once. The figure bottomed out in 2000, when only 16.6 million enthusiasts hoisted a racket. It has since rebounded substantially; 18.3 million Americans played tennis in 2004. One factor in the resurgence of tennis is a conscious effort to democratize the sport. Once played primarily by the wealthy at country clubs, tennis is now available to people at all socioeconomic levels. The United States Tennis Association (http://www.usta.com/home/default.sps) has helped this trend along by investing heavily in programs aimed at growing the sport, including a $50 million initiative launched in 1997 called "USA Tennis Plan for Growth," which offered free lessons around the country; and a Diversity Plan aimed at encouraging multicultural participation in a sport that has long been dominated by white players, coaches, and officials. Gains in minority participation have received a boost from the success and popularity of such African-American stars as Serena and Venus Williams and James Blake. Other racquet sports, including badminton and racquetball, while much less popular than tennis, are also widely played, with 6.4 million and 5.5 million participants respectively in 2004.

Among the personal contact sports, martial arts are by far the most popular, according to the *Topline Report*. Their 6.9 million participants were well over three times as many as engaged in wrestling, and more than seven times the number who participated in boxing.

Recreational swimming has been America's most popular sporting activity since at least 1998. In 2004, 95.2 million Americans participated. Canoeing was the next most popular water sport in the United States in 2004, with 11.4 million participants, according to the *Topline Report*. Snorkeling, at 11.1 million, was next and growing fast in popularity; kayaking was third at 6.1 million, and has been gaining adherents at a brisk pace, though 2004 represented a small decline in participants from the previous year.

Recreational walking and bicycling are two other sporting activities that are very popular with Americans. Walking has been gaining in popularity. Its 92.6 million participants in 2004 made it the second-most-popular sports activity and represented a 14.6% gain since 1998. Cycling is headed in the opposite direction, with a 4.7% decline over the same period. However, with fifty-two million participants in 2004 it remains the fourth-most-popular sport in the country.

National Sporting Goods Association Survey

The National Sporting Goods Association (NSGA; not to be confused with the SGMA International, discussed above) also conducts a broad nationwide survey on sports participation. Following are some highlights from the 2004 NSGA survey.

TABLE 2.3

Sports participation, 2004 vs. 1999

[Participated more than once (in millions). Seven (7) years of age and older.]

Sport	2004	1999	Percent change
Total U.S.	258.5	245.3	5.4%
Snowboarding	6.6	3.3	98.3%
Paintball games	9.4	5.1	84.7%
Skateboarding	10.3	7.0	48.6%
Target shooting	19.2	13.0	47.7%
Workout at club	31.8	24.1	32.0%
Hockey (ice)	2.4	1.9	28.9%
Mountain biking (off road)	8.0	6.8	18.2%
Exercising with equipment	52.2	45.2	15.4%
Backpack/wilderness camp	17.3	15.3	13.0%
Aerobic exercising	29.5	26.2	12.2%
Camping (vacation/overnight)	55.3	50.1	10.3%
Running/jogging	24.7	22.4	10.3%
Muzzleloading	3.8	3.5	9.4%
Archery (target)	5.3	4.9	7.6%
Billiards/pool	34.2	32.1	6.5%
Hunting with firearms	17.7	16.6	6.4%
Skiing (cross country)	2.4	2.2	5.3%
Bowling	43.8	41.6	5.3%
Exercise walking	84.7	80.8	4.9%
Canoeing	7.5	7.3	1.9%
Hiking	28.3	28.1	0.9%
Soccer	13.3	13.2	0.5%
Baseball	15.9	16.3	−2.9%
Hunting with bow & arrow	5.8	6.0	−3.4%
Bicycle riding	40.3	42.4	−4.9%
Football (tackle)	8.2	8.7	−5.8%
Basketball	27.8	29.6	−6.0%
Sailing	2.6	2.8	−6.1%
Boating, motor/power	22.8	24.4	−6.8%
Swimming	53.4	57.9	−7.7%
Volleyball	10.8	11.7	−7.9%
Martial arts	4.7	5.1	−8.7%
Golf	24.5	27.0	−9.4%
Fishing	41.2	46.7	−11.8%
Tennis	9.6	10.9	−11.9%
Football (touch)	9.6	11.1	−14.1%
Softball	12.5	14.7	−15.0%
Skiing (alpine)	5.9	7.4	−20.3%
Kick boxing	2.8	3.8	−26.8%
Water skiing	4.7	6.6	−28.1%
In-line roller skating	11.7	24.1	−51.5%

SOURCE: "2004 Participation—2004 vs. 1999," National Sporting Goods Association, 2005, http://www.nsga.org/public/pages/index.cfm?pageid=152 (accessed September 22, 2005)

Table 1.2 in Chapter 1 ranks sports and other physical activities by total participation and provides a useful snapshot of what Americans choose to do when they want to move their bodies.

Table 2.3 provides a sport-by-sport glance at changes in participation between 1999 and 2004, ranking the sports in terms of their growth in participation over that span. Overall, there was a 5.4% increase in the number of Americans who participated in a sport more than once over the course of the year. The sport that enjoyed the biggest increase in participants between 1999 and 2004 was snowboarding. The number of snowboarders roughly doubled during that period. Paintball is another sport that experienced dramatic growth between those years. Among the sports whose participants decreased were in-line roller-skating (−51.5%), water skiing (−28.1%), and kick boxing (−26.8%). A ten-year history of selected sports is shown in Table 2.4. From this graphic, one can observe the contrast between, for example, the surging popularity of skateboarding and the waning participation in skiing, as Americans exchange one board sport for another.

YOUTH SPORTS. According to a 2004 survey sponsored by Velocity Sports Performance (http://www.velocitysp.com/), an independent training program for athletes of all ages and skill levels, American adults believe it is important for children to participate in sports. Velocity found that 36% of respondents believed that sports participation has the greatest impact on a youth's character, ranking ahead of such activities as after-school programs, travel, and summer camp. This sentiment was even more prevalent among the affluent, those with full-time jobs, and those under age fifty-five.

However, youth participation in team sports is on the decline. An August 2004 article in the industry magazine *Sporting Goods Dealer* notes that the population of seven- to eleven-year-olds grew 7% between 1993 and 2003, and the twelve to seventeen age group grew 15.7% during that span. Therefore, a sport that grows in participation any less than that among those age groups is not keeping up with population growth. Baseball participation, the article says, dropped by double-digit percentages in both age groups. Basketball participation increased in the younger group, but dropped by nearly 16% among twelve- to seventeen-year-olds. Soccer, in contrast, saw increases in participation among both age groups. The article, which is based on NSGA survey data, also notes that equipment purchases for those sports mirror these trends. It is reasonable to suggest that the trimming of school sports programs in the face of education budget crises is aggravating these trends. Table 2.5 shows ten-year trends (1994–2004) in youth participation in selected sports. Golf, skateboarding, and snowboarding were among the small number of sports that enjoyed substantial increases in participation among youth between 1994 and 2004.

SPORTS PARTICIPATION AND GENDER. According to NSGA survey data, the sports that drew the greatest number of female participants in 2004 (if you exclude exercise and recreational activities such as camping and aerobics) were swimming (28.6 million), bowling (21.3 million), and bicycling (18.7 million). (See Table 2.6.) Basketball, at 8.7 million participants, topped the list among team sports, with softball and volleyball not far behind at more than six million each. Golf, soccer, and tennis each attracted over five million female participants in 2004. Women represent a greater share of participants in some sports than in others. For example, 58.5% of the nation's volleyball players and 52.9% of tennis players in

TABLE 2.4

Ten-year history of selected sports participation, 1994–2004, selected years

[Participated more than once (in millions). Seven (7) years of age and older.]

Sport	2004	2002	2000	1998	1996	1994
Aerobic exercising	29.5	29.0	26.7	25.8	24.1	23.2
Archery (target)	5.3	4.2	4.5	4.8	5.3	na
Backpack/wilderness camp	17.3	14.8	15.4	14.6	11.5	9.8
Baseball	15.9	15.6	15.6	15.9	14.8	15.1
Basketball	27.8	28.9	27.1	29.4	31.8	28.2
Bicycle riding	40.3	39.7	43.1	43.5	53.3	49.8
Billiards/pool	34.2	33.1	32.5	32.3	34.5	34.0
Boating, motor/power	22.8	26.6	24.2	25.7	28.8	26.4
Bowling	43.8	42.4	43.1	40.1	42.9	37.4
Camping (vacation/overnight)	55.3	55.4	49.9	46.5	44.7	42.9
Exercise walking	84.7	82.2	81.3	77.6	73.3	70.8
Exercising with equipment	52.2	46.8	44.8	46.1	47.8	43.8
Fishing	41.2	44.2	47.2	43.6	45.6	45.7
Football (tackle)	8.2	7.8	8.0	8.1	9.0	na
Football (touch)	9.6	10.3	9.8	10.8	11.6	na
Golf	24.5	27.1	26.4	27.5	23.1	24.6
Hiking	28.3	27.2	24.3	27.2	26.5	25.3
Hockey (ice)	2.4	2.1	1.9	2.1	2.1	1.9
Hunting with firearms	17.7	19.5	19.1	17.3	18.3	16.4
Hunting with bow & arrow	5.8	4.6	4.7	5.6	5.5	na
Ice/figure skating	na	na	6.7	7.8	8.4	7.8
Kayaking/rafting	na	na	3.1	3.2	3.6	na
Kick boxing	2.8	na	3.9	2.3	na	na
Martial arts	4.7	4.2	5.4	4.6	4.7	na
Mountain biking (off road)	8.0	7.8	7.1	8.6	7.3	5.7
Muzzleloading	3.8	3.6	2.9	3.1	3.2	na
Paintball games	9.4	6.9	5.3	na	na	3.7
Roller skating (in-line)	11.7	18.8	19.2			23.9
Running/jogging	24.7	24.7	22.8	22.5	22.2	20.6
Sailing	2.6	na	2.5	3.6	4.0	4.1
Scooter riding	12.9	13.4	11.6	na	na	na
Skateboarding	10.3	9.7	9.1	5.8	4.7	4.9
Skiing (alpine)	5.9	7.4	7.4	7.7	10.5	10.6
Skiing (cross country)	2.4	2.2	2.3	2.6	3.4	3.6
Snorkeling	na	na	5.5	7.3	7.1	5.9
Soccer	13.3	13.7	12.9	13.2	13.9	12.5
Softball	12.5	13.6	14.0	15.6	19.9	18.1
Swimming	53.4	53.1	58.8	58.2	60.2	60.3
T'ai Chi/yoga	6.7	6.1	na	na	na	na
Target shooting	19.2	18.9	16.9	18.9	21.2	na
Tennis	9.6	11.0	10.0	11.2	11.5	11.6
Volleyball	10.8	11.5	12.3	14.8	18.5	17.4
Water skiing	4.7	6.9	5.9	7.2	7.4	7.4
Weight lifting	26.2	25.1	22.8	na	na	na
Workout at club	31.8	28.9	24.1	26.5	22.5	20.4

Note: na=not available

SOURCE: "Ten-Year History of Selected Sports Participation," National Sporting Goods Association, 2005, http://www.nsga.org/public/pages/index.cfm?pageid=153 (accessed September 22, 2005)

2004 were female. Not surprisingly, a huge majority of cheerleading participants (95.1%) are female. Table 2.7 shows changes in participation among women between 1999 and 2004. Skateboarding, archery, and tennis all showed substantial gains in participation over that interval. Among the team sports, soccer and softball showed the greatest growth among women. While many sports are still dominated by one or the other gender, there is no question that participation in many others is moving toward greater parity. The Women's Sports Foundation (http://www.womenssportsfoundation.org/), for example, reported that 54% of American children aged six to seventeen played on at least one organized sports team in 2002 and of that group 44% were girls.

U.S. Census Bureau Statistical Abstract

The U.S. Census Bureau provides data on participation in selected sports, collected from a variety of sources, in its *Statistical Abstract of the United States: 2004–2005*. According to the *Abstract*, there were thirty million amateur softball players in the United States in 2003, after a slow, steady decline from forty-one million in 1985. Youth participants represented 1.35 million of that total, and while that number had decreased over the last few years, it was still nearly twice the 712,000 youth softball players counted in 1985. The *Abstract* recorded a steady increase in the number of tennis players nationwide, showing 23.2 million players in 2002, up from thirteen million in 1985.

TABLE 2.5

Youth sports participation, 2004 vs. 1994

[Participated more than once (in millions). Seven (7) years of age and older.]

	Year	Total	Change vs 1994	Total 7–11	Change vs 1994	Total 12–17	Change vs 1994
Total U.S.	1994	232,986		18,773		21,579	
Total U.S.	2004	258,533	11.0%	19,650	4.7%	24,988	15.8%
Sport							
Baseball	1994	232,986		18,773		21,579	
Baseball	2004	258,533	11.0%	19,650	4.7%	24,988	15.8%
Basketball	1994	28,191		5,554		7,951	
Basketball	2004	27,847	−1.2%	5,867	5.6%	7,175	−9.8%
Bicycle riding	1994	49,818		11,403		9,363	
Bicycle riding	2004	40,317	−19.1%	9,196	−19.4%	7,770	−17.0%
Fishing	1994	40,477		4,883		4,632	
Fishing	2004	36,265	−10.4%	3,583	−26.6%	4,103	−11.4%
Golf	1994	24,551		670		1,885	
Golf	2004	24,479	−0.3%	1,027	53.3%	2,487	31.9%
Ice hockey	1994	1,914		388		408	
Ice hockey	2004	2,423	26.6%	292	−24.7%	544	33.3%
In-line skating	1994	19,468		6,998		5,273	
In-line skating	2004	11,677	−40.0%	3,313	−52.7%	3,913	−25.8%
Skateboarding	2004	10,388	111.0%	3,439	82.4%	4,262	111.8%
Skiing (alpine)	1994	10,620		646		1,966	
Skiing (alpine)	2004	5,903	−44.4%	659	2.0%	979	−50.2%
Snowboarding	1994	2,061		210		853	
Snowboarding	2004	6,572	218.9%	971	362.4%	2,356	176.2%
Soccer	1994	12,508		5,494		3,536	
Soccer	2004	13,287	6.2%	5,411	−1.5%	3,578	1.2%

SOURCE: "2004 Youth Participation in Selected Sports with Comparisons to 1994," National Sporting Goods Association, 2005, http://www.nsga.org/public/pages/index.cfm?pageid=158 (accessed September 22, 2005)

Emerging Sports

EXTREME SPORTS. As participation in traditional team sports like baseball and basketball declines, especially among youth and young adults, a generation of sports participants is turning instead to a class of activities collectively known as "extreme sports." While there is no consensus on exactly which sports qualify as extreme, most lists include skateboarding, rock climbing, snowboarding, mountain biking, BMX bicycling, and windsurfing. The boldest of extreme sportspersons will engage in such daredevilry as riding a motorcycle off of a ski jump. Many of these sports, according to *Superstudy* data, are among the fastest growing in the country.

According to SGMA International's analysis of *Superstudy* data, inline skating is by far the most popular extreme sport. (See Table 2.8.) In 2004, 17.3 million people age six and over donned inline skates at least once—more than the number of baseball and tackle football players combined. Skateboarding was second, with 11.6 million participants. SGMA notes that most of these skateboarders were not just folks who went out once and then tucked their board back into the deep recesses of the garage. They rode their boards an average of forty-eight days during the year. According to an article in *American Demographics* (Joan Raymond, "Going to Extremes—Marketing and Extreme Sports—Statistical Data," June 1, 2002), the shift among young people from classic team sports to the rugged individualism of extreme sports was related to changing values among that population. The article points to a rejection of such traditional values as "working together, character-building and group competition" and quotes ASD's Lauer as saying that alternative sports are "rooted in a diametrically opposite set of values," including alienation and defiance. Nevertheless, the sheer numbers of people engaging in these sports suggest that the word "alternative" may no longer be appropriate. Extreme sports are no longer solely the domain of tattooed and pierced daredevils under thirty; they have become utterly mainstream.

LACROSSE. Among the fastest-growing team sports in the United States is lacrosse. Lacrosse is similar in form to hockey or soccer. It is played on a field by two teams of ten players. Players use netted sticks to throw and catch a small rubber ball and, ultimately, to propel the ball into the opponents' goal, which resembles a hockey goal. Lacrosse may be the oldest sport in North America. It originated among Native Americans and has been played in one form or another for at least five hundred years.

U.S. Lacrosse, the organization that coordinates lacrosse activity nationwide, estimates that there were 364,835 active lacrosse players in the United States in 2004, up from 253,931 in 2001. (See Table 2.9.) According to U.S. Lacrosse's most recent nationwide survey,

TABLE 2.6

Sports participation among women, by total participation, 2004

[Participated more than once (in millions). Seven (7) years of age and older.]

Sport	Total female	Percent female
Exercise walking	52.4	61.8%
Swimming	28.6	53.6%
Exercising with equipment	28.0	53.7%
Camping (vacation/overnight)	26.5	47.9%
Aerobic exercising	21.7	73.8%
Bowling	21.3	48.7%
Bicycle riding	18.7	46.5%
Workout at club	17.8	55.9%
Hiking	13.7	48.3%
Billiards/pool	13.6	39.8%
Fishing	12.9	31.4%
Running/jogging	11.5	46.6%
Boating, motor/power	9.9	43.7%
Weight lifting	8.9	33.8%
Basketball	8.7	31.2%
Backpack/wilderness camp	7.3	42.3%
Softball	6.5	51.8%
Volleyball	6.3	58.5%
In-line roller skating	5.9	50.3%
Scooter riding	5.9	45.3%
T'ai Chi/yoga	5.8	87.2%
Golf	5.7	23.4%
Soccer	5.5	41.7%
Tennis	5.1	52.9%
Target shooting	4.3	22.5%
Cheerleading	3.9	95.1%
Baseball	3.5	22.1%
Canoeing	3.4	45.1%
Mountain biking (off road)	2.7	33.8%
Skateboarding	2.6	25.3%
Skiing (alpine)	2.6	44.4%
Football (touch)	2.2	22.7%
Hunting with firearms	2.0	11.2%
Water skiing	1.9	40.3%
Kick boxing	1.9	68.0%
Paintball games	1.8	19.5%
Snowboarding	1.7	26.6%
Martial arts	1.6	35.3%
Archery (target)	1.5	27.8%
Sailing	1.2	44.5%
Skiing (cross country)	1.0	42.3%
Football (tackle)	1.0	11.9%
Hockey (ice)	0.6	24.8%
Hunting with bow & arrow	0.5	8.6%
Muzzleloading	0.4	10.9%

SOURCE: "2004 Women's Participation—Ranked by Total Female Participation," National Sporting Goods Association, 2005, http://www .nsga.org/public/pages/index.cfm?pageid=154 (accessed September 22, 2005)

about half of current players are in the youth category (186,048 in 2004). Another 133,857 played high school lacrosse, and 25,671 played at the collegiate level. Lacrosse has long been popular in the Northeast and in the mid-Atlantic states, but in the 2000s has been surging in popularity in many parts of the country, including the Pacific Northwest and the Rocky Mountain states.

SOCCER. As mentioned above, soccer is the only well-established team sport that does not appear to be losing players, largely due to its growing popularity among young people. As of 2005 the U.S. Youth Soccer Web site reported membership of over three million players between the ages of five and nineteen—an impressive number when compared to the 100,000 registered members the organization had in 1974, the year it was founded (http://www.usyouthsoccer.org/). Moreover, two other smaller nationwide youth soccer agencies—the American Youth Soccer Organization (AYSO; http://soccer.org/) and the Soccer Association for Youth (http://www.saysoccer. org/)—have a combined 1.5 million members. The presence of these young soccer players on America's fields, as well as growing populations of people from places like Latin America, where soccer has long reigned supreme among sports, is likely to lift soccer into prominence among adults in the coming years.

CONSUMER PURCHASES OF SPORTING GOODS

In addition to asking individuals about their sports participation, NSGA also tracks nationwide retail sales of sporting goods. (See Table 2.10.) According to NSGA data, Americans spent about $84.7 billion on sports-related items in 2004, and were projected to spend $86.8 billion in 2005. Of that total, about $35.8 billion was spent on what NSGA calls "recreational transport," a category that includes bicycles, pleasure boats, RVs, and snowmobiles. The other $48.9 billion was spent on what most people consider "sporting goods," including specialized equipment, footwear, and clothing. Footwear accounted for about $15 billion of that spending, and clothing $11 billion. The $48.9 total represented a 3% increase over the previous year.

Excluding apparel, footwear, and exercise equipment, golf equipment accounted for the largest share of sports equipment purchased by Americans in 2004. Consumer purchases of golf gear tallied $3.1 billion that year. According to the National Golf Foundation, "avid golfers" (i.e., those who play at least twenty-five rounds a year) account for nearly two-thirds of the spending, even though they make up less than a quarter of the nation's golfers. Hunting and firearms, one of the fastest-growing categories of consumer purchases, was close behind at $2.9 billion. Fishing tackle ($2.0 billion) and camping equipment ($1.5 billion) also experienced strong gains in 2004. Of the twenty-one sporting goods categories NSGA surveyed, only three declined in sales in 2004: wheeled sports (including scooters), water skis, and hockey and ice skates. (See Table 1.3 in Chapter 1.)

Where do people go to make these purchases? The top two retail sellers in the country are large general retail chains rather than sporting goods specialists. Wal-Mart was the biggest sporting goods retailer, though it is difficult to tell by how much, since they report sporting goods and toys together. According to the annual rankings in *Sporting Goods Business Retail Top 100* (http://www.sgbmag.com, June 2005), Wal-Mart sold $17.1 billion worth of sporting goods and toys in 2004.

TABLE 2.7

Female sports participation, 2004 vs. 1999

[Participated more than once (in millions). Seven (7) years of age and older.]

Sport	Total	2004 total female	2004 percent female	1999 total female	1999 percent female	Percent changed
Aerobic exercising	29.5	21.7	73.8%	19.6	74.5%	−0.7%
Archery (target)	5.3	1.5	27.8%	1.0	20.5%	7.4%
Backpack/wilderness camp	17.3	7.3	42.3%	6.0	39.2%	3.1%
Baseball	15.9	3.5	22.1%	3.5	21.6%	0.5%
Basketball	27.8	8.7	31.2%	8.6	29.1%	2.1%
Bicycle riding	40.3	18.7	46.5%	18.9	44.5%	2.0%
Billiards/pool	34.2	13.6	39.8%	12.0	37.3%	2.6%
Boating, motor/power	22.8	9.9	43.7%	10.7	43.7%	0.0%
Bowling	43.8	21.3	48.7%	20.3	48.9%	−0.2%
Camping (vacation/overnight)	55.3	26.5	47.9%	23.3	46.5%	1.5%
Canoeing	7.5	3.4	45.1%	3.1	42.2%	2.9%
Exercise walking	84.7	52.4	61.8%	50.0	61.9%	−0.1%
Exercising with equipment	52.2	28.0	53.7%	23.1	51.1%	2.6%
Fishing	41.2	12.9	31.4%	12.9	31.5%	−0.1%
Football (tackle)	8.2	1.0	11.9%	0.7	8.2%	3.8%
Football (touch)	9.6	2.2	22.7%	2.0	17.9%	4.8%
Golf	24.5	5.7	23.4%	5.6	20.9%	2.4%
Hiking	28.3	13.7	48.3%	12.8	45.6%	2.8%
Hockey (ice)	2.4	0.6	24.8%	0.5	24.7%	0.0%
Hunting with bow & arrow	5.8	0.5	8.6%	0.6	9.6%	−1.0%
Hunting with firearms	17.7	2.0	11.2%	1.9	11.4%	−0.2%
In-line roller skating	11.7	5.9	50.3%	12.2	50.6%	−0.4%
Kick boxing	2.8	1.9	68.0%	2.7	71.2%	−3.1%
Martial arts	4.7	1.6	35.3%	2.0	40.1%	−4.8%
Mountain biking (off road)	8.0	2.7	33.8%	2.1	30.8%	3.0%
Muzzleloading	3.8	0.4	10.9%	0.2	7.0%	3.8%
Paintball games	9.4	1.8	19.5%	1.0	19.6%	0.0%
Running/jogging	24.7	11.5	46.6%	10.1	45.2%	1.4%
Sailing	2.6	1.2	44.5%	1.2	42.3%	2.2%
Skateboarding	10.3	2.6	25.3%	1.2	17.9%	7.5%
Skiing (alpine)	5.9	2.6	44.4%	2.9	39.3%	5.0%
Skiing (cross country)	2.4	1.0	42.3%	1.2	51.6%	−9.3%
Snowboarding	6.6	1.7	26.6%	0.9	25.7%	0.8%
Soccer	13.3	5.5	41.7%	4.8	36.6%	5.0%
Softball	12.5	6.5	51.8%	6.9	46.8%	5.0%
Swimming	53.4	28.6	53.6%	30.8	53.2%	0.4%
Target shooting	19.2	4.3	22.5%	2.3	17.9%	4.6%
Tennis	9.6	5.1	52.9%	5.0	46.1%	6.8%
Volleyball	10.8	6.3	58.5%	6.4	54.5%	4.0%
Water skiing	4.7	1.9	40.3%	2.8	42.3%	−2.0%
Workout at club	31.8	17.8	55.9%	12.9	53.6%	2.3%

Note: na=not available

SOURCE: "Female Sports Participation: 2004 vs. 1999," National Sporting Goods Association, 2005, http://www.nsga.org/public/pages/index.cfm?pageid=156 (accessed September 22, 2005)

Second on the list was Target, with sporting goods-only sales of $2.6 billion. That total enabled Target to pass the previous year's runner-up, Sports Authority, whose $2.4 billion in sporting goods sales was good for third place in 2004. Dick's Sporting Goods was the only other chain to register over $2 billion in sporting goods sales ($2.1 billion) for the year.

SPORTS FANS

Since 2000 the Gallup Organization has been asking Americans whether or not they are sports fans. A strong majority—between 56% and 66%—has said yes each year, with 63% responding positively in February 2005. (See Figure 2.1.) Table 1.1 in Chapter 1 ranks each sport according to the percentage of people who say they are fans. Gallup data show that men and young people are more likely to be sports fans than women and older people. (See Table 2.11 and Table 2.12.) About three-quarters of men describe themselves as sports fans, while the rate for women is only about one-half. People seem to become less interested in sports as they grow older. Among Americans between the ages of eighteen and twenty-nine, nearly three-fourths (72%) were fans. For the thirty to forty-nine age group, the figure drops to 64%; it decreased further to 58% for those age fifty and above.

While baseball has long been called the national pastime, less than half (48%) of the population considered themselves fans of the professional version of the sport as of February 2005, though the figure has fluctuated quite a bit since Gallup started asking about it in 1993. (See Figure 2.2.) Men are far more likely than

TABLE 2.8

Extreme sports participation, 2004

[U.S. population; six years or older]

Rank	Sport	Number of participants (participated at least once in 2004)
1	Inline skating	17,348,000
2	Skateboarding	11,592,000
3	Paintball	9,640,000
4	Artificial wall climbing	7,659,000
5	Snowboarding	7,110,000
6	Trail running	6,486,000
7	Mountain biking	5,334,000
8	Wakeboarding	2,843,000
9	BMX bicycling	2,642,000
10	Mountain/rock climbing	2,161,000
11	Roller hockey	1,788,000
12	Boardsailing/windsurfing	418,000

SOURCE: "Most Popular Extreme Sports in the USA," in *Extreme Sports: Ranking High in Popularity*, SGMA International, May 31, 2005, http://www.sgma.com/press/2005/press1117636042-19826.html (accessed September 22, 2005)

TABLE 2.9

Lacrosse participation, 2001, 2003 and 2004

Level	2001	2003	2004	% growth
Youth	125,000	150,000	186,048	24.0%
High school	100,925	119,079	133,857	12.4%
College	20,293	24,331	25,671	5.5%
College club	N/A	N/A	10,474	N/A
Professional	150	150	150	Same
Post-collegiate	7,563	8,000	8,635	7.9%
Total	**253,931**	**301,560**	**364,835**	**21.1%**

NA=Not available.

SOURCE: "US Lacrosse Estimate on Number of Lacrosse Players Nationally," in *US Lacrosse Participation Survey: A Review of National Lacrosse Participation in 2004*, US Lacrosse National Headquarters, 2005, http://www.uslacrosse.org/pdf/usl_participationsurvey04.pdf (accessed September 22, 2005)

---

women to be baseball fans, by a 58% to 46% margin. Age is less of a factor; only a slightly higher percentage of eighteen- to twenty-nine-year-olds called themselves fans than in the older brackets. Basketball, meanwhile, has gained on baseball over the years of the survey, with a high of 46% saying they were basketball fans in 1998 and 2000. However, that percentage has decreased; only 38% of those polled in December 2004 said they were basketball fans. (See Figure 2.3.)

Race

Table 2.13 shows that football is the leading sport among both white and nonwhite fans. From there, however, tastes diverge. Nonwhites are nearly twice as likely to call themselves professional basketball fans (63%) as are whites (32%). More than twice as many nonwhites as whites say they are fans of professional wrestling, while whites are nearly twice as likely to identify themselves as hockey fans.

As the percentage of black players in Major League Baseball has declined—from 27% in 1975 to about 10% in 2003, according to a 2003 *Sports Illustrated* article—so has the percentage of African-Americans who consider themselves baseball fans (Tom Verducci, "Blackout: The African-American Baseball Player Is Vanishing. Does He Have a Future?" July 7, 2003). Meanwhile, the number of blacks who play professional football and professional basketball has held steady or grown; in fact, black players now make up majorities in both of those sports.

While Gallup polls over the years have shown a general shift among American sports fans away from baseball and toward basketball and football, the pace of this shift has been even more pronounced among African-Americans. According to Gallup, 43% of blacks named baseball as their favorite sport in 1960, compared to 33% of the overall American public.

TABLE 2.10

Sporting goods sales, by category, 1998–2005

	1998	1999	2000	2001	2002	2003	2004	2005[b]	Change 04 vs 03
Equipment	19,170	20,319	21,603	21,599	21,699	22,394	22,934	23,390	2%
Footwear	13,068	12,546	13,026	13,814	14,144	14,446	14,752	15,002	2%
Clothing	12,884	10,307	11,030	10,217	9,801	10,543	11,201	11,649	6%
Subtotal	45,082	43,172	45,659	45,630	45,644	47,382	48,887	50,041	3%
Recreational transport[a]	24,743	27,965	28,779	28,712	32,106	32,396	35,797	36,733	10%
Total	**69,825**	**71,137**	**74,438**	**74,342**	**77,750**	**79,778**	**84,684**	**86,774**	**6%**

[a]Bicycles, pleasure boats, RVs and snowmobiles; projections provided by other associations.
[b]Projected.

SOURCE: "2004 Consumer Purchases by Category, Sales of Sporting Goods (in millions of dollars), 1998 to 2004 with Projections for 2005," National Sporting Goods Association, 2005, http://www.nsga.org/public/pages/index.cfm?pageid=161 (accessed September 22, 2005)

FIGURE 2.1

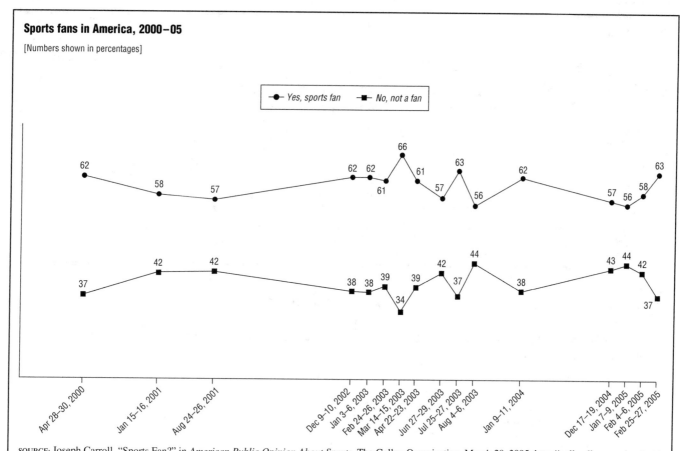

Sports fans in America, 2000–05

[Numbers shown in percentages]

SOURCE: Joseph Carroll, "Sports Fan?" in *American Public Opinion About Sports*, The Gallup Organization, March 29, 2005, http://poll.gallup.com/content/default.aspx?ci=15421&pg=1 (accessed September 22, 2005). Copyright © 2005 by The Gallup Organization. Reproduced by permission of The Gallup Organization.

TABLE 2.11

Sports fans, by gender, 2004

Men	Fans %	Women	Fans %
Professional football	77	Figure skating	60
College football	70	Professional football	51
Professional baseball	58	Professional baseball	46
College basketball	49	College football	39
Professional basketball	42	Professional basketball	36
Professional golf	40	College basketball	32
Auto racing	39	Professional tennis	25
Professional ice hockey	28	Auto racing	22
Professional tennis	24	Professional golf	20
Figure skating	21	Professional ice hockey	18
Professional wrestling	14	Professional wrestling	7

SOURCE: Jeffrey M. Jones, "Sports Fans, by Gender," in *Six in 10 Americans Are Pro Football Fans*, The Gallup Organization, February 4, 2005, http://www.gallup.com/poll/content/?ci=14812&pg=1 (accessed September 22, 2005). Copyright © 2005 by The Gallup Organization. Reproduced by permission of The Gallup Organization.

This strong preference among African-Americans may have been the result of the integration of professional baseball over the previous decade, beginning with Jackie Robinson's 1947 crossing of baseball's "color line," followed by the emergence of such black stars as Willie Mays, Henry Aaron, Ernie Banks, and Frank Robinson.

A Gallup analysis found that by 1985 the percentage of African-Americans calling baseball their favorite sport had fallen to just 17%, a drop that far outpaced the decline among white fans, from 32% to 19% (Jeffrey M. Jones, "The Disappearing Black Baseball Fan," July 15, 2003). Combined polls from 2000 to 2002 demonstrated a continuation of the decline of baseball's popularity among African-Americans. By this time, only 5% said baseball was their favorite sport. Meanwhile, both basketball and football had gained substantial popularity among African-American sports fans: football was the favorite of 31%, and basketball of 37%.

The trend among white fans has been similar in some respects, different in others. According to the Gallup data, the percentage of white fans who reported baseball as their favorite sport dropped from 32% in 1960 to just 13% in 2000–02, while football grew in popularity. The percentage of whites saying football was their favorite

TABLE 2.12

Sports fans, by age, 2004

18- to 29-year-olds		30- to 49-year-olds		50- to 64-year-olds		65 years and older	
Sport	**%**	**Sport**	**%**	**Sport**	**%**	**Sport**	**%**
Professional football	65	Professional football	65	Professional football	63	Professional football	60
College football	56	College football	55	Professional baseball	58	Figure skating	59
Professional basketball	53	Professional baseball	51	College football	52	Professional baseball	56
College basketball	45	College basketball	39	Figure skating	43	College football	54
Professional baseball	41	Auto racing	37	College basketball	39	College basketball	40
Figure skating	29	Figure skating	37	Professional basketball	36	Professional golf	40
Professional ice hockey	27	Professional basketball	34	Auto racing	29	Professional basketball	38
Auto racing	24	Professional golf	28	Professional golf	29	Professional tennis	28
Professional golf	23	Professional ice hockey	27	Professional tennis	24	Auto racing	22
Professional wrestling	23	Professional tennis	26	Professional ice hockey	21	Professional ice hockey	13
Professional tennis	16	Professional wrestling	10	Professional wrestling	7	Professional wrestling	5

SOURCE: Jeffrey M. Jones, "Sports Fans, by Age Group," in *Six in 10 Americans Are Pro Football Fans*, The Gallup Organization, February 4, 2005, http://www.gallup.com/poll/content/?ci=14812&pg=1 (accessed September 22, 2005). Copyright © 2005 by The Gallup Organization. Reproduced by permission of The Gallup Organization.

FIGURE 2.2

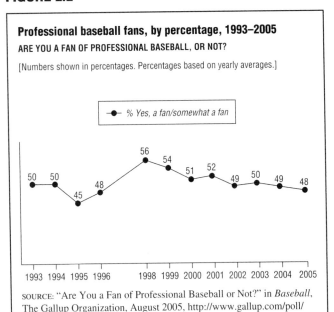

Professional baseball fans, by percentage, 1993–2005

ARE YOU A FAN OF PROFESSIONAL BASEBALL, OR NOT?

[Numbers shown in percentages. Percentages based on yearly averages.]

SOURCE: "Are You a Fan of Professional Baseball or Not?" in *Baseball*, The Gallup Organization, August 2005, http://www.gallup.com/poll/content/?ci=1696&pg=1 (accessed September 22, 2005). Copyright © 2005 by The Gallup Organization. Reproduced by permission of The Gallup Organization.

FIGURE 2.3

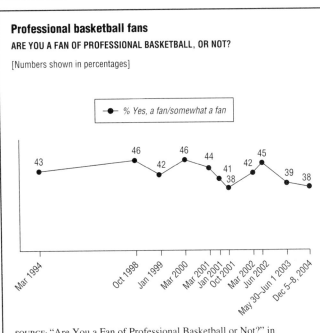

Professional basketball fans

ARE YOU A FAN OF PROFESSIONAL BASKETBALL, OR NOT?

[Numbers shown in percentages]

SOURCE: "Are You a Fan of Professional Basketball or Not?" in *Basketball*, The Gallup Organization, December 2004, http://www.gallup.com/poll/content/?ci=1699&pg=1 (accessed September 22, 2005). Copyright © 2004 by The Gallup Organization. Reproduced by permission of The Gallup Organization.

sport rose from 22% in 1960 to 33% by 2000–02. Unlike African-Americans, white sports fans did not flock to basketball in huge numbers during the same period. Gallup polls show that from 1960 to 2002, the percentage of whites calling basketball their favorite sport has remained fairly level, increasing from just 10% to 12% over that span.

Despite some similarities in these trends, the contrast between the sports preferences of white and black fans is fairly striking. Combined Gallup data from 2002 and 2003 show that when asked simply whether they are baseball fans and whether they are basketball fans, white respondents gave baseball an edge over basketball, 39% to 28%. Nearly twice as many African-American respondents said they were basketball fans (60%) as said they were baseball fans (33%). Jones's analysis of these results suggests two possible reasons for the differences:

- The dominance of professional basketball by African-American players; and

- The relative lack of baseball facilities and programs in urban areas with predominantly African-American populations.

TABLE 2.13

Sports fans, by race, 2004

Whites	%	Nonwhites	%
Professional football	62	Professional football	71
College football	53	Professional basketball	63
Professional baseball	52	College football	60
Figure skating	41	College basketball	53
College basketball	37	Professional baseball	52
Professional basketball	32	Figure skating	42
Auto racing	32	Professional tennis	35
Professional golf	30	Professional golf	27
Professional ice hockey	25	Auto racing	23
Professional tennis	21	Professional wrestling	20
Professional wrestling	8	Professional ice hockey	13

SOURCE: Jeffrey M. Jones, "Sports Fans, by Race," in *Six in 10 Americans Are Pro Football Fans*, The Gallup Organization, February 4, 2005, http://www.gallup.com/poll/content/?ci=14812&pg=1 (accessed September 22, 2005). Copyright © 2005 by The Gallup Organization. Reproduced by permission of The Gallup Organization.

Geography

Professional football is at or near the top in every part of the country. In the South, nearly as many people like college football as follow the professionals. In the West, baseball ranks a very close second to pro football. Interestingly, auto racing, considered a southern sport in the public imagination, is more or less equally popular across the country, though its fan base lags slightly in the West. (See Table 2.14.)

SPORTS ATTENDANCE

Attendance trends vary considerably from one sport to another, and in general one sport's loss, whether due to scandal or declining interest, translates into another sport's gain. Professional sports teams rely on revenue from ticket sales to cover much of the cost of the huge salaries they pay their players. At the college level, ticket sales are a big part of what keeps university athletic programs solvent.

Major Sports

BASEBALL. While the national pastime seems to have lost some of its luster in terms of participation and self-identified fan base, the public is still taking itself out to the ballgame in big numbers, according to statistics reported on ESPN.com. (See Table 2.15.) Nearly seventy-five million fans attended Major League Baseball games during the 2005 regular season, a new record and a 2.6% jump from the previous year. Average attendance at MLB games for the year was 30,970, which amounted to 559 more spectators per game than in 2004. Six different teams topped the three-million mark; one of them, the St. Louis Cardinals, accomplished this in one of the leagues smaller markets. One team, the New York Yankees, drew more than four million fans during the season, and averaged better than 50,000 per game, only the third team in history to crack the four-million barrier. No other team has achieved a higher season total or per-game average since 1993. Other top drawers were the Los Angeles Dodgers, whose season attendance figure was 3.6 million; the Los Angeles Angels, at 3.4 million; and the San Francisco Giants and Chicago Cubs, each of which drew 3.1 million paying customers. Only two teams drew fewer than 20,000 fans per game to the stadium. The Tampa Bay Devil Rays recorded attendance of only 1.1 million for the season, for a per-game average of just over 14,000, making them the only team whose stadium was less than half full for an average game. In addition, the Kansas City Royals drew only 1.4 million spectators over the course of the 2005 regular season, averaging a crowd of 17,356 per game. Nevertheless, it was a strong showing for a league still reeling from bad publicity related to revelations of steroid use among top players—a topic that will be discussed in more detail in Chapters 4 and 9.

BASKETBALL. Professional basketball is enjoying strong ticket sales in the 2000s. Attendance at NBA games

TABLE 2.14

Sports fans, by region, 2004

East		Midwest		South		West	
Sport	**%**	**Sport**	**%**	**Sport**	**%**	**Sport**	**%**
Professional football	68	Professional football	68	College football	62	Professional football	60
Professional baseball	58	College football	55	Professional football	60	Professional baseball	57
College football	47	Figure skating	44	Professional baseball	52	Professional basketball	50
Figure skating	40	Professional baseball	43	College basketball	45	College football	49
College basketball	34	College basketball	40	Professional basketball	38	Figure skating	46
Professional basketball	32	Professional basketball	35	Figure skating	37	College basketball	40
Auto racing	32	Auto racing	31	Auto racing	32	Professional golf	31
Professional golf	30	Professional ice hockey	29	Professional golf	30	Professional tennis	26
Professional ice hockey	25	Professional golf	27	Professional tennis	25	Auto racing	25
Professional tennis	24	Professional tennis	22	Professional ice hockey	17	Professional ice hockey	22
Professional wrestling	10	Professional wrestling	11	Professional wrestling	11	Professional wrestling	9

SOURCE: Jeffrey M. Jones, "Sports Fans, by Region," in *Six in 10 Americans Are Pro Football Fans*, The Gallup Organization, February 4, 2005, http://www.gallup.com/poll/content/?ci=14812&pg=1 (accessed September 22, 2005). Copyright © 2005 by The Gallup Organization. Reproduced by permission of The Gallup Organization.

TABLE 2.15

Major League Baseball attendance, 2005

Rank	Team	Home			Road		Overall	
		Games	Total	Average	Games	Average	Games	Average
1	NY Yankees	81	4,090,440	50,499	80	37,036	161	43,809
2	LA Dodgers	81	3,603,680	44,489	80	32,498	161	38,531
3	St. Louis	80	3,491,837	43,647	81	30,611	161	37,089
4	LA Angels	81	3,404,686	42,033	79	30,684	160	36,429
5	San Francisco	80	3,140,781	39,259	80	31,695	160	35,477
6	Chicago Cubs	80	3,100,262	38,753	80	36,389	160	37,571
7	San Diego	80	2,832,039	35,400	80	31,642	160	33,521
8	NY Mets	79	2,782,212	35,217	81	35,023	160	35,119
9	Boston	80	2,813,354	35,166	81	37,735	161	36,459
10	Houston	80	2,762,472	34,530	80	30,652	160	32,591
11	Washington	80	2,692,123	33,651	80	32,055	160	32,853
12	Seattle	80	2,689,529	33,619	81	27,604	161	30,593
13	Philadelphia	80	2,665,301	33,316	80	29,147	160	31,232
14	Baltimore	81	2,624,804	32,404	80	30,441	161	31,429
15	Atlanta	80	2,521,534	31,519	80	32,811	160	32,165
16	Texas	79	2,486,925	31,480	81	27,126	160	29,275
17	Chicago Sox	81	2,342,834	28,923	79	28,004	160	28,470
18	Milwaukee	81	2,211,023	27,296	80	29,421	161	28,352
19	Oakland	81	2,109,298	26,040	80	29,814	161	27,915
20	Arizona	81	2,059,331	25,423	79	32,229	160	28,783
21	Detroit	80	2,024,505	25,306	78	26,437	158	25,864
22	Minnesota	80	2,013,453	25,168	81	27,368	161	26,275
23	Toronto	80	1,977,949	24,724	81	29,899	161	27,328
24	Cleveland	80	1,973,185	24,664	81	27,432	161	26,057
25	Cincinnati	81	1,943,157	23,989	79	32,246	160	28,066
26	Colorado	80	1,915,586	23,944	80	31,175	160	27,559
27	Pittsburgh	78	1,794,237	23,003	81	33,016	159	28,104
28	Florida	80	1,823,388	22,792	80	32,856	160	27,824
29	Kansas City	79	1,371,181	17,356	80	25,906	159	21,658
30	Tampa Bay	80	1,124,189	14,052	81	29,235	161	21,691

SOURCE: "MLB Attendance Report: 2005," ESPN, 2005, http://sports.espn.go.com/mlb/attendance (accessed October 7, 2005)

during the 2004–05 regular season reached nearly 21.3 million, breaking the league's previous record of 20.5 million, set during the 1995–96 season according to *USA Today*. Figures from ESPN.com indicate that the defending champion Detroit Pistons (who surrendered their crown to the San Antonio Spurs in 2005) led the pack in home attendance for the season, drawing a total home-court crowd of 905,119, or an average of 22,076 over the course of their forty-one home games. (See Table 2.16.) The Chicago Bulls and Dallas Mavericks were second and third respectively, each enjoying average home game attendance of more than 20,000. The New Orleans Hornets finished at the bottom of the league in attendance numbers. Hornets crowds averaged 14,221 per game, for a season total of 583,070. Also near the bottom were the Charlotte Bobcats, which averaged 14,431 attendees per game; and the Atlanta Hawks, at 14,456.

On a team-by-team basis, attendance in the NBA has a lot to do with the success of the team and the size of the city. It is not difficult to predict that a winning team in a large city is likely to sell more tickets than a lousy team in a small market. Perhaps more than any other sport, however, professional basketball attendance is influenced by personalities. The acquisition of a truly high-profile player—a Shaquille O'Neal or Tracy McGrady, for instance—can lead to a spike in ticket sales for the star's

new team. Periodically, a player or set of players emerges with such charisma that the entire league's attendance numbers benefit. This was the case in the 1980s, when the ongoing rivalry between Magic Johnson's Los Angeles Lakers and Larry Bird's Boston Celtics spurred a surge of interest throughout the league.

FOOTBALL. The NFL also set a new overall attendance record for the 2004 regular season. League-wide, an average of 66,409 fans attended NFL games, for a total paid attendance of 17,000,811 for the season, according to United Press International. This total barely surpassed 2003's mark of 16,913,584.

According to attendance figures reported on ESPN.com, the Washington Redskins led the league in attendance. (See Table 2.17.) The pride of the nation's capital attracted 702,670 paying customers over the course of its eight home games in 2004, for an average of 87,833 fans per game. New York City is a big enough market not only to have two NFL squads—the Jets and the Giants—but to have those two teams place second and third in attendance. (Both the Jets and the Giants play their home games at The Meadowlands stadium in East Rutherford, New Jersey, just across the Hudson River from New York City.) The Jets drew a total of 623,181 fans to their 2004 home games, for an average of 77,897

TABLE 2.16

NBA attendance, 2004–05 season

Rank	Team	Home			Road			Overall		
		Games	Total	Average	Games	Total	Average	Games	Total	Average
1	Detroit	41	905,119	22,076	41	732,588	17,868	82	1,637,707	19,972
2	Chicago	41	828,384	20,204	41	710,733	17,334	82	1,539,117	18,769
3	Dallas	41	822,533	20,061	41	707,622	17,259	82	1,530,155	18,660
4	Miami	41	815,143	19,881	41	774,551	18,891	82	1,589,694	19,386
5	New York	41	800,144	19,515	41	719,159	17,540	82	1,519,303	18,528
6	Cleveland	41	784,249	19,128	41	749,302	18,275	82	1,533,551	18,701
7	LA Lakers	41	770,494	18,792	41	771,217	18,810	82	1,541,711	18,801
8	Utah	41	769,014	18,756	41	693,864	16,923	82	1,462,878	17,839
9	San Antonio	41	750,970	18,316	41	714,207	17,419	82	1,465,177	17,868
10	Philadelphia	41	732,686	17,870	41	735,288	17,933	82	1,467,974	17,902
11	Phoenix	41	726,066	17,708	41	720,410	17,570	82	1,446,476	17,639
12	Denver	41	723,949	17,657	41	717,775	17,506	82	1,441,724	17,582
13	Sacramento	41	709,997	17,317	41	725,815	17,702	82	1,435,812	17,509
14	Washington	41	705,069	17,196	41	691,351	16,862	82	1,396,420	17,029
15	Minnesota	41	704,438	17,181	41	732,847	17,874	82	1,437,285	17,527
16	Toronto	41	703,388	17,155	41	683,787	16,677	82	1,387,175	16,916
17	Indiana	41	696,764	16,944	41	692,711	16,895	82	1,389,475	16,944
18	LA Clippers	41	696,181	16,980	41	686,139	16,735	82	1,382,320	16,857
19	Memphis	41	691,362	16,862	41	681,487	16,621	82	1,372,849	16,742
20	Portland	41	680,374	16,594	41	683,013	16,658	82	1,363,387	16,626
21	Seattle	41	675,490	16,475	41	698,216	17,029	82	1,373,706	16,752
22	Golden State	41	670,368	16,350	41	685,060	16,708	82	1,355,428	16,529
23	Houston	41	663,444	16,181	41	745,536	18,183	82	1,408,980	17,182
24	Boston	41	656,081	16,001	41	705,864	17,216	82	1,361,945	16,609
25	Milwaukee	41	637,009	15,536	41	689,065	16,806	82	1,326,074	16,171
26	New Jersey	41	618,677	15,089	41	681,623	16,624	82	1,300,300	15,857
27	Orlando	41	597,942	14,583	41	717,914	17,510	82	1,315,856	16,047
28	Atlanta	41	592,729	14,456	41	685,959	16,730	82	1,278,688	15,593
29	Charlotte	41	591,701	14,431	41	685,409	16,717	82	1,277,110	15,574
30	New Orleans	41	583,070	14,221	41	684,323	16,690	82	1,267,393	15,456

SOURCE: Adapted from "NBA Attendance," ESPN, 2005, http://sports.espn.go.com/nba/attendance?year=2005 (accessed September 22, 2005)

customers per game. The Giants drew 629,874 paying customers during the regular season, an average of 78,734 per game. As with all spectator sports, one of the most important factors in an NFL team's attendance—along with market size and personalities—is team performance. The Arizona Cardinals, with a lackluster six wins and ten losses for the season, finished last in terms of attendance: they averaged 37,533 spectators per game, by far the worst in the National Football League. In addition, their seasonal paid attendance figure of 300,267 was less than half that of the league's leaders.

The Super Bowl, which determines the NFL champion from among the champions of its two conferences, is much more about TV viewing than about live attendance. Its paid attendees are limited by the size of the venue, which changes each year. Super Bowl XXXIX brought 78,125 ticket-holders to Alltel Stadium in Jacksonville, Florida, in 2005 to see the New England Patriots win their second consecutive NFL title. This was nowhere near record attendance for a Super Bowl; in 1980, 103,985 spectators packed the Rose Bowl in Pasadena, California, to watch the Pittsburgh Steelers defeat the Los Angeles Rams in Super Bowl XIV.

HOCKEY. National Hockey League attendance for the 2004–05 season was zero; the season was cancelled due to labor turmoil (see Chapter 4 for details). ESPN reported total attendance for the 2003–04 NHL season as just over 20.3 million. The total was about 13,000 less than in 2000–01 and has decreased slightly in each season since. The average paid crowd for an NHL game in 2003–04 was 16,534. The top draw was the Montreal Canadiens with 842,767 spectators over the course of the season, for an average of 20,555 per home game. The only other team to attract more than 20,000 fans per game was the Detroit Red Wings, a perennial powerhouse. The Red Wings' total paid attendance for the season was 802,640. The Pittsburgh Penguins had the poorest turnout for the season, with total attendance of 486,961. Two of the league's newer markets—located in southern states not known for interest in winter sports—fared only slightly better than the Penguins. The Carolina Hurricanes actually drew fewer fans than the Penguins, but did so with one fewer home game, giving them a better per-game average. The Nashville Predators just managed to surpass the half-million mark for the season, with 527,091 total paid attendance. (See Table 2.18.)

The NHL owners' lockout of the players and subsequent cancellation of the 2004–05 season could potentially have a long-term devastating impact on professional hockey attendance. Players and owners

TABLE 2.17

National Football League attendance, 2004

Rank	Team	Home			Road			Overall		
		Games	Total	Average	Games	Total	Average	Games	Total	Average
1	Washington	8	702,670	87,833	8	537,559	67,194	16	1,240,229	77,514
2	NY Giants	8	629,874	78,734	8	530,816	66,352	16	1,160,690	72,543
3	NY Jets	8	623,181	77,897	8	509,622	63,702	16	1,132,803	70,800
4	Kansas City	8	623,010	77,876	8	527,718	65,964	16	1,150,728	71,920
5	Denver	8	601,031	75,128	8	539,587	67,448	16	1,140,618	71,288
6	Carolina	8	586,259	73,282	8	545,850	68,231	16	1,132,109	70,756
7	Cleveland	8	584,840	73,105	8	556,930	69,616	16	1,141,770	71,360
8	Miami	8	580,808	72,601	8	563,061	70,382	16	1,143,869	71,491
9	Buffalo	8	574,399	71,799	8	538,132	67,266	16	1,112,531	69,533
10	Houston	8	565,192	70,649	8	544,857	68,107	16	1,110,049	69,378
11	Atlanta	8	564,829	70,603	8	568,377	71,047	16	1,133,206	70,825
12	Green Bay	8	564,400	70,550	8	548,169	68,521	16	1,112,569	69,535
13	Baltimore	8	558,594	69,824	8	564,694	70,586	16	1,123,288	70,205
14	Jacksonville	8	555,464	69,433	8	496,092	62,011	16	1,051,556	65,722
15	Tennessee	8	551,210	68,901	8	500,522	62,565	16	1,051,732	65,733
16	New England	8	550,048	68,756	8	558,162	69,770	16	1,108,210	69,263
17	Philadelphia	8	540,870	67,608	8	561,973	70,246	16	1,102,843	68,927
18	Seattle	8	533,436	66,679	8	506,911	63,363	16	1,040,347	65,021
19	St. Louis	8	527,384	65,923	8	533,617	66,702	16	1,061,001	66,312
20	Cincinnati	8	524,248	65,531	8	575,138	71,892	16	1,099,386	68,711
21	Tampa Bay	8	522,720	65,340	8	523,354	65,419	16	1,046,074	65,379
22	San Francisco	8	518,271	64,783	8	506,704	63,338	16	1,024,975	64,060
23	New Orleans	8	513,178	64,147	8	471,918	58,989	16	985,096	61,568
24	Minnesota	8	512,969	64,121	8	532,536	66,567	16	1,045,505	65,344
25	Dallas	8	510,892	63,861	8	575,112	71,889	16	1,086,004	67,875
26	Pittsburgh	8	507,385	63,423	8	574,856	71,857	16	1,082,241	67,640
27	Detroit	8	499,162	62,395	8	544,319	68,039	16	1,043,481	65,217
28	Chicago	8	495,706	61,963	8	541,641	67,705	16	1,037,347	64,834
29	San Diego	8	485,462	60,682	8	542,242	67,780	16	1,027,704	64,231
30	Indianapolis	8	456,791	57,098	8	560,040	70,005	16	1,016,831	63,551
31	Oakland	8	405,936	50,742	8	551,687	68,960	16	957,623	59,851
32	Arizona	8	300,267	37,533	8	538,290	67,286	16	838,557	52,409

SOURCE: Adapted from "NFL Attendance," ESPN, 2005, http://sports.espn.go.com/nfl/attendance?year=2004 (accessed September 22, 2005)

managed to reach an agreement on their labor issues in time to start the 2005–06 season on schedule, but few involved in the game seemed convinced that hockey fans were ready to forgive and forget. As players and management prepared for the new season, a number of measures were taken designed to entice fans back into the arenas. One fan-friendly rule change was the elimination of ties. Games still deadlocked after the completion of overtime are now to be decided by shootout. Other rule changes were designed to boost scoring, including a reduction in the size of goalie equipment and deeming certain areas in the corner of the rink off-limits to goalies. Above all, most teams reduced their ticket prices, a move made possible in part by a substantial lowering of salary caps, a clear-cut victory for the team owners.

SOCCER. Even as soccer emerges as a major sport in the United States, attendance at Major League Soccer games has stagnated over the last several years. MLS games drew crowds totaling 2.3 million for the 2004 regular season, according to MLS data as reported on SI.com, the Web site of *Sports Illustrated* magazine. This figure represented an improvement over the previous year, when 2.2 million spectators attended MLS games, but was still well below the 2.7 million paying customers

that watched professional soccer annually during most of the late 1990s. Overall attendance fell more than 10% between 1996 and 2004. MLS games attracted an average crowd of 15,559 in 2004. The top drawing team that year was the Los Angeles Galaxy, whose attendance for fifteen home games reached a total of 357,137 or an average 23,809 per game. The league's poorest drawing team was the Dallas Burn, whose games were attended by only 136,319 fans over the course of the entire 2004 regular season.

AUTO RACING. Auto racing has been enjoying a surge in popularity during the 2000s. The most prominent auto racing event in the United States is the Indianapolis 500, which is run Memorial Day weekend each year at Indianapolis Motor Speedway. The 2005 race was the 89th Indy 500. The Indy 500 does not release official attendance figures, but the *Indianapolis Star* estimated that about 250,000 fans packed the grandstand for the 2005 event. MSNBC predicted turnout closer to 300,000. The 2005 Indy 500 was probably better attended than most, in part due to the presence of female rookie Danica Patrick, a driver with both the skills to interest hardcore racing fans and the personal appeal to interest countless additional fans who are usually lukewarm to racing.

TABLE 2.18

NHL attendance, 2003–04 season

Rank	Team	Home			Road		Overall	
		Games	Total	Average	Games	Average	Games	Average
1	Montreal	41	842,767	20,555	41	17,482	82	19,018
2	Detroit	40	802,640	20,066	40	17,911	80	18,988
3	Toronto	41	794,439	19,376	39	16,893	80	18,165
4	Philadelphia	41	794,388	19,375	40	16,372	81	17,892
5	Vancouver	39	726,607	18,630	40	16,815	79	17,711
6	St. Louis	41	760,976	18,560	39	16,558	80	17,584
7	Minnesota	40	741,208	18,530	41	16,206	81	17,353
8	Dallas	40	734,024	18,350	41	16,446	81	17,386
9	NY Rangers	37	668,737	18,073	41	17,011	78	17,515
10	Colorado	40	720,280	18,007	38	17,664	78	17,839
11	Los Angeles	40	714,215	17,855	39	16,220	79	17,048
12	Tampa Bay	41	730,634	17,820	40	16,021	81	16,932
13	Ottawa	41	728,101	17,758	41	15,771	82	16,764
14	Edmonton	40	707,941	17,698	38	16,549	78	17,138
15	Columbus	38	658,897	17,339	41	16,065	79	16,678
16	Calgary	40	664,038	16,600	40	16,982	80	16,791
17	Florida	40	636,176	15,904	40	15,708	80	15,806
18	San Jose	41	649,261	15,835	39	16,069	80	15,949
19	Phoenix	37	576,914	15,592	41	15,799	78	15,701
20	Buffalo	40	613,726	15,343	41	16,010	81	15,680
21	Atlanta	41	619,965	15,121	39	16,299	80	15,695
22	Boston	39	587,744	15,070	41	16,594	80	15,851
23	Anaheim	41	614,476	14,987	40	16,710	81	15,838
24	New Jersey	39	581,599	14,912	40	16,715	79	15,825
25	Washington	41	603,528	14,720	41	16,319	82	15,519
26	NY Islanders	40	537,264	13,431	40	16,537	80	14,984
27	Chicago	41	543,374	13,253	40	16,763	81	14,986
28	Nashville	40	527,091	13,177	40	16,667	80	14,922
29	Carolina	40	486,870	12,171	40	16,219	80	14,195
30	Pittsburgh	41	486,961	11,877	40	16,652	81	14,235

SOURCE: Adapted from "NHL Attendance Leaders," ESPN, 2004, http://sports.espn.go.com/nhl/attendance?year=2004 (accessed September 22, 2005)

However, the Indy Racing League (IRL) is only one faction of the broader auto racing scene. There is also NASCAR, which has become such a phenomenon that its followers (a.k.a. NASCAR Dads) are now viewed by political analysts as a powerful voting bloc alongside "soccer moms." The Super Bowl of the NASCAR circuit is the Daytona 500, run in February at the Daytona International Speedway in Florida. Like the Indy 500, exact attendance figures for Daytona are not released, but ESPN estimates that 200,000 people attend the event annually. In addition to the IndyCar and NASCAR circuits, there are the Champ Car (formerly known as CART) Series, Formula One Grand Prix series, the National Hot Rod Association (NHRA), and various smaller racing circuits. NASCAR has by far the greatest overall attendance numbers, drawing 4.4 million spectators in 2004 according to Kagan Research, a major tracker of sports market numbers. Table 2.19 shows attendance figures for the various auto racing circuits.

OTHER SPORTS. One can assume that what draws those hundreds of thousands of spectators to auto races like the Indy 500 each year is the speed—the experience of watching people hurtle around a track at well over two hundred miles per hour. However, people also jam the

TABLE 2.19

Auto racing attendance, 2004

Race cars	2004 attendance (in millions)
NASCAR Nextel Cup	4.4
NHRA drag cars*	2.1
Champ Car	1.9
NASCAR Busch	2.5
SCCA Trans Am	0.6
IRL (Indy Racing League)	1.2
NASCAR Trucks	1.0
American Le Mans	0.5
Auto Racing Club	0.4
Toyota Atlantic	1.1

*NHRA is National Hot Rod Association.

SOURCE: "Rolling It In," Kagan Research, LLC, sidebar in John W. Schoen, "Auto Racing Revs Up Revenues, Profits," *MSNBC Online,* May 28, 2005, http://www.msnbc.msn.com/id/8007370 (accessed September 12, 2005)

streets of Boston each year to watch a race in which the fastest entrant averages a mere twelve miles an hour. That race, of course, is the Boston Marathon, the most famous marathon in the world. Each year, according to the Boston Athletic Association, about half a million spectators line the streets along the marathon's 26.2–mile route to encourage the racers to ignore their agony and persevere. Few other sports in the world are witnessed live by as many people as is the Boston Marathon.

Table 2.20 presents information on frequency of attendance at sporting events by adults as reported in the Census Bureau's *Statistical Abstract of the United States: 2004–2005*. These figures are based on data from Mediamark Research, Inc., and drawn on survey data compiled in 2003. Baseball was the sport that by far the most respondents said they had attended: 12.64% said they had attended baseball, yet about two-thirds of those who had attended baseball had gone to a baseball game less then once a month. High school sports were also popular: 5.49% of respondents reported attending high school sporting events at least once a month, and another 3.76% said they watched high school sports though less than once a month. College football and college basketball were also attended in large numbers: 7.15% attended college football, and 5.17% attended college basketball. Such individual sports as bowling, golf, and tennis may be popular games to play, but they do not draw large attendance. Just over 2% of survey respondents had attended a bowling event; about 2.7% had attended golf; and 1.75% attended tennis matches. Soccer attendance was surprisingly low, given the number of youth soccer players nationwide. Only 3.16% of adults reported having attended a soccer match in 2003. Table 2.21 puts some of this information in historical perspective, comparing 2003 attendance at selected sports with attendance during previous years dating back to 1985.

TABLE 2.20

Adult attendance at sports events, by frequency, 2003

[In thousands (9,438 represents 9,438,000), except percent]

Event	Attend one or more times a month		Attend less than once a month	
	Number	Percent	Number	Percent
Baseball	9,438	4.50	17,063	8.14
Basketball				
College games	4,264	2.03	6,583	3.14
Professional games	3,517	1.68	7,767	3.70
Bowling	1,721	0.82	2,849	1.36
Boxing	865	0.41	2,335	1.11
Equestrian events	857	0.41	2,456	1.17
Figure skating	626	0.30	2,407	1.15
Fishing tournaments	685	0.33	2,210	1.05
Football				
College games	5,620	2.68	9,371	4.47
Monday night professional games	2,038	0.97	3,458	1.65
Weekend professional games	3,939	1.88	7,936	3.79
Golf	1,642	0.78	4,167	1.99
High school sports	11,501	5.49	7,892	3.76
Horse racing				
Flats, runners	1,004	0.48	2,920	1.39
Trotters/harness	455	0.22	2,109	1.01
Ice hockey	2,542	1.21	6,717	3.20
Motorcycle racing	792	0.38	2,392	1.14
Pro beach volleyball	338	0.16	1,903	0.91
Rodeo	633	0.30	4,304	2.05
Soccer	3,220	1.54	3,403	1.62
Tennis	810	0.39	2,847	1.36
Truck and tractor pull/mud racing	606	0.29	3,450	1.65
Wrestling—professional	1,071	0.51	2,781	1.33

SOURCE: "No. 1237. Adult Attendance at Sports Events by Frequency: 2003," in *Statistical Abstract of the United States: 2004–2005*, U.S. Census Bureau, August 2005, http://www.census.gov/prod/2004pubs/04statab/arts.pdf (accessed September 22, 2005).

TABLE 2.21

Attendance at selected spectator sports, 1985–2003

[47,742 represents 47,742,000]

Sport	Unit	1985	1990	1995	1999	2000	2001	2002	2003
Baseball, major leagues									
Attendance	1,000	47,742	55,512	51,288	71,558	74,339	73,881	69,428	69,501
Regular season	1,000	46,824	54,824	50,469	70,139	72,748	72,267	67,859	67,568
National League	1,000	22,292	24,492	25,110	38,323	39,851	39,558	36,949	36,661
American League	1,000	24,532	30,332	25,359	31,817	32,898	32,709	30,910	30,908
Playoffs[a]	1,000	591	479	533	1,202	1,314	1,247	1,262	1,568
World Series	1,000	327	209	286	216	277	366	306	365
Players' salaries									
Average	$1,000	371	598	1,111	1,607	1,896	2,139	2,296	2,372
Basketball[b]									
NCAA—Men's college									
Teams	Number	753	767	868	926	932	937	936	967
Attendance	1,000	26,584	28,741	28,548	28,505	29,025	28,949	29,395	30,124
NCAA—Women's college									
Teams	Number	746	782	864	940	956	958	975	1,009
Attendance	1,000	2,072	2,777	4,962	8,010	8,698	8,825	9,533	10,164
Pro									
Teams	Number	23	27	27	29	29	29	29	29
Attendance, total[c]	1,000	11,534	18,586	19,883	13,450	21,503	21,436	21,571	21,760
Regular season	1,000	10,506	17,369	18,516	12,135	20,059	19,956	20,182	20,074
Average per game	Number	11,141	15,690	16,727	16,738	16,870	16,784	16,974	16,883
Playoffs	1,000	985	1,203	1,347	1,315	1,427	1,460	1,370	1,685
Average per game	Number	14,479	16,704	18,457	19,926	19,202	20,565	19,296	19,152
Football									
NCAA college									
Teams	Number	509	533	565	601	606	608	617	617
Attendance	1,000	34,952	35,330	35,638	39,483	39,059	40,481	44,556	46,145
National Football League									
Teams	Number	28	28	30	32	31	31	32	32
Attendance, total[d]	1,000	14,058	17,666	19,203	20,763	20,954	20,590	21,505	21,639
Regular season	1,000	13,345	13,960	15,044	16,207	16,387	16,166	16,833	16,914
Average per game	Number	59,567	62,321	62,682	65,349	66,078	65,187	65,755	66,328
Postseason games[e]	1,000	711	848	(NA)	794	809	767	782	806
Players' salaries									
Average	$1,000	217	354	584	708	787	986	1,180	1,259
Median base salary	$1,000	160	275	301	400	441	501	568	590
National Hockey League[f]									
Regular season attendance	1,000	11,634	12,580	9,234	17,152	18,800	20,373	20,615	20,409
Playoffs attendance	1,000	1,108	1,356	1,329	1,472	1,525	1,584	1,691	1,636
Horseracing[g]									
Racing days	Number	13,745	13,841	13,243	11,398	11,348	(NA)	(NA)	(NA)
Attendance	1,000	73,346	63,803	38,934	(NA)	(NA)	(NA)	(NA)	(NA)
Pari-mutuel turnover	Million dollars	12,222	7,162	14,592	15,828	16,040	(NA)	(NA)	(NA)
Revenue to government	Million dollars	625	624	456	392	368	(NA)	(NA)	(NA)
Greyhound									
Total performances	Number	9,590	14,915	16,110	14,455	14,403	(NA)	(NA)	(NA)
Attendance	1,000	23,853	28,660	(NA)	(NA)	(NA)	(NA)	(NA)	(NA)
Pari-mutuel turnover	Million dollars	2,702	3,422	2,730	2,130	2,054	(NA)	(NA)	(NA)
Revenue to government	Million dollars	201	235	157	101	98	(NA)	(NA)	(NA)

TABLE 2.21

Attendance at selected spectator sports, 1985–2003 [CONTINUED]

[47,742 represents 47,742,000]

Sport	Unit	1985	1990	1995	1999	2000	2001	2002	2003
Jai alai									
Total performances	Number	2,736	3,620	2,748	2,119	2,034	(NA)	(NA)	(NA)
Games played	Number	32,260	(NA)	37,052	28,706	27,461	(NA)	(NA)	(NA)
Attendance	1,000	4,722	5,329	3,208	(NA)	(NA)	(NA)	(NA)	(NA)
Total handle	Million dollars	664	546	296	119	1,959	(NA)	(NA)	(NA)
Revenue to government	Million dollars	50	39	13	5	4	(NA)	(NA)	(NA)
Professional rodeo									
Rodeos	Number	617	754	739	700	688	668	666	657
Performances	Number	1,887	2,159	2,217	2,128	2,081	2,015	2,207	1,949
Members	Number	5,239	5,693	6,894	7,403	6,255	5,913	6,209	6,158
Permit-holders (rookies)	Number	2,534	3,290	3,835	3,511	3,249	2,544	2,543	3,121
Total prize money	Million dollars	15.1	18.2	24.5	31.1	32.3	33.1	33.3	34.3

Note: NA=Not available.
[a]Beginning 1997, two rounds of playoffs were played. Prior years had one round.
[b]Season ending in year shown.
[c]Includes All-Star game, not shown separately.
[d]Beginning 1987 includes preseason attendance, not shown separately.
[e]Includes Pro Bowl, a nonchampionship game and Super Bowl.
[f]For season ending in year shown.
[g]Includes thoroughbred, harness, quarter horse, and fairs.

SOURCE: "No. 1239. Selected Spectator Sports: 1985 to 2003," in *Statistical Abstract of the United States: 2004–2005*, U.S. Census Bureau, August 2005, http://www.census.gov/prod/2004pubs/04statab/arts.pdf (accessed September 22, 2005)

CHAPTER 3
SPORTS AND THE MEDIA

Sports and media are so thoroughly intertwined in the United States that it is difficult to think of them as two distinct industries. The financial relationship is complex and reciprocal. Media enterprises, mostly broadcast and cable television stations but also Web-based, pay the sports leagues millions of dollars for the rights to broadcast their games. Leagues distribute this money to their member teams—the distribution formula varies from sport to sport—which then transfer much of that money to their players in the form of salaries. Those media outlets, which have just paid a great deal of money for the rights to broadcast sports, try to recoup those expenditures by selling advertising time during sports broadcasts to companies that believe their products will appeal to the kinds of people who like to watch sports on television. These consumer product companies also pay large sums to individual athletes to endorse their products, or in some cases to teams to display their company logos on their uniforms or, in the case of auto racing, on their cars. Consumers then purchase these products, providing the money the companies use to buy advertising and pay for celebrity endorsements. The more people who watch a sport, the more the station can charge for advertising. The more the station can charge for advertising, the more they can offer the league for broadcast rights. The more the league gets for broadcast rights, the more the teams can pay their players. It would be nice, at least from the team owners' perspective, if it followed that the more the team pays its players, the better the players play; but unfortunately, it does not always work out that way.

THE HISTORY OF SPORTS ON TELEVISION

According to pioneering television sports director Harry Coyle, "Television got off the ground because of sports. Today, maybe, sports need television to survive, but it was just the opposite when it first started. When we (NBC) put on the World Series in 1947, heavyweight fights, the Army-Navy football game, the sales of televi-

sion sets just spurted" ("Sports and Television," Museum of Broadcast Communications, http://www.museum.tv/).

While it may be an exaggeration to credit the explosive growth of television in its early days solely to sports, sports certainly played a significant role. The first-ever televised sporting event was a 1939 baseball game between Columbia and Princeton universities. It was covered by one camera, positioned along the third base line. The first network-wide sports broadcast came five years later with the premier of NBC's *Gillette Cavalcade of Sports*, the first installment of which featured a featherweight championship boxing match between Willie Pep and Chalky Wright. Sports quickly became a staple of primetime network fare, accounting for up to one-third of primetime programming, but other genres began to catch up in the 1950s, perhaps spurred on by an increase in female viewers. The *Gillette Cavalcade of Sports* remained on the air for twenty years, before giving way to a new model in which sports programs were sponsored by multiple buyers of advertising spots rather than by a single corporation, as the cost of sponsorship became prohibitively expensive in the mid-1960s. The number of hours of sports programming on the networks continued to increase dramatically well into the 1980s, when advertising dollars generated by sports began to decline, making them less profitable for the networks to carry.

The amount of money involved in televising sports was growing fast by the 1970s. In 1970, according to the Museum of Broadcast Communications article, the networks paid $50 million for the right to broadcast National Football League games, $2 million to air the National Basketball Association, and $18 million for Major League Baseball broadcast rights. By 1985 those numbers had grown to $450 million for football, $45 million for basketball, and $160 million for baseball. This explosive growth was fueled by a combination of growing public interest, better—and therefore more expensive—coverage of events by the networks, and an effort on the part of the networks to lock in their position of dominance in sports programming in the face of challenges from emerging cable TV networks. These skyrocketing fees did not cause much of a problem during the 1970s, as the networks were able to pass the high cost of producing sports programs along to their advertisers. However, things began to change in the early 1980s. Between 1980 and 1984, professional football lost 7% of its viewing audience, and baseball lost 26% of its viewers, according to the Museum of Broadcast Communications. Advertisers, meanwhile, became hesitant to pay increasing prices for commercials that would be seen by fewer people. The networks responded by airing more hours of sports. By 1985 the three major networks combined broadcast 1,500 hours of sports, about twice as many as in 1960. However, by the mid-1980s the market for sports programming appeared saturated, and the presence of more shows made it harder for the networks to sell ads at top prices.

The first half of the 1980s marked the rise of sports coverage on cable. According to the Museum of Broadcast Communications, the all-sports station ESPN, first launched in 1979, was reaching four million households by the middle of 1980. Superstations such as WTBS and WGN, as well as the premium channel HBO, were also airing a substantial number of sporting events. By 1986, thirty-seven million households were subscribing to ESPN.

Between the early 1990s and early 2000s, broadcast television ratings for the four major professional sports generally trended downward. There is no real consensus as to why this happened. Some experts point to a fragmentation of interest in sports among Americans. Jere Longman noted in "Pro Leagues' Ratings Drop; Nobody Is Quite Sure Why" (Scott R. Rosner and Kenneth L. Shropshire, eds., *The Business of Sports*, Sudbury, MA: Jones and Bartlett, 2004) that the development of a golf cable channel, the emergence of women's professional basketball and soccer leagues, and the rise of extreme sports and auto racing have all contributed to a dilution of the viewing audience for major team sports. According to Longman, possible contributing factors in the decline of ratings also include "a growing dislocation between fans and traditional sports, as players, coaches and teams move frequently, as athletes misbehave publicly, as salaries skyrocket, and as ticket prices become prohibitively expensive."

The key challenge for all of the major sports leagues—beyond the obvious challenge of attracting as many viewers and listeners as possible—is to balance exposure and distribution of their product against consumer demand. In other words, in an era witnessing the emergence of such new media as the Internet and satellite radio, at what point does the coverage of a sport avail-

able for consumption outstrip the public's interest in that sport, thereby becoming a losing financial proposition? As of 2006 it is still too early in the new media era to understand precisely the extent to which the Internet competes with television, or subscription-only cable competes with a live feed beamed directly into one's cell phone.

BASEBALL AND TELEVISION: THE CONVERGENCE OF OUR TWO NATIONAL PASTIMES

By 1939 baseball was already known as America's national pastime. Television was still a novelty at the time. The only option for those who could not attend a baseball game in person was to listen to a live broadcast on the radio. The first televised baseball game, between the Brooklyn Dodgers and the Cincinnati Reds, took place on August 26 of that year. The broadcast utilized two cameras: a main one positioned high above home plate, and a second one along the third base line. Such a broadcast would appear primitive by twenty-first-century standards. To cover a typical World Series game in the modern era, broadcasters use perhaps a couple dozen cameras, some of them operated electronically, and at least one mounted on an airborne blimp. In addition, early broadcasts offered none of the additional features contemporary viewers take for granted, including color, instant replays, and statistics superimposed on the screen.

NBC was the network that first brought televised baseball to the American public. Because NBC used home-team announcers to call the World Series, and because the New York Yankees were in the World Series nearly every year, Yankees announcer Mel Allen became the first coast-to-coast voice of baseball. Hall of Fame pitcher Dizzy Dean became the first genuine nationwide TV baseball announcer when the network premiered the *Game of the Week* in 1953, thus initiating the long parade of former ball players who have transformed themselves into commentators when their playing careers have ended.

By the 1960s baseball had lost a large share of its audience to other sports, particularly football. Baseball nevertheless remains a solid ratings draw, especially when teams with big stars located in large markets square off in the postseason. While ratings for World Series broadcasts have been declining overall for years, the numbers have rebounded somewhat since bottoming out in 2002. According to Nielsen data, the 2004 World Series received a 15.8 rating (meaning 15.8% of all households were tuned in) and a 25 share (meaning 25% of those watching something were watching the World Series). These figures marked a significant improvement over 2002, when the Series registered an 11.9 rating and a 20% share. They were still well below

1980, however, when the World Series was on the screens of 32.8% of all households and 56% of those whose televisions were turned on at the time. Playoff ratings have been benefiting in the last couple years from grudge matches between two big-market teams, the New York Yankees and the Boston Red Sox. Game Seven of the 2004 American League Championship Series between those two teams was watched by an average of 27.5 million viewers, the biggest viewing audience for a league championship game since 1991, and the fourth-highest major league baseball rating ever on Fox up to that time. Game Four of that series, according to Nielsen, marked the first time a league championship game had beaten out *Monday Night Football* in the ratings war.

Major League Baseball announced a new round of television deals in 2005. ESPN agreed to pay $2.37 billion to start a series of Monday night baseball broadcasts as part of an eight-year contract, which runs from 2006 through 2013. Under the terms of the deal, ESPN may televise up to eighty regular season games per season. The agreement also affords ESPN substantial flexibility to move some of the games to Sunday nights. The previous contract with ESPN, which ended in 2005, included a television component that was worth about $815 million over six years. MLB is also nearing the end of a six-year, $2.5 billion deal with Fox that runs through 2006 and includes the regular season, the All-Star game, and the playoffs. Ongoing negotiations will determine whether Fox will continue to carry professional baseball or if another broadcast network will take over beginning in 2007. MLB is also developing its own cable network, akin to what professional basketball has initiated in NBA-TV. Professional baseball has increased its media income substantially in recent years, according to the Associated Press in "ESPN and Baseball Agree to Eight-Year Deal" (September 14, 2005). The 2005 season marked the first year of a six-year contract with ESPN radio worth an average of $11 million per year; a six-year Internet deal with ESPN for an annual average of $30 million; and a $60 million-per-year deal with XM satellite radio covering eleven years' worth of baseball transmission.

In "Is MLB Extending Its Reach or Overreaching?" (March 2005) *SportsBusiness Journal* observed that the 2005 MLB season marked "a critical juncture for MLB officials, who are charged with managing a perfect storm of peaking demand for content, the emergence of new technologies for delivering it, and the growing number of media outlets demanding a larger piece of both." The article describes a situation in which baseball clubs' local television partners are clamoring for more content from a sport that has more games to offer than any other. Opportunities abound, many of them in new media, for a sport that has long been criticized for "underutilizing its product"; that is, not showing enough games in sophisticated

enough ways, and for neglecting the younger portion of its potential audience. This neglect and underutilization no longer seem to be the case. According to *Sports Business Journal*, the Internet division of MLB, known as MLB Advanced Media, has built a thriving subscription business by streaming live video of well over 2,000 regular season games and live audio of all games, and by packaging and selling video on an on-demand basis once the game has ended. TV contracts do not apply to these sales, since broadcast rights revert to the league once the game has taken place.

FOOTBALL: BIGGEST ATHLETES, BIGGEST AUDIENCE

Professional Football

It is not an exaggeration to say that television put football where it is today. As Steve Sabol wrote in *NFL Insider* (http://www.superbowl.com/insider/story/6116959), "Before the coming of television, professional football was, in comparison to baseball, virtually a minor league. ... Radio, with its leisurely word pictures, was perfect for baseball, but it did not convey the drama and fury of football." According to Sabol, it was the 1958 Super Bowl, a thrilling overtime victory by the Baltimore Colts over the New York Giants, that convinced America that football made great television, though the first televised professional football game had taken place seven years earlier. Within a few years the relationship was cemented. When *Time* put Green Bay Packers coach Vince Lombardi on its cover in 1962—accompanied by the pronouncement that football was "The Sport of the '60s"—it was clear that the sport had come of age as a media phenomenon.

Table 1.4 in Chapter 1 shows the most recent round of NFL television contracts. In April 2005 the National Football League signed a deal for a staggering $1.1 billion a year to move *Monday Night Football* from its longstanding home on ABC—which was paying about half that sum under its expiring contract—to ESPN from 2006 through the 2013 season. Under the terms of the deal, ESPN will continue to make its NFL games available on regular broadcast TV in the markets of the participating teams each week. However, unlike basketball, which experienced a loss of casual viewers when games were moved to cable in 2002 (see discussion below), regular network television will continue to play a large role in bringing football to the viewing public.

The same day they shook hands with ESPN, the league reached a broadcast agreement with NBC, which had not broadcast NFL games since 1997. The NBC contract provides $600 million per year for the rights to carry seventeen Sunday night games each season through 2011. Meanwhile, the NFL had agreed in November 2004 to extend its existing relationships with CBS and Fox to carry regular season AFC and NFC games respectively. The new CBS agreement included two Super Bowls and guaranteed $622.5 million a year through 2011; the new Fox contract called for five years at $712.5 million a year, with two Super Bowls included in the deal. The league received another $700 million from DirectTV in a five-year agreement covering satellite transmission rights.

What do the networks get for all that money? They get plenty because advertisers know how firmly football is entrenched in America's households and sports bars. Football is by far the most popular sport to watch on television in the United States. In a December 2004 poll by the Gallup Organization, 37% of Americans named football as their top choice among sports on television. This is nothing new; football has topped the poll consistently since the early 1970s, when it overtook baseball as the public's favorite sport to watch. In the 2004 survey basketball was a distant second at 13%, meaning football is the favorite of more than three times as many people as its nearest competitor. The only other sport to receive the vote of a double-digit portion of the population was baseball, chosen by 10% of respondents. The preference for watching baseball has been on the decline since its peak in 1948, when 39% said it was their favorite sport to watch, according to Gallup. (See Figure 3.1, Table 3.1, and Table 3.2.)

Five of the ten top-rated television shows of all time have been sports programs, and of those five, four were Super Bowls. Super Bowl XVI in 1982 is the fourth-highest-rated show of all time, according to Nielsen Media Research. About forty million households tuned in to that game. The highest ranking non–Super Bowl sporting event was women's figure skating at the 1994 Winter Olympics. This broadcast, which was viewed by 45.7 million households, received the sixth-highest ratings of any show in history. By comparison, Super Bowl XXXIX in February 2005 drew a rating of 43.4, a respectable statistic, but down slightly from the 44.3 rating achieved the previous year.

College Football

Televised college sports have nearly as much appeal as professional sports for American audiences, and since the 1980s have become the subject of large media contracts as well. In the early days of televised sports, the NCAA determined which college teams could play on television. Officially, the NCAA's goal in making these decisions was to protect the schools from the loss of ticket-buying fans who were lured by the glowing screen in a warm home. The NCAA's dominance over the right to broadcast football games went virtually unquestioned for years. According to a July 2004 article in the *Chronicle of Higher Education*, the only case of a college losing its membership in the NCAA came in 1951, when the University of Pennsylvania was dismissed for attempting to

FIGURE 3.1

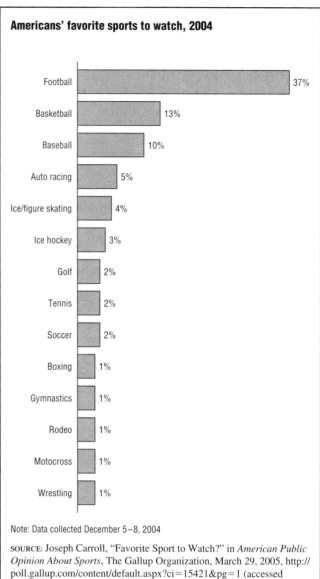

Americans' favorite sports to watch, 2004

Note: Data collected December 5–8, 2004

SOURCE: Joseph Carroll, "Favorite Sport to Watch?" in *American Public Opinion About Sports*, The Gallup Organization, March 29, 2005, http://poll.gallup.com/content/default.aspx?ci=15421&pg=1 (accessed September 16, 2005). Copyright © 2005 by The Gallup Organization. Reproduced by permission of The Gallup Organization.

schedule its own broadcasts in defiance of the NCAA. The school quickly repented, and its membership was restored.

The networks, however, aware of the potential audience for games between big-name universities with esteemed football programs, kept courting college athletic departments. By the 1970s several universities with top football programs had become frustrated with the limits the NCAA was placing on their television exposure. In 1977 five major conferences, along with a handful of high-profile independents, formed their own group, the College Football Association, in order to fight for their interests within the NCAA. A few years later the Association signed its own television agreement with NBC, the second largest sports television contract ever signed up to that time. Naturally, the NCAA was unhappy about this development and moved

TABLE 3.1

Sports Americans like to watch most, 1998–2004

	2004 Dec %	2003 Dec %	2002 Dec %	2001 Mar %	2000 Mar %	1998 Nov %
Football	37	37	37	28	33	36
Basketball	13	14	13	16	16	12
Baseball	10	10	12	12	13	16
Auto racing	5	5	5	6	5	3
Ice/figure skating	4	6	4	4	4	2
Ice hockey	3	5	3	3	5	3
Golf	2	3	2	4	5	3
Tennis	2	1	2	2	1	2
Soccer	2	2	2	2	2	2
Boxing	1	2	1	2	2	1
Gymnastics	1	1	1	1	1	1
Rodeo	1	*	1	1	—	*
Motocross	1	*	—	1	—	—
Wrestling	1	1	1	1	1	1
Fishing	*	*	1	*	*	1
Swimming	*	*	1	*	*	—
Bowling	*	*	1	*	*	1
Volleyball	—	*	—	1	—	—
Other	4	4	2	4	3	6
None	12	9	10	12	8	9
No opinion	1	*	1	1	1	1
	100	100	100	100	100	100

SOURCE: "What is Your Favorite Sport to Watch?" in *Football*, The Gallup Organization, 2005, http://www.gallup.com/poll/content/?ci=1705&pg=1 (accessed September 22, 2005). Copyright © 2005 by The Gallup Organization. Reproduced by permission of The Gallup Organization.

TABLE 3.2

Sports Americans like to watch most, long-term trend, selected years, 1937–2004

	Football (percent)	Baseball (percent)	Basketball (percent)	Auto racing (percent)	Ice/ figure skating (percent)	Ice hockey (percent)
2004 Dec 5–8	37	10	13	5	4	3
2003 Dec 11–14	37	10	14	5	6	5
2002 Dec 5–8	37	12	13	5	4	3
2001 Mar 26–28	28	12	16	6	4	3
2000 Mar 30–Apr 2	33	13	15	5	4	5
1998 Nov 20–22	36	16	12	3	2	3
1997 Apr 18–20[a]	30	14	17	7	2	3
1995 Apr 17–19	32	16	15	2	2	3
1994 Sep 16–20	37	16	13	2	3	1
1994 Aug 8–9	35	21	11	2	3	3
1992 Sept	38	16	12	2	2	4
1990 Feb	35	16	15	1	2	3
1981 Jan	38	16	9	1	2	2
1972 Oct	32	24	9	2	1	4
1960 Dec	21	34	9	[b]	1	3
1948	17	39	10	NA	NA	NA
1937 Mar 24–29	23	34	8	1	1	2

Note: NA=Not available.

SOURCE: "Long Term Trend," in *Football*, The Gallup Organization, January 30, 2004, http://www.gallup.com/poll/content/?ci=1705&pg=1 (accessed September 22, 2005). Copyright © 2004 by The Gallup Organization. Reproduced by permission of The Gallup Organization.

to ban the teams involved from all championship events. The University of Georgia and Oklahoma University sued the NCAA, and the case was eventually decided by the U.S. Supreme Court in 1984 in *NCAA v. Board of Regents of the University of Oklahoma, et al.* (468, U.S. 85). In the end, the NCAA was found to be in violation of antitrust laws. Thus the NCAA's stranglehold on television broadcast of college football was broken.

In the wake of the Supreme Court decision, the College Football Association took on the role of coordinating television coverage of most of the nation's leading football conferences. Still, some teams found the arrangement too restrictive. Following the defection of a handful of teams and conferences, the CFA folded in 1994, and the conferences were on their own to negotiate television contracts with the networks. The dollars began to flow in ever-greater volume during this period. According to the

Chronicle article, the Southeastern Conference (SEC) signed a contract in 1990 that brought in $16 million to be divided among its members; in 2004 SEC teams, including the University of Alabama, University of Arkansas, University of Georgia, and Louisiana State University, split nearly seven times that amount.

With about 1,000 universities participating in over 150,000 sporting events each year by 2006, competition for the right to put these events on television has become fierce. In 2003 a new station devoted strictly to collegiate athletics was launched under the name College Sports Television (CSTV). As of March 2005 CSTV was available in more than twenty million homes, according to Ken Kerschbaumer ("Battle for College Sports Fans: ESPNU, CSTV Deploy a Variety of Media Platforms," *Broadcasting & Cable*, March 14, 2005). CSTV also streams audio and/or video for over five thousand events a year to subscribers via high-speed Internet. The additional revenue from this medium is substantial; Kagan Media, which operates CSTV, has estimated that subscription fees and online advertising accounted for more than half of the company's $23.7 million in revenue in 2004. As often happens in the media world, success has bred competition. In March 2005 ESPN launched ESPNU, its own version of a college-only sports station. ESPNU was expected to show about three hundred college sporting events during 2005.

BASKETBALL: ON THE REBOUND, OR IN NEED OF AN ASSIST?

NBA regular season games have never drawn the kind of television audiences that NFL games routinely attract, simply because there are so many of them—the NBA season lasts eighty-two games, while the NFL's lasts just sixteen. In basketball, viewership increases significantly during the playoffs and is greatly influenced by the specific teams or personalities involved in a game. According to a January 2003 *Media Life* article, the highest-rated regular season NBA game ever shown on cable was a 1996 match-up between Michael Jordan's Chicago Bulls and the Los Angeles Lakers, in what was the Lakers' Magic Johnson's second game back from retirement. The game was viewed by 4.74 million people on TNT. A 2003 game pitting two of professional basketball's biggest and best centers against each other—Shaquille O'Neal of the Lakers and Yao Ming of the Houston Rockets—earned a household rating of 3.82 for ESPN, the network's best basketball rating ever up to that time. It is likely that ratings were boosted by the tension created when O'Neal insulted Ming in a mock Chinese accent in front of reporters shortly before the game took place.

Many in the basketball industry were mystified by the mediocre ratings generated by ABC's broadcast of the 2005 Championship Finals, which matched up the champions from the previous two years, the Detroit Pistons and the San Antonio Spurs. While each of the games in the seven-game series was the top-rated television show for that night, the series averaged only an 8.2 household rating, just the second time since 1981 that the NBA Finals have scored a rating below ten, according to *Variety*. Average ratings for the Finals were 30% below those of the previous year's final, which *Variety* attributed to the presence of the Los Angeles Lakers, featuring superstars Shaquille O'Neal and Kobe Bryant, as the Pistons' foes that year.

However, according to Erik Spanberg in "NBA: Why Aren't You Watching?" (*Christian Science Monitor*, June 23, 2005), basketball's television ratings had been plummeting long before the beginning of the Finals. Spanberg quotes industry analyst David Carter of the Los Angeles–based consulting firm The Sports Business Group, blaming a charisma gap: "The NBA is lacking chemistry and the style and personalities that drove it during the 1980s and 1990s." According to Carter, the slower pace of the game, which has been dominated by stifling defenses in recent years, also has a negative effect on ratings. The article also raises the issue of the widening gulf between players and fans. Peter Roby, director of the Center for the Study of Sport in Society at Northeastern University, notes, "There is a lack of connection between players and fans because the players make so much money now. . . . Players in the 1960s and 1970s used to live in the same neighborhoods as the fans. Now there is a wedge between fans and players, so there is no empathy."

The preference for watching basketball over other sports displays a significant race gap. Over the last few decades, the percentage of African-Americans who count basketball as their favorite sport to watch has grown explosively. The same is not true for white viewers. Figure 3.2 and Figure 3.3 show the contrast in how viewing preferences have changed between white and African-American audiences.

Table 3.3 shows the history of the NBA's television contracts since 1953. The rate at which the money involved has increased is striking. The set of deals the league signed in 1990 with TNT and NBC were worth well under $1 billion for four years. The most recent contracts, signed in 2002 with TNT and ABC/ESPN, cover six years (from the 2002–03 season through 2007–08) and have a total value of $4.6 billion. Under these contracts, AOL/Time Warner (now Time Warner) agreed to pay nearly $2.2 billion to show fifty-two regular season telecasts on TNT, and up to forty-five postseason games. ESPN signed on to broadcast seventy-five regular season games for $2.4 billion. The 2002 deal represented a key shift that saw the majority of games moved from network television to cable. The terms of the latest contract call for ABC to air fifteen regular season games per year, less than half of what NBC was airing under the previous contract. During that contract period, which lasted from 1998–99 through 2001–02, the

FIGURE 3.2

Favorite sport to watch among African-Americans, 1960–2002
WHAT IS YOUR FAVORITE SPORT TO WATCH?

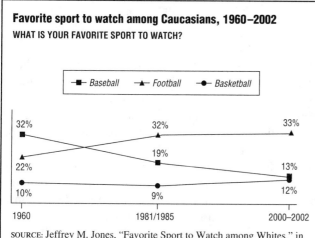

SOURCE: Jeffrey M. Jones, "Favorite Sport to Watch among Blacks," in *The Disappearing Black Baseball Fan*, The Gallup Organization, July 15, 2003, http://www.gallup.com/content/?ci=8854&pg=1 (accessed September 22, 2005). Copyright © 2003 by The Gallup Organization. Reproduced by permission of The Gallup Organization.

FIGURE 3.3

Favorite sport to watch among Caucasians, 1960–2002
WHAT IS YOUR FAVORITE SPORT TO WATCH?

SOURCE: Jeffrey M. Jones, "Favorite Sport to Watch among Whites," in *The Disappearing Black Baseball Fan*, The Gallup Organization, July 15, 2003, http://www.gallup.com/content/?ci=8854&pg=1 (accessed September 22, 2005). Copyright © 2003 by The Gallup Organization. Reproduced by permission of The Gallup Organization.

TABLE 3.3

NBA television contracts, by cable channel or broadcast network, 1953–2008

Seasons	Station	Contracts amount
1979–80 to 1981–82	USA	$1.5 million/3 years
1982–83 to 1983–84	USA/ESPN	$11 million/2 years
1984–85 to 1985–86	TBS	$20 million/2 years
1986–87 to 1987–88	TBS	$25 million/2 years
1988–89 to 1989–90	TBS/TNT	$50 million/2 years
1990–91 to 1993–94	TNT	$275 million/4 years
1994–95 to 1997–98	TNT/TBS	$397 million/4 years
1998–99 to 2001–02	TNT/TBS	$840 million/4 years
2002–03 to 2007–08	TNT	$2.2 billion/6 years
1953–54	DUMONT	$39,000/13 games
1954–55 to 1961–62	NBC	N/A
1962–63 to 1972–73	ABC	N/A
1973–74 to 1975–76	CBS	$27 million/3 years
1976–77 to 1977–78	CBS	$21 million/2 years
1978–79 to 1981–82	CBS	$74 million/4 years
1982–83 to 1985–86	CBS	$91.9 million/4 years
1986–87 to 1989–90	CBS	$173 million/4 years
1990–91 to 1993–94	NBC	$601 million/4 years
1994–95 to 1997–98	NBC	$892 million/4 years
1998–99 to 2001–02	NBC	$1.616 billion/4 years
2002–03 to 2007–08	ABC/ESPN	$2.4 billion/6 years

N/A=Not available.

SOURCE: "NBA Cable Television Contracts" and "NBA Network Television Contracts," in *NBA TV Contracts*, InsideHoops.com, 2005, http://www.insidehoops.com/nba-tv-contracts.shtml (accessed September 22, 2005)

In 2003 Time Warner Cable, Cox Communications, and Cablevision Systems teamed up on a multi-year agreement with the NBA for distribution of NBA-TV, the league's own twenty-four-hour network, which as of 2005 was available in about sixty-seven million households according to the NBA.

HOCKEY: BOUNCING BACK AFTER A SEASON ON ICE

Interest in the National Hockey League has sagged badly over the past decade. So apathetic was the viewing public in 2004 that the conference finals of the Stanley Cup Playoffs did not even draw a large enough share of the potential viewing audience to crack the top-fifteen program list for the week of May 17 through May 23. Both a regular season WNBA game and the Indianapolis 500 outscored the playoffs in the ratings race, each garnering more than 1% of viewing households.

Not surprisingly, the NHL has by far the least lucrative national television deals among the major sports. According to the 2005 *ESPN Sports Almanac*, NBC currently pays no fee for broadcast rights, and the NHL gets no money at all until NBC recoups all of its costs. Once that happens, the two entities share advertising revenues equally. This deal was set to expire at the end of 2006; NBC retains the option to renew the agreement for two additional years. The NHL also signed a one-year contract with ESPN, which paid $60 million for broadcast

league's television ratings had fallen more than 35%, according to Rudy Martzke in *USA Today* ("NBA Finalizes TV Deals: Goodbye NBC," January 22, 2002) . As a result, NBC was not inclined to make a particularly generous offer to extend its NBA contract; their bid of $300 million per year came in well below the $400 million offered by ESPN. Another factor in the shift from network to cable is the availability to cable stations of revenue from subscription fees. This additional source of income gives cable stations a negotiating advantage over traditional networks, which depend on solely advertising fees for their income.

rights through 2004–05, a season that was cancelled due to a labor dispute between owners and players. ESPN also had the right to extend the deal for another two years for $70 million per year, but declined to exercise that option going into the 2005–06 season. The NHL instead signed a new agreement with the Comcast-owned Outdoor Life Network (OLN), in which the league is guaranteed $65 million for the first year and $70 million for the second. An optional third year would be worth $72.5 million; the contract includes options for three additional years, at prices to be determined based on OLN subscription sales. While OLN reaches only sixty-four million households compared to ESPN's ninety million, the NHL expressed the hope that OLN subscriptions would pick up once hockey telecasts began.

As the 2005–06 season began, there was reason to believe the league's hope would be fulfilled. OLN's inaugural hockey telecast, an opening night match-up between the New York Rangers and the Philadelphia Flyers, drew an average viewing audience of 353,439, nearly triple the network's Wednesday average for the year to date. For the first week of the season, OLN hockey telecasts averaged a 1.8 rating, according to *Variety*.

Hockey has never received huge television ratings in the United States. Even at the sport's most popular point in the mid-1990s, NHL broadcasts on Fox only drew Nielsen ratings of about 2.0, meaning 2% of American households were watching. Under the NHL's five-year contract with ABC that expired in 2004, the best yearly average was 1.4. For the three seasons preceding the 2004–05 lockout, ratings for regular season games on ESPN were 0.49, 0.46, and 0.47. Ratings for the Stanley Cup Finals—the NHL's championship series—have fallen as well. In 1997 the series between the Detroit Red Wings and the Philadelphia Flyers earned a 4.0 rating for Fox. The Tampa Bay Lightning–Calgary Flames match-up of 2004 on ABC yielded a rating of only 2.6. It was therefore not surprising that ESPN opted not to extend its NHL contract.

AUTO RACING

NASCAR's $2.4 billion television package gives NBC and Fox the rights to broadcast races through 2006. As that contract nears its end, it has been reported that several networks are positioning themselves to vie for broadcast rights the next time around. The six-year deal was the largest ever for the sport. Before this contract went into effect, individual racing facilities negotiated their own agreements with the television networks, meaning a NASCAR race might be on CBS one week and ABC the next.

NASCAR's twenty-six races on NBC and Fox in 2004 received average Nielsen ratings of 5.6, which means that 5.6% of the nation's households were viewing the show. When these figures were released, NASCAR began to boast that stock car racing was now the number two sport in the country in terms of viewership, second only to professional football. This claim sparked a controversy, as Major League Baseball disputed the way NASCAR tallied the Nielsen numbers. Baseball officials pointed out that the NASCAR ratings used to support the claim included the races that make up the "Chase for the Nextel Cup," a playoff-style championship introduced in 2004. Meanwhile, NASCAR's calculation conveniently excluded the baseball playoffs and the All-Star game, which boosted MLB's average ratings to 6.9 for the forty-three games telecast on Fox in 2004. According to Chris Jenkins in *USA Today*, MLB executive vice president Tim Brosnan believes baseball's lead over NASCAR would be even greater if viewers of locally televised games were included in the mix ("Baseball Says NASCAR's TV Claims Are Off Track," September 22, 2005). If NASCAR has not surpassed baseball yet, it may do so soon enough. *Mediaweek* reported in September 2005 that NBC was averaging a 4.5 rating for the season to date for its Nextel Cup telecasts, a 10% increase over its previous season. TNT coverage of its seven-race NASCAR season showed an 11% increase, to a record 3.9 household rating.

EXTREME SPORTS

While television ratings for extreme sports still have a long way to go before they are in the same league as professional football and basketball, the audience is growing. More important, at least from the perspective of advertisers, the audience watching extreme sports is youthful and predominantly male, with a lot of buying power. Not many sports can take credit for completely altering the public image of a soft drink, but extreme sports have done just that for Mountain Dew. Once perceived as a "hillbilly" drink, Mountain Dew is now almost universally associated with youth culture as personified by practitioners of extreme sports. The transformation started in 1992 with the appearance of the "Do the Dew" advertising campaign, according to Joan Raymond in "Going to Extremes" (*American Demographics*, June 1, 2002). The campaign, which featured attractive young people engaging in a variety of extreme activities, helped make Mountain Dew the fastest-growing soft drink during the 1990s.

By the turn of the millennium, while *Monday Night Football*'s ratings were plummeting—viewership dropped from an average of 12.7% of the nation's households in 2000 to 11.5% in 2001—ratings for the two premier extreme sports events, the X Games and the Gravity Games, were skyrocketing. About two million households tuned in to the 2001 Gravity Games, up from 1.6 million the previous year, according to *American Demographics*. However, an online *CNN/Money* column by Chris Isidore

("X-treme Marks the Spot," August 6, 2004) noted that while the best ratings for the 2003 Summer X-Games on ABC showed 2.2% of the nation's households watching, that number was still barely half the rating ABC achieved for the final game of NHL's Stanley Cup finals, which were themselves considered a ratings disappointment. Broadcasters and advertisers are nevertheless very optimistic about the future of extreme sports programming. The sport's median viewership age is twenty-seven, according to Isidore, compared to a median age of forty-two for ESPN's NFL football broadcasts. The ages for some other sports are even higher; baseball's median is forty-eight, and golf's is fifty-five. Media companies are scrambling to ride this youthful wave. Fox has launched a new digital cable channel called FuelTV, devoted to extreme sports and other programming that targets the under-forty demographic.

ADVERTISING

Street & Smith's *SportsBusiness Journal* estimates that sports in the United States are a $213 billion industry, making it twice as large as the U.S. auto industry. Of that $213 billion, 14.1%, or $27.43 billion, falls into the advertising category. Surprisingly, television does not account for the largest share of that total. The biggest chunk, $16.39 billion, is spent on billboards and signage at arenas and stadiums. National network television is the second largest expenditure, at $4.69 billion, followed by radio at $2.34 billion. Another $1.78 billion is spent on advertising on national cable television, and sports magazines account for $1.45 billion of the sports advertising total. The rest is spent on regional television, both network and cable, and national syndicated television. Internet spending is a completely separate category in Street & Smith's scheme. The $229.9 million spent on Internet advertising is not part of the $213 billion sports advertising total described above.

A significant portion of sports advertising spending is on commercials aired during big games. The most expensive television advertisements of any kind are those placed during the NFL's Super Bowl. A thirty-second spot during the 2005 Super Bowl cost advertisers $2.4 million, up from $86,000 in 1972, according to author Phil Schaaf in *Sports, Inc.* (Amherst, NY: Prometheus, 2004). For that kind of money, advertisers want maximum impact, and they create innovative and sometimes controversial ads just for the occasion. Super Bowl commercials have in fact become something of a genre in themselves. In 2005, however, advertisers appeared to have toned down the shock factor in the wake of the previous year's infamous halftime incident in which Janet Jackson's breast was exposed during the live broadcast. Advertising during baseball's World Series is a bargain in comparison, but it still yields large sums of money for the broadcaster. Fox charged $325,000 for a thirty-second spot during the 2002 World Series, and

took in nearly $20 million per game over the course of the series. This meant that in just five games, Fox was able to recoup about a quarter of its $400 million yearly investment in Major League Baseball, according to Schaaf. It is worth noting that advertising spots during the first five games were sold out even before it was known which two teams would be participating.

Advertising rates for non-championship sporting events are usually negotiated in packages rather than for individual time-slots. However, when broken down into thirty-second spots for comparison purposes, other estimated advertising rates published in *Sports, Inc.* include: ESPN's *SportsCenter*, $11,000; U.S. Open tennis finals, $175,000; *Monday Night Football*, $325,000; and baseball divisional championship series, $90,000.

Sports Advertising and Alcohol

Sports advertising is dominated by products that appeal to young adult males. However, one product in particular, beer, is the undisputed king of the sports advertising jungle. The top sports advertiser in 2004 was Anheuser-Busch Companies, Inc., which spent over $293 million—83% of the company's total advertising budget—on sports advertising, according to *Sports Business Journal* ("A-B Paces Ad Spending, Olympic Sponsors Climb List," March 21, 2005). Its rival, Miller Brewing Co., was seventh on the list, down from fourth place the previous year. Miller spent $131.8 million, representing 69% of its advertising total, on sports advertising. Coors Brewing Co. spent $82.25 million, about a quarter of its total for all advertising, on sports advertising, which made it fifteenth on the list. Coors had placed sixth the previous year. The biggest non-beer sports advertiser in 2004 was General Motors Corporation's Chevrolet division, which spent $220 million of its $370 million advertising budget to advertise to sports fans.

The Center on Alcohol Marketing and Youth (CAMY) has studied extensively the relationship between sports programming and alcohol advertising. The CAMY report *Alcohol Advertising on Sports Television, 2001 to 2003* found that while sports programming accounted for only 16% to 18% of overall TV advertising spending and only about 4% of all ads in those years, over 60% of the alcohol industry's advertising spending and around 30% of its ads were on sports programs. Overall, the alcohol industry spent $541 million to place 90,817 ads on television sports programming in 2003. (See Table 3.4.) Table 3.5 shows on which brands the most money was spent. The report also notes that the percentage of commercials on sports shows that are for alcohol products is triple the percentage of ads on all programming that are for alcohol products. While beer advertisements have long been omnipresent on sports television, in recent years ads for hard liquor have been appearing with greater frequency.

TABLE 3.4

Alcohol advertising on sports TV, 2001–03

	2001		2002		2003	
	Dollars	Ads	Dollars	Ads	Dollars	Ads
Alcohol						
Total sports	$491,695,626	59,461	$597,337,222	80,548	$540,841,358	90,817
Total all programs	$811,166,404	208,909	$990,225,497	289,381	$879,143,274	298,054
Sports as % of all programs	60.6%	28.5%	60.3%	27.8%	61.5%	30.5%
All categories						
Total sports	$7,435,202,670	2,166,842	$9,074,508,240	2,675,648	$8,212,413,180	2,777,224
Total all programs	$44,840,147,250	55,756,506	$49,384,436,500	66,399,304	$50,729,026,920	69,063,279
Sports as % of all programs	16.6%	3.9%	18.4%	4.0%	16.2%	4.0%

SOURCE: "Table 2. Alcohol Sports TV Advertising Relative to All Sports TV Advertising: 2001 to 2003," in *Alcohol Advertising on Sports Television 2001 to 2003*, The Center on Alcohol Marketing and Youth, October 2004, http://camy.org/factsheets/pdf/AlcoholAdvertisingSportsTelevision2001–2003.pdf (accessed September 22, 2005). Data from TNS Media Intelligence/CMR 2001–2003.

TABLE 3.5

Top alcohol brands advertised on sports TV, 2003

Top 20 brands	Sports dollars	Sports units	Total dollars	Total units	Sports dollars percent of total	Sports units percent of total
Bud Light	$93,016,511.00	9,106	$120,455,157	17,526	77.2%	52.0%
Miller Lite	$85,151,843.00	10,210	$96,780,974	15,796	88.0%	64.6%
Budweiser Beer	$81,730,252.00	8,411	$99,729,867	16,021	82.0%	52.5%
Coors Light	$73,321,437.00	5,679	$113,993,173	26,278	64.3%	21.6%
Miller Genuine Draft	$30,537,836.00	2,466	$35,361,247	6,538	86.4%	37.7%
Michelob Ultra Light Beer	$19,559,777.00	665	$28,842,426	2,978	67.8%	22.3%
Coors	$9,775,447.00	1,688	$18,537,916	9,267	52.7%	18.2%
Labatt Blue Beer	$9,432,084.00	2,983	$15,010,891	7,270	62.8%	41.0%
Miller High Life	$9,402,900.00	2,865	$9,625,806	3,089	97.7%	92.7%
Smirnoff Ice Triple Black	$9,290,251.00	1,936	$20,393,757	4,840	45.6%	40.0%
Michelob Light Beer	$8,999,633.00	798	$15,168,140	3,545	59.3%	22.5%
Heineken Beer	$8,930,868.00	2,577	$31,366,448	10,010	28.5%	25.7%
Amstel Light Beer	$8,823,001.00	5,251	$18,469,429	9,891	47.8%	53.1%
Samuel Adams Boston Lager	$8,522,978.00	1,190	$19,101,508	4,846	44.6%	24.6%
Guinness Beers	$7,763,630.00	2,055	$11,664,122	4,361	66.6%	47.1%
Busch	$7,512,434.00	1,575	$7,582,442	1,685	99.1%	93.5%
Smirnoff Ice Malt Beverage	$7,027,879.00	976	$12,421,423	1,817	56.6%	53.7%
Bacardi Silver Malt Beverage	$5,600,549.00	224	$12,817,100	856	43.7%	26.2%
Rolling Rock Beer	$5,240,343.00	1,543	$7,079,941	3,288	74.0%	46.9%
Zima Clear Malt Beverage	$4,753,121.00	372	$8,377,089	3,363	56.7%	11.1%

SOURCE: Adapted from "Table 4. Top Brands on Sports TV: 2001 to 2003 (Based on Expenditures)," in *Alcohol Advertising on Sports Television 2001 to 2003*, The Center on Alcohol Marketing and Youth, October 2004, http://camy.org/factsheets/pdf/AlcoholAdvertisingSportsTelevision2001-2003.pdf (accessed September 22, 2005). Data from TNS Media Intelligence/CMR 2001–2003.

Sports television advertising for distilled spirits increased 350% between 2001 and 2003.

The CAMY report also found that alcohol advertising increased for "big games," like the Super Bowl and *Monday Night Football*. Table 3.6 shows advertising expenditures for selected big games from 2001 to 2003. In terms of percentage, however, soccer outranked all other sports in terms of the percentage of its advertising that is for alcohol products; 8.3% of the commercials on televised soccer games were for alcohol. Hockey was second at 7.2%, followed by professional basketball at 6.8%. Overall, a little over 3% of all ads shown during televised sporting events are for alcohol products. Among professional sports, hockey games had the highest number of alcohol ads per broadcast. A typical televised hockey game featured 5.5 alcohol ads in 2003 according to CAMY. Boxing matches averaged 4.5 alcohol ads, followed closely by pro basketball with 4.4. (See Table 3.7.)

Advertising on college sports presentations is at least as alcohol-oriented as on professional sports programming. According to CAMY, alcohol companies spent $52.2 million to place nearly 5,000 ads on college sports programs. College basketball, at over $28 million, accounted for more than half of that spending. (See Table 3.8.)

SPORTS VIEWING AND GENDER

Women and men watch sports for different reasons, according to journalist Toni Fitzgerald ("Women Have

TABLE 3.6

Alcohol advertising on "Big Game" broadcasts, 2001–03

	2001		2002		2003		2003 vs. 2002 percent change	
Program	Dollars	Ads	Dollars	Ads	Dollars	Ads	Dollars	Ads
Super Bowl total	$16,335,984	28	$24,526,587	170	$29,642,426	279	21%	64%
World Series total	$9,549,716	116	$9,240,729	138	$7,825,840	101	−15%	−27%
NCAA basketball total	$23,550,039	849	$27,614,409	934	$21,056,952	395	−24%	−58%
Bowl games total	$5,265,622	100	$5,706,897	234	$5,670,640	206	−1%	−12%
NFL Monday Night Football total	$40,361,952	522	$42,701,345	477	$38,424,393	459	−10%	−4%
X-Games total	$55,425	27	$60,209	34	$47,584	48	−21%	41%
Women's sports total	$540,892	261	$751,902	541	$1,236,208	648	64%	20%
Big sports total	**$95,659,630**	**1,903**	**$110,602,078**	**2,528**	**$103,904,043**	**2,136**	**−6%**	**−16%**

SOURCE: "Table 6. Alcohol Advertising on Big Sports Games: 2001 to 2003," in *Alcohol Advertising on Sports Television 2001 to 2003*, The Center on Alcohol Marketing and Youth, October 2004, http://camy.org/factsheets/pdf/AlcoholAdvertisingSportsTelevision2001-2003.pdf (accessed September 22, 2005). Data from TNS Media Intelligence/CMR 2001–2003.

TABLE 3.7

Average number of alcohol ads per game, 2001–03

	2001	2002	2003
Non-professional football—game	3.0	6.5	5.5
Hockey—game	5.0	4.9	5.3
Boxing	2.2	4.9	4.5
Professional basketball—game	4.2	3.7	4.4
Professional baseball—game	4.3	4.2	4.3
Non-professional basketball—game	2.9	4.7	4.2
Golf	2.0	2.4	3.4
Bowling	1.5	1.7	3.2
College baseball—game	3.1	2.8	3.1
Olympics	6.5	1.9	3.0
Auto racing	2.1	2.3	3.0
Other specific event—game	2.5	2.5	2.9
Soccer	2.1	2.4	2.8
College basketball—game	2.4	2.0	2.6
College football—game	2.9	2.2	2.5
Professional football—game	2.3	2.3	2.5
Non-professional basketball—game	5.0	2.2	2.5
Tennis	1.7	2.1	2.3
Horse racing	2.3	2.1	2.1
College baseball—pre-game	NA	2.0	1.7
College football—pre-game	2.6	1.9	1.6
Professional football—pre-game	1.4	1.2	1.5
Professional football—post-game	1.2	1.1	1.3
Professional basketball—pre-game	1.1	1.1	1.2
Professional baseball—post-game	NA	1.0	1.2
Professional basketball—post-game	1.5	1.1	1.1
Professional baseball—pre-game	1.1	1.0	1.1
College basketball—post-game	1.1	1.2	1.1
College basketball—pre-game	2.7	1.0	1.0
College football—post-game	1.0	NA	1.0
Non-professional basketball—pre-game	NA	NA	1.0

Note: NA=Not available.

SOURCE: "Table 8. Average Number of Alcohol Ads per Sports Game: 2001 to 2003," in *Alcohol Advertising on Sports Television 2001 to 2003*, The Center on Alcohol Marketing and Youth, October 2004, http://camy.org/factsheets/pdf/AlcoholAdvertisingSportsTelevision2001-2003.pdf (accessed September 22, 2005). Data from Source: TNS Media Intelligence/CMR 2001-2003.

Turned Chilly to TV Sports," *Media Life*, April 20, 2004). Women, Fitzgerald suggested, watch sports for the story lines, meaning their primary interest is in the drama and personalities. Men, on the other hand, are interested in the skills and statistics. Fitzgerald points to a report from the media research firm Magna Global USA, which found that sports viewership by women had declined significantly between 1998 and 2003, as measured both by ratings and total weekly hours spent watching sports. According to the Magna Global data, average broadcast (i.e., non-cable) television ratings among women decreased by 18% during that period. The ratings drop was even more precipitous (44%) for women watching basic cable television sports. The total number of hours women spent watching sports on television—either broadcast or basic cable—dropped by 17%, from 1.45 hours per week in 1998 (with Olympic coverage excluded from the total) to 1.20 in 2003. For men, meanwhile, broadcast ratings decreased only 9% during that span, while cable ratings fell 36%. Men's viewing hours dropped only 6%, from 2.76 hours per week to 2.58. Fitzgerald argues that these numbers are the result of what was happening in the sports world. When the sports that women like to watch, such as figure skating and tennis, have relatively few appealing story lines in motion, women hit the off button. Therefore, injuries to the Williams sisters in tennis and the gradual erosion of figure-skater Michelle Kwan's dominating ability have a measurable impact on viewership among women.

GAMING

Not long ago there were only two options for sports enthusiasts: playing a sport yourself or watching others play it live or onscreen. In recent years, a third way has emerged in the form of sports gaming.

Sports-oriented video games have been around for a long time, but until the mid-1980s the graphics were mediocre and the action unexciting for a true sports buff. A big change took place in the late 1980s when Electronic Arts (EA), at the time a relatively new company making interactive entertainment software, introduced the first-ever football video game to offer realistic

TABLE 3.8

Alcohol advertising on college sports TV, 2001–03

Sports program type	Alcohol			All categories			Alcohol as percent of all		
	2001 dollars	2002 dollars	2003 dollars	2001 dollars	2002 dollars	2003 dollars	2001 dollars	2002 dollars	2003 dollars
College baseball—game	$48,923	$108,159	$80,132	$2,115,000	$3,071,800	$2,976,840	2.3%	3.5%	2.7%
College baseball—pre-game	$0	$1,358	$11,243	$37,000	$124,000	$331,050	0.0%	1.1%	3.4%
College basketball—game	$32,440,775	$34,097,498	$28,260,794	$537,041,660	$569,391,450	$586,241,120	6.0%	6.0%	4.8%
College basketball—post-game	$191,370	$1,554,636	$1,179,731	$6,489,800	$13,363,200	$18,633,630	2.9%	11.6%	6.3%
College basketball—pre-game	$142,178	$34,247	$14,173	$5,086,000	$1,921,700	$3,381,930	2.8%	1.8%	0.4%
College football—game	$19,859,427	$21,947,490	$22,484,038	$447,809,650	$509,732,040	$531,923,940	4.4%	4.3%	4.2%
College football—post-game	$19,000	$0	$17,857	$1,849,400	$1,073,000	$1,485,350	1.0%	0.0%	1.2%
College football—pre-game	$258,128	$365,892	$180,387	$10,143,930	$6,200,370	$6,015,040	2.5%	5.9%	3.0%
College sports total	**$52,959,801**	**$58,109,280**	**$52,228,355**	**$1,010,572,440**	**$1,104,877,560**	**$1,150,988,900**	**5.2%**	**5.3%**	**4.5%**

SOURCE: "Table 9. Alcohol Advertising on College Sports TV: 2001 to 2003," in *Alcohol Advertising on Sports Television 2001 to 2003*, The Center on Alcohol Marketing and Youth, October 2004, http://camy.org/factsheets/pdf/AlcoholAdvertisingSportsTelevision2001-2003.pdf (accessed September 22, 2005). Data from TNS Media Intelligence/CMR 2001–2003.

eleven-on-eleven action. To make the game as realistic as possible, the company consulted extensively with former NFL coach and current football commentator John Madden. They ended naming the game after Madden, and in 1989 the first version of *John Madden Football* was released for Apple II computers. The game was an instant sensation. A version for the Sega Genesis home entertainment system was introduced the following year. Over the next few years the gaming industry grew exponentially, split about evenly between computer games and television-based systems. By the release of the 1995 version of the game, *Madden NFL '95*, EA had hashed out licensing deals with the NFL and the NFL Players Association allowing them to use likenesses of real players and the official league and team logos and uniforms. *Madden NFL* was eventually made available for every major gaming system. By 2004 *Madden NFL* had sold nearly thirty-seven million units since its 1989 launch, according to the *Washington Post*; it was the best-selling video game of any kind, not just sports, in both 2003 and 2004.

Madden NFL, however, is just one of a number of highly successful sports games. According to an industry analysis by Clint Swett in the *Sacramento Bee* ("Video Gaming Is On a Roll, as NBA, NFL Lend Reality to Look," April 2, 2005), sports game sales in the United States totaled $1.2 billion in 2004, representing nearly one-fifth of the entire $6.2 billion video game market. According to GameSpot.com sports editor Brian Ekberg in Swett's article, the appeal of sports games is that the games offer not only fun competition but the ability to identify with your favorite teams and players. The latest development in sports gaming is the appearance of exclusive licensing contracts between sports leagues and individual game manufacturers. Swett reported that in December 2004, EA—which in addition to the *Madden NFL* series also makes *NBA Live*—signed a $400 million deal with the NFL giving it exclusive rights to the like-

nesses of NFL players, uniforms, and stadiums for five years, effectively freezing out competitors like Take-Two Interactive Software, Inc., which had eroded sales of *Madden NFL* by offering its *ESPN NFL 2K5* at sharply reduced prices. Take-Two's consolation prize was a seven-year, $250 million contract with Major League Baseball. EA was also one of five game companies to agree to pay a combined $400 million to the NBA for use of its imagery. In yet another such licensing deal, EA is paying ESPN $850 million for fifteen years for use of ESPN features, including announcers and scoreboards.

CURRENT ISSUES IN SPORTS AND MEDIA

The Influence of Advertising on Young Sports Fans

The prevalence of alcohol in sports advertising noted above, and the potential harm it could cause to young viewers, is just one of many key issues in how sports are delivered to the American public via the media. A 1999 study by the Amateur Athletic Foundation of Los Angeles found that 98% of U.S. boys between the ages of eight and seventeen consumed some form of sports-related media; 90% of them watched sports on television. Children Now, a national, nonpartisan advocacy group, analyzed the content of sports programming during the late 1990s and combined that information with data from polling and focus groups of young people. Their intent was to connect the messages youths receive when watching sports programming—and the commercials placed therein—with their attitudes and behaviors. The resulting report, *Boys to Men: Sports Media* (September 1999), noted that aggression and violence are often depicted in a positive light, and war metaphors are regularly employed. Children Now also found that much of the advertising on sports programs was for fast food and other snacks that may be unhealthy. The report was particularly concerned with how sports programming and advertising portrayed masculinity, and how that portrayal may affect boys. A common theme in commercials was the notion that purchasing a particular product will make one more "manly," playing on boys' insecurities about being cool or attractive to girls. The Children Now report also highlighted issues related to race and gender in sports. According to *Boys to Men*, more than three-quarters of sports announcers are white males. White females and African-American males each account for only 10% of sports commentators on American broadcasts. While the report did not find significant evidence of overt racist content, sports programs sometimes reinforced racial stereotypes, such as lauding African-American players for their "natural athleticism" or remarking on the intelligence of white athletes. Women on sports programs are often treated as no more than props with sex appeal.

Native American Mascots

For the last fifty years, the Native American community has expressed opposition to the use by sports teams of Native American names and mascots. Organizations such as the National Coalition on Racism in Sports and Media have embarked on a campaign to convince teams to discard cartoonish Native American mascots and to encourage teams with such names as the Braves, Chiefs, and Redskins to rename themselves. The movement has met with some success. In the 1970s activists convinced Stanford and Dartmouth Universities to change their names from Indians to race-neutral names, to the Cardinals and the Big Green respectively. In 1994 Marquette University shed its Warriors nickname and became the Golden Eagles. The St. Johns University Redmen became the Red Storm the same year. However, many more teams have resisted calls to retire their traditional mascots, and the debate continues.

Sports Violence

Scholars, such as Professor Lynn Jamieson of Indiana University, have studied the connection between sports and violence extensively. "Sport tends to reflect society, and we live in a violent era," Jamieson is quoted as saying in an Indiana University news release (July 24, 2002). "We have a violent society where people use violence to solve problems instead of using other means.... The violence issue is not limited to professional sports. It filters down to the high schools and even to recreational activities.... This is because if it occurs at the professional level, it is likely to be imitated at the lower levels like Little League and city recreational programs."

Recent events seem to support Jamieson's thesis about the prevalence of violence in sports today. The 2004–05 NBA season was marred by a huge brawl in Detroit during a game between the Pistons and the Indiana Pacers; the fracas spilled into the stands, resulting in the involvement of spectators in addition to players. Several players received lengthy suspensions, and the entire season took place under the cloud of the melee. The intense media coverage surrounding Kobe Bryant's trial on sexual assault charges in 2003 and 2004 contributed to the NBA's image problems as well. Violence in the NBA is nothing new. In 1997 Latrell Sprewell of the Golden State Warriors was suspended and fined for choking coach P. J. Carlesimo. Basketball is not alone in contending with image problems stemming from the actions of its own players. In October 2005 several members of the NFL's Minnesota Vikings were allegedly involved in a wild party aboard a chartered boat that erupted into a drunken sex orgy. These events are just the most publicized examples. Practically every day a new report appears detailing unseemly acts by a high-profile athlete. This kind of news usually receives widespread coverage, which is absorbed by the young people who view these players as role models.

CHAPTER 4

PROFESSIONAL TEAM SPORTS

For decades, baseball, football, basketball, and hockey have been considered the four "major" professional team sports in the United States. While other sports, such as auto racing and soccer, are gaining ground in terms of popularity, and hockey is struggling to maintain its status, it most likely will be some time before "major league sports" in the United States means anything other than the four core sports.

In addition to being popular spectator events, professional league sports are also major industries that generate huge amounts of money—for team owners and managers, companies that sponsor teams, equipment and athletic gear manufacturers, and the athletes themselves.

MAJOR LEAGUE BASEBALL (MLB)

Major league baseball is no longer as popular as professional football and is losing ground to other sports (particularly auto racing), yet it remains firmly ingrained in the American imagination, retaining the title of "national pastime." In 2004 and 2005 two teams with long histories of futility, the Boston Red Sox and the Chicago White Sox, saw World Series victories. Their success evoked an emotional response in fans across the United States and seemed to spark renewed interest in a sport that has had more than its share of bad publicity since the 1990s, mostly due to steroid scandals. It remains to be seen if this renewed interest will translate into long-term gains in attendance and television viewership in the face of stiff competition from other sports, old and new.

The Structure of Major League Baseball

As of 2005 thirty teams made up Major League Baseball. These teams are divided into two leagues: sixteen in the National League and fourteen in the American League. Each of these leagues is further split into three divisions—East, Central, and West—loosely based on geography. (See Table 4.1.) The MLB season normally runs from early April through late September, and consists of 162 games. This season length was established in 1961, prior to which teams played a 154-game schedule. Most games are played against teams within each league, though not necessarily within each own division.

Following the regular season, the champions of each division (three teams in each league) plus a wild-card team—the team with the best record among those not winning their division—from each league compete in the playoffs. The playoffs consist of three rounds: two best-of-five Division Series in each league; a best-of-seven Championship Series in each league; and finally, the World Series, a best-of-seven game series between the champions of each league to determine the Major League champion team.

According to Plunkett Research, Ltd., Major League Baseball took in $4.1 billion in revenue in 2005. The average player salary was $2.5 million. Table 4.2 shows the latest team values and revenue figures for each MLB team, as compiled by *Forbes*. Street & Smith's *Sports Business Journal* (http://www.sportsbusinessjournal.com/) estimates that of the $10.5 billion worth of officially licensed sports merchandise sold annually, from banners to bobbleheads, $2.3 billion is spent on goods licensed by Major League Baseball and its member teams, second only to the NFL among the major sport leagues. Technically speaking, "Major League Baseball" (MLB) refers to the entity that operates the National and American Leagues, the two top professional baseball leagues in North America. MLB operates these two leagues under a joint organizational structure that was established in 1920 with the creation of the Major League Constitution. The Constitution has been overhauled numerous times since then. MLB team owners appoint a Commissioner, under whose direction MLB hires and maintains umpiring crews, negotiates marketing and television deals, and

TABLE 4.1

Major League Baseball teams and divisions

American League	National League
East Division	**East Division**
Baltimore Orioles	Atlanta Braves
Boston Red Sox	Florida Marlins
New York Yankees	New York Mets
Tampa Bay Devil Rays	Philadelphia Phillies
Toronto Blue Jays	Washington Nationals
Central Division	**Central Division**
Chicago White Sox	Chicago Cubs
Cleveland Indians	Cincinnati Reds
Detroit Tigers	Houston Astros
Kansas City Royals	Milwaukee Brewers
Minnesota Twins	Pittsburgh Pirates
	St. Louis Cardinals
West Division	**West Division**
Los Angeles Angels	Arizona Diamondbacks
Oakland Athletics	Colorado Rockies
Seattle Mariners	Los Angeles Dodgers
Texas Rangers	San Diego Padres
	San Francisco Giants

SOURCE: Created by Information Plus using data from Major League Baseball, http://www.mlb.com

TABLE 4.2

Baseball team values and revenue, 2005

Rank	Team	Current value[a] ($million)	Revenues ($million)	Operating income[b] ($million)
1	New York Yankees	950	264	−37.1
2	Boston Red Sox	563	201	−11.3
3	New York Mets	505	180	−11.2
4	Los Angeles Dodgers	424	166	−7.4
5	Seattle Mariners	415	173	10.8
6	Chicago Cubs	398	170	11.4
7	Philadelphia Phillies	392	167	6.1
8	Atlanta Braves	382	162	15.4
9	San Francisco Giants	381	159	6.9
10	St Louis Cardinals	370	151	−3.9
11	Houston Astros	357	155	9.6
12	Baltimore Orioles	341	148	34.0
13	San Diego Padres	329	150	17.1
14	Texas Rangers	326	142	2.9
15	Cleveland Indians	319	139	27.2
16	Washington Nationals (formerly the Montreal Expos)	310	80	−3.0
17	Los Angeles Angels of Anaheim	294	147	−30.0
18	Colorado Rockies	290	132	−7.8
19	Arizona Diamondbacks	286	136	−18.7
20	Chicago White Sox	262	131	8.1
21	Cincinnati Reds	255	127	22.6
22	Detroit Tigers	239	126	7.9
23	Pittsburgh Pirates	218	109	12.2
24	Toronto Blue Jays	214	107	7.8
25	Milwaukee Brewers	208	112	24.2
26	Florida Marlins	206	103	3.0
27	Kansas City Royals	187	104	3.0
28	Oakland Athletics	185	116	5.9
29	Minnesota Twins	178	102	−0.5
30	Tampa Bay Devil Rays	176	110	27.2

Note: Revenues and operating income are for 2004 season.

[a]Value of team based on current arena deal (unless new arena is pending) without deduction for debt (other than arena debt).

[b]Earnings before interest, taxes, depreciation and amortization.

SOURCE: Adapted from "MLB Team Valuations," in *Forbes Special Report: The Business of Baseball*, April 6, 2005, http://www.forbes.com/2005/04/06/05mlbland.html (accessed September 22, 2005)

negotiates labor agreements with the Major League Baseball Players' Association.

MLB maintains a level of control over baseball that is somewhat unique among the major sports. This comes as a result of a 1922 U.S. Supreme Court decision in which baseball was deemed not to be "interstate commerce," and therefore not subject to federal antitrust law. Consequently, MLB is allowed to operate in monopolistic ways that would not be legal in most other industries. This privileged status allowed baseball to stave off player free agency, and the high salaries that accompanied it, until the mid-1970s.

MLB History

The first professional baseball team was the Cincinnati Red Stockings, founded in 1869. That year the team—which still exists as the Cincinnati Reds—embarked on a fifty-seven-game national tour, and went undefeated against local amateur teams. Their success led to the 1871 creation of the first professional baseball league, the nine-team, eight-city National Association of Professional Baseball Players. Various other competing leagues were formed over the next decade, including a precursor to the modern National League. The American League was founded in 1901. The champions of the American and National Leagues faced off in what became the first World Series in 1903. The popularity of professional baseball continued to grow over the next several years. A crisis unfolded in 1919, when several members of the Chicago White Sox were paid by gamblers to throw the World Series, in what became known as the "Black Sox scandal." In the wake of the scandal, club owners hired baseball's first commissioner, Judge Kenesaw Mountain Landis, to clean up the game. Baseball's commissioner as of 2005 was Bud Selig, a founder of the Milwaukee Brewers. Selig, the ninth commissioner in MLB history, was appointed to the post by the team owners in 1998.

Baseball's golden era took place between the two World Wars, marked by the rise of such all-time greats as Babe Ruth, Ty Cobb, and Lou Gehrig. The major leagues survived the Depression by introducing night games, which soon became the norm for games played during the week; weekend games were still played during the day. From its beginnings through World War II, major league baseball was racially segregated. That changed in 1947, when African-American player Jackie Robinson joined the Brooklyn Dodgers. Such legends as Willie Mays and Hank Aaron followed over the next decade, and by the middle of the 1950s black players were fairly common on major league rosters. More recently, the number of African-American players in baseball has plummeted, as young black athletes have flocked to other sports. The 2005 World Series roster of the Houston

Astros did not include a single black player; it was the first team to compete for the MLB championship without an African-American player in half a century.

After fifty years of stability, the 1950s brought changes to MLB in response to demographic shifts in the United States. The Boston Braves moved to Milwaukee in 1953. Two New York teams moved to the West Coast in 1957: the Brooklyn Dodgers departing for Los Angeles and the New York Giants to San Francisco.

Baseball started losing fans, especially younger ones, in big numbers in the 1960s and 1970s, as labor conflicts and other challenges plagued the sport, while football ascended in popularity. In 1966 the Major League Baseball Players' Association was formed. The Players' Association's main goal was to end the "reserve clause," a contractual provision that essentially gave teams "ownership" of players, meaning they were bound to a particular team until they were traded or released. The reserve clause was finally overturned in 1975, ushering in the era of free agency in baseball, wherein players were free to negotiate with any team they wanted once their existing contract had expired. Labor squabbles continued over the next twenty years, and parts of several seasons were lost to work stoppages. The worst of these took place in 1994, when the final third of the season, including the World Series, was cancelled.

The sport survived in spite of these distractions, however, thanks partly to a handful of individual accomplishments. These included Cal Ripken, Jr.'s destruction of Lou Gehrig's longstanding record for consecutive games played; and Mark McGwire's and Sammy Sosa's 1998 competition to break the record for home runs in a season—a record that was broken again by Barry Bonds just three years later. Unfortunately, enthusiasm over these feats has since been muted by ongoing scandals involving performance-enhancing drugs, which called into question the validity of the exploits of Bonds, McGwire, Sosa, and others who just a few years earlier had been credited with reviving public interest in the sport.

Players vs. Owners: The Labor History of Major League Baseball

MLB's first major strike took place in 1981, as owners sought to blunt the impact of free agency. The owners wanted to receive compensation when one of their players was signed by another team. The players went on strike in protest, and more than seven hundred games were cancelled before the two sides agreed on a limited form of compensation for free agent signings.

In 1990 owners proposed a sort of salary cap and the elimination of the arbitration system in place for resolving salary disputes. A thirty-two-day lockout ensued, resulting in the cancellation of spring training that year.

The owners finally dropped their demands, and the full regular season took place, though its start was postponed by one week.

In June 1994 the owners proposed a salary cap that would have limited the players to 50% of total industry revenues. This represented a pay cut of about 15% for the players; not surprisingly, they declined the offer and went on strike in August. This strike resulted in the cancellation of the 1994 postseason, including the World Series. A ruling by federal judge Sonia Sotomayor ended the strike in March 1995. The 1995 and 1996 seasons were played under the terms of the expired contract.

In 2002 MLB appeared to be on the brink of another strike, the causes of which were mainly rooted in imbalances around the league resulting from financial disparities between teams in large and small markets. The team owners lobbied for salary caps, but of course the players were opposed to this. Instead, the owners came up with the idea of a luxury tax, which would be imposed on any team that spent more than a predetermined amount on player salaries. A strike was thus averted. The impact of the luxury tax, however, has been questionable. The New York Yankees, for example, have continued to spend vast sums to lure top players; in 2005 the Yankees became the first team in the history of sports to spend more than $200 million on salaries in a season. This was about $80 million over the luxury tax threshold, triggering a $25 million tax bill for team owner George Steinbrenner. On the other hand, only two other teams, the Los Angeles Angels and the Boston Red Sox, had to pay the luxury tax in 2005, so the tax is generally believed to work as a deterrent to reckless spending for most teams.

The other part of the 2002 deal was increased revenue sharing, meaning a greater share of each team's revenue was put into a pot to be divided among the entire major leagues. The biggest difference between baseball's revenue sharing system and football's is that baseball teams earn significant revenue from local television broadcasts, while almost all football coverage is national. MLB's 2002 contract brought a sharp increase in the amount of local revenue teams must share. The 2002 collective bargaining agreement runs through the 2006 season. The biggest question facing team owners and the players union as negotiations for the next contract heat up is whether to change the revenue-sharing formula to more closely follow the NFL model.

Current Issues in Baseball

In addition to the question of adjusting MLB's revenue-sharing formula, a key issue facing baseball is how to respond to recent revelations of the rampant use of performance-enhancing drugs among top players (see Chapter 9 for more detailed information). As news comes to light about the use of steroids and other substances by some of the very players credited with reviving the sport in the 1990s, professional baseball's credibility has come under fire. Important questions inevitably arise, such as how to account for records broken by players who were probably using banned substances. The ability of the league to handle such questions in a way that satisfies disgruntled fans will have a huge impact on the future of professional baseball in the United States.

NATIONAL FOOTBALL LEAGUE (NFL)

The National Football League (NFL) is the premier U.S. professional football league. The United States is the only place where the term "football" refers to the game played by NFL teams; in most other parts of the world, "football" refers to the sport Americans call "soccer." Plunkett Research estimates the NFL's total league-wide revenue at $4.8 billion in 2005. The average player earned a salary of $1.25 million for that season. According to *SportsBusiness Journal*, sales of merchandise licensed by the NFL or its teams total about $2.5 billion a year, highest among the major sports. Table 4.3 shows current team values and revenue as compiled by *Forbes*.

Figure 4.1 shows the gradual growth between 1998 and 2004 in the percentage of Americans who identify themselves as fans of professional football, according to Gallup polling. The NFL's success can be credited in part to breakthroughs in the 1960s and 1970s in packaging the sport for television. No other sport has managed to capture the kind of spectacle that NFL broadcasts generate. The league has also benefited from labor relations that have been relatively stable compared to those of the other major sports (a state some commentators have attributed to the fact that the NFL players' union is weak and ineffectual compared to those in other sports). The NFL's revenue-sharing system is also generally considered the best among the major sports in terms of keeping small-market teams competitive.

NFL Structure and Administration

As of 2005 there were thirty-two teams in the NFL, sixteen each in the National and American Conferences. Each conference is divided into four divisions: East, North, South, and West. Each division has four teams. (See Table 4.4.) NFL teams play a sixteen-game regular season, which begins the weekend of Labor Day. Each team also has a "bye" weekend during the season; the full regular season therefore lasts seventeen weeks. Sunday afternoons have long been the traditional time for pro football games. The exceptions have been one game per week on Sunday night and one on Monday night, though in recent years the league has begun scheduling occasional games on Thursday nights as well.

TABLE 4.3

Football team values and revenue, 2004

Rank	Team	Current value[a] ($million)	Revenues ($million)	Operating income[b] ($million)
1	Washington Redskins	1,104	245	69.6
2	Dallas Cowboys	923	205	37.5
3	Houston Texans	905	201	55.5
4	New England Patriots	861	191	30.5
5	Philadelphia Eagles	833	198	44.3
6	Denver Broncos	815	183	42.8
7	Cleveland Browns	798	183	59.0
8	Chicago Bears	785	175	33.1
9	Tampa Bay Buccaneers	779	175	25.0
10	Baltimore Ravens	776	172	34.8
11	Miami Dolphins	765	170	32.1
12	Carolina Panthers	760	169	17.3
13	Green Bay Packers	756	168	23.4
14	Detroit Lions	747	168	25.1
15	Tennessee Titans	736	164	22.2
16	Pittsburgh Steelers	717	159	35.3
17	Seattle Seahawks	712	158	6.0
18	Kansas City Chiefs	709	159	24.0
19	St Louis Rams	708	157	21.8
20	New York Giants	692	154	20.2
21	Jacksonville Jaguars	688	153	16.6
22	New York Jets	685	152	26.5
23	Cincinnati Bengals	675	150	14.2
24	Buffalo Bills	637	152	28.5
25	San Francisco 49ers	636	151	29.4
26	New Orleans Saints	627	157	7.8
27	Oakland Raiders	624	149	26.1
28	San Diego Chargers	622	148	22.5
29	Indianapolis Colts	609	145	13.6
30	Minnesota Vikings	604	144	4.1
31	Atlanta Falcons	603	144	6.4
32	Arizona Cardinals	552	131	−4.9

Note: Revenues and operating income are for 2003 season.
[a]Value of team based on current arena deal (unless new arena is pending) without deduction for debt (other than arena debt).
[b]Earnings before interest, taxes, depreciation and amortization.

SOURCE: Adapted from "NFL Team Valuations," in *Forbes Special Report: The Business of Football*, September 1, 2004, http://www.forbes.com/2004/09/01/04nfland.html (accessed September 22, 2005)

At the end of the regular season, six teams from each conference qualify for the playoffs—the four division champions, and two "wild card" teams (those with the best record that did not win their division). The champions of the two conferences square off in the Super Bowl. For much of its history, the Super Bowl has taken place in January; since 2002 it has been played in early February.

In the NFL revenue from television contracts and product licensing is shared equally among the teams. The idea behind this approach is to create parity, in contrast to Major League Baseball, where teams located in bigger markets generally have a lot more money to spend than their rivals in smaller towns. Football teams also split money from ticket sales. Generally, the home team gets 60% of the money from the gate and the visiting team gets 40%. The exception is luxury boxes; the home team gets to keep all of the money it makes selling its luxury box seating to corporations and other wealthy customers. This is one of the main reasons why

FIGURE 4.1

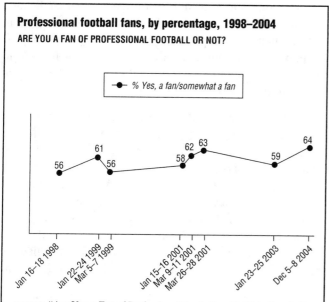

Professional football fans, by percentage, 1998–2004

ARE YOU A FAN OF PROFESSIONAL FOOTBALL OR NOT?

```
  ●── % Yes, a fan/somewhat a fan
```

| 56 | 61 | 56 | 58 | 62 | 63 | 59 | 64 |

Jan 16–18 1998, Jan 22–24 1999, Mar 5–7 1999, Jan 15–16 2001, Mar 9–11 2001, Mar 26–28 2001, Jan 23–25 2003, Dec 5–8 2004

SOURCE: "Are You a Fan of Professional Football or Not?" in *Football*, The Gallup Organization, January 30, 2004, http://www.gallup.com/poll/content/?ci=1705&pg=1 (accessed September 22, 2005). Copyright © 2004 by The Gallup Organization. Reproduced by permission of The Gallup Organization.

TABLE 4.4

National Football League teams and divisions

American Football Conference (AFC)	National Football Conference (AFC)
East Division	**East Division**
Buffalo Bills	Dallas Cowboys
Miami Dolphins	New York Giants
New England Patriots	Philadelphia Eagles
New York Jets	Washington Redskins
North Division	**North Division**
Baltimore Ravens	Chicago Bears
Cincinnati Bengals	Detroit Lions
Cleveland Browns	Green Bay Packers
Pittsburgh Steelers	Minnesota Vikings
South Division	**South Division**
Houston Texans	Atlanta Falcons
Indianapolis Colts	Carolina Panthers
Jacksonville Jaguars	New Orleans Saints
Tennessee Titans	Tampa Bay Buccaneers
West Division	**West Division**
Denver Broncos	Arizona Cardinals
Kansas City Chiefs	St. Louis Rams
Oakland Raiders	San Francisco 49ers
San Diego Chargers	Seattle Seahawks

SOURCE: Created by Information Plus using data from the National Football League, http://www.nfl.com

so many teams have been campaigning for new stadiums containing fewer regular seats and more premium boxes. Owners of teams that generate more money find the NFL's revenue-sharing system unfair, arguing that teams that draw more fans and sell more merchandise should benefit the most. Others contend that if revenue sharing is abolished, the NFL as a whole will suffer as team records begin to reflect the disparity between wealthier teams and those that generate less money.

The NFL is administered by the Office of the Commissioner. The first Commissioner of the NFL was Elmer Layden, who had been a star player and later a coach at the University of Notre Dame. Layden held the post from 1941 until 1946, guiding the league through the difficult years of World War II, when most able-bodied American men had either joined or were drafted into the armed services. Layden was succeeded by Bert Bell, co-founder of the Philadelphia Eagles. Under Bell, whose term as commissioner lasted until his death in 1959, NFL attendance grew every year. Bell is famous for his oft-quoted statement, "On any given Sunday, any team can beat any other team."

However, it was Bell's successor, Pete Rozelle, who led the league through its period of dramatic growth in the 1960s and 1970s. Rozelle introduced the concept of long-term network broadcast contracts and applied sophisticated marketing techniques to sell the NFL brand to the American public. Rozelle oversaw the merger between the American Football League (AFL) and the NFL and guided the league to what is generally considered a victory over the players' union during the 1987 labor strike. Rozelle retired in 1989 and was replaced by Paul Tagliabue, who remains commissioner as of late 2005. Under Tagliabue, the NFL has been marked by a great deal of team movement between cities, as owners seek to maximize the revenue they can generate from the sale of stadium naming rights and luxury sky-box seating. The NFL under Tagliabue has largely avoided the labor disputes that have plagued the other major sports. One of the key issues the commissioner must deal with before 2010 is the future of the NFL's revenue-sharing system, a debate that may pit owners of big-market teams against owners of teams who play in less populous cities.

History of the NFL

The NFL came to life in 1920 as the American Professional Football Association (APFA). The league adopted its current name two years later, but professional football actually dates back to 1892, when a Pittsburgh club paid William "Pudge" Heffelfinger $500 to play in a game.

The APFA—which was based in a Canton, Ohio, automobile dealership—consisted of eleven teams, all but one of them located in the Midwest. In its original form, the APFA was not really a league in the modern sense; it was essentially an agreement among member teams not to steal players from each other. While professional football remained secondary to the college version in its early years, it gradually gained in popularity when former college stars like Red Grange and Benny

Friedman turned professional. An annual championship game was established in 1933. By this time, most of the league's teams, with the notable exception of the Green Bay Packers, had left the small towns of their birth for bigger cities.

Professional football began to challenge college football's dominance in the years following World War II, as a faster-paced, higher-scoring style drew new fans. The NFL expanded to the West Coast in 1945, when the Cleveland Rams relocated to Los Angeles. By the 1950s pro football was firmly entrenched as a major sport in the United States, as television effectively captured the heroics of such glamorous stars as Bobby Layne, Paul Hornung, and Johnny Unitas. The explosive growth of professional football led to the creation of a rival league, the American Football League (AFL), in 1960, resulting in a costly bidding war for the services of top players. By the mid-1960s professional football had eclipsed baseball as America's favorite sport by some measures. In 1970 the two football leagues merged. The AFL's ten teams plus three NFL teams became the American Football Conference (AFC); the remaining thirteen NFL teams became the National Football Conference (NFC). The champions of the two conferences would meet in the newly created Super Bowl to determine the world champion of professional football.

The NFL was the biggest spectator sport in America in the 1970s and 1980s. The Super Bowl was the most watched television show of any kind most years, and *Monday Night Football* set a new standard for sports broadcasting with its innovative mixture of sports and entertainment. Since the 1990s the popularity of football has spread internationally. In 1993 the NFL launched the World League of American Football, now called NFL Europe, which, with teams in Germany and the Netherlands, serves as a sort of development league in which a player's skills can be honed to reach NFL standards.

Labor Squabbles in the NFL

The NFL Players Union was formed in 1956 when players on the Green Bay Packers and Cleveland Browns organized to demand minimum salaries, team-paid uniforms and equipment, and other benefits from owners. The owners refused to respond to any of these demands. The union threatened to sue, a threat strengthened by a 1957 U.S. Supreme Court ruling (*Radovich v. National Football League*, 352 U.S. 445) that the NFL did not enjoy the same special status as Major League Baseball did with regard to antitrust laws. The owners eventually gave in to most of the players' demands but did not formally recognize the union for collective bargaining purposes. The NFL Players Association (NFLPA), as it was by then named, did not become the official bargaining agent for players until 1968, following a short lockout and strike.

After the merger of the NFL and AFL, the Players' Association focused on antitrust litigation that challenged the so-called Rozelle Rule, which required a team signing a free agent to compensate the team losing the player, thereby severely limiting players' ability to benefit from free agency. The union succeeded in getting the Rozelle Rule eliminated in 1977.

When the NFLPA went on strike for a month in 1987, the owners responded by carrying on with the schedule using replacement players and a handful of veterans who chose to cross the picket line. With support weakening, the union ended its strike on October 15, 1987. Free agency finally came to the NFL in 1992, and this was balanced by the introduction of salary caps in the mid-1990s. The NFL has experienced relatively smooth labor relations since then. The current collective bargaining agreement is active through the 2007 season.

Unlike Major League Baseball and the National Basketball Association (NBA), the NFL has a hard salary cap, meaning teams cannot spend more than a specified amount on salaries under any circumstances. For players and their union, free agency is considered an acceptable trade-off for the introduction of salary caps. With each new contract, the size of the salary cap is a subject of intense negotiation, but there have not to date been any work stoppages over it. Salary caps are considered an important way to insure competition across the league: they stop the large-market teams from buying their way to the Super Bowl, and they give smaller-market teams like Kansas City, Cincinnati, and Green Bay the ability to afford high-performing players.

Studies in sports economics have shown a strong correlation between total team salary and winning percentage. In "Buying Success: Team Performance and Wage Bills in U.S. and European Sports Leagues" (European Association of Labor Economists, February 2003), Robert Simmons and David Forrest analyzed salary and percentages of wins of seven professional sports leagues in the 1980s and 1990s—three European soccer leagues, Major League Baseball, the National Hockey League, National Basketball Association, and the NFL. The results showed that, in general, a higher overall team salary was associated with a greater likelihood of higher point scoring (in the European leagues) and of entering playoffs (in the North American leagues). Salary caps were invented precisely to mitigate this effect, and by and large they have been effective at balancing the wealth within leagues. The NFL's cap is the "hardest" (it has the fewest loopholes), and as such has had the biggest balancing effect. Of course, wealth parity does not always translate into winning percentage parity, since there are so many other variables involved, such as whether management makes good decisions about what players to spend their limited payroll on.

NATIONAL BASKETBALL ASSOCIATION (NBA)

Professional basketball has changed drastically since its early days; in fact, its evolution has perhaps been more pronounced than that of any other major sport—in dress, style of play, and, most noticeably, the racial composition of teams. Once a sport that featured white men in close-fitting uniforms hoisting up set shots from chest level, by the late twentieth century basketball was largely an African-American phenomenon, featuring loose-fitting fashions, a hip-hop sensibility, and an emphasis on the shortest-range shot of all—the slam dunk. While a sport like hockey, for example, has always been dominated by white fans and players, basketball's racial shift has led to an identity crisis of sorts, with the issue of race becoming a major feature of discussion about the game.

History of the NBA

Basketball was invented in 1891 by a Canadian physical education instructor and physician named James Naismith (1861–1939). Working at a YMCA in Springfield, Massachusetts, Naismith was directed by the head of the physical education department to create an indoor athletic game that would keep a class of young men occupied during the winter months. In two weeks Naismith had developed the game, including the original thirteen rules of basketball. While he never sought recognition for his invention, Naismith was present at the 1936 Olympic Games in Berlin, Germany, basketball's first appearance as an Olympic event.

Basketball was first played professionally in 1896, when members of a YMCA team in Trenton, New Jersey, left to form a squad that would play for money. Two years later, a group of New Jersey sports journalists founded the National Basketball League (NBL), which consisted of six teams based in Pennsylvania and New Jersey. The NBL petered out after several years, but in the mid-1930s a new league with the same name was founded. A second professional league, the Basketball Association of America (BAA), was formed by a group of New York businessmen. The BAA, which was in direct competition against the NBL, had teams in New York, Boston, Philadelphia, Chicago, and Detroit. Right before the start of the 1948–49 season, four NBL teams—Minneapolis, Rochester, Fort Wayne, and Indianapolis—joined the BAA, and the following year, the NBL's six surviving teams followed suit. The BAA was then divided into three divisions and renamed the National Basketball Association. One division was eliminated the following year, leaving the two that became the forerunners of the modern Eastern and Western Conferences of the NBA.

The NBA had no competition for the next two decades. That changed in 1967 with the formation of the American Basketball Association (ABA). The ABA lured fans, and quite a few players, away from the NBA with a flashier style of play, featuring a red, white, and blue ball. The ABA disbanded in 1976, and several of its teams became part of the NBA. However, by the late 1970s pro basketball's popularity was sagging. Revenue and TV ratings were down, and the game had become dull. The league received a huge boost with the emergence of two new stars, Magic Johnson of the Los Angeles Lakers and Larry Bird of the Boston Celtics, who together are credited with ushering in a new era of popularity and prosperity to the NBA. Behind Johnson and Bird, the Lakers and Celtics completely dominated the NBA through the 1980s. The 1990s belonged to Michael Jordan and the Chicago Bulls. With the charismatic Jordan leading the way, the NBA continued to thrive through most of the decade.

After the 1997–98 season, tensions between players and owners began to heighten, as the salary cap and other issues came to a head. The owners instituted a player lockout, and the two sides did not reach an agreement until January of 1999, by which time more than a third of the regular season had been cancelled.

The first part of the twenty-first century saw a dramatic increase in the number of foreign-born players in the NBA. The American Olympic basketball team's mediocre performance in 2004 demonstrated that the rest of the world was starting to catch up with the United States in terms of basketball talent. Players from Europe appeared to have a better grounding in such basketball fundamentals as passing and long-range shooting. In a September 6, 2002, ESPN.com article ("Solving USA Basketball's Long List of Problems"), reporter David Aldridge noted that top NBA coaches George Karl and Larry Brown (who coached the American team to a bronze medal in the 2002 World Championships) have complained for years that there is less emphasis on skill development and fundamentals on American teams than on teams in other countries. Bringing foreign-born players into the NBA is believed to be one possible solution to the problem. As of February 2005, NBA rosters included seventy-seven foreign-born players from thirty-four different countries and territories. Some of them, including German-born Dirk Nowitzky of the Dallas Mavericks, Argentinean-born Manu Ginobili of the San Antonio Spurs, and Yugoslavian-born Peja Stojakovic of the Sacramento Kings, are among the best players in the league.

League Structure

The thirty-team National Basketball Association is divided into two conferences: the Eastern Conference, which is in turn made up of the Atlantic, Central, and Southeast Divisions; and the Western Conference, made up of the Northwest, Pacific, and Southwest Divisions. Each division is composed of five teams. (See Table 4.5.)

TABLE 4.5

National Basketball Association teams and divisions

Eastern Conference	Western Conference
Atlantic Division	**Southwest Division**
Boston Celtics	Dallas Mavericks
New Jersey Nets	Houston Rockets
New York Knicks	Memphis Grizzlies
Philadelphia 76ers	New Orleans Hornets
Toronto Raptors	San Antonio Spurs
Central Division	**Northwest Division**
Chicago Bulls	Denver Nuggets
Cleveland Cavaliers	Minnesota Timberwolves
Detroit Pistons	Portland Trailblazers
Indiana Pacers	Seattle Supersonics
Milwaukee Bucks	Utah Jazz
Southeast Division	**Pacific Division**
Atlanta Hawks	Golden State Warriors
Charlotte Bobcats	Los Angeles Clippers
Miami Heat	Los Angeles Lakers
Orlando Magic	Phoenix Suns
Washington Wizards	Sacramento Kings

SOURCE: Created by Information Plus using data from the National Basketball Association, http://www.nba.com

The NBA regular season begins in early November. A season consists of eighty-two games for each team, divided evenly between home and away games. Teams play each of the other teams in their own division four times per season; they play teams in the other divisions of their own conference three or four times, and teams in the other conference twice each. The NBA is currently the only one of the major sport leagues in which all teams play each other over the course of the regular season.

The NBA Playoffs begin in late April. Eight teams from each conference qualify: the winners of each of the three divisions plus the five teams with the next best records. Each round of the playoffs is a best-of-seven series. The third round of the playoffs is for the Conference Championship, and the winners of these two series compete against each other in the NBA Finals, the winner receiving the Larry O'Brien Trophy.

According to Plunkett Research, the NBA generates a total of $3.1 billion in revenue. The average player salary throughout the league is $4.92 million, the highest among the major sports in the United States. Sales of NBA-licensed merchandise bring in about $1 billion a year, according to *SportsBusiness Journal*. Table 4.6 shows the current values of NBA teams and their most recent revenue figures, as compiled by *Forbes*.

Current Issues in the NBA

SALARY CAPS. Basketball has a "soft" salary cap, meaning the amount a team can spend on salaries is limited, but there are loopholes and complications. As a result, there are still great disparities in how much the teams spend. For example, the New York Knicks ended

TABLE 4.6

Basketball team values and revenue, 2004

Rank	Team	Current value[a] ($million)	Revenues ($million)	Operating income[b] ($million)
1	Los Angeles Lakers	510	170	35.8
2	New York Knicks	494	170	−14.3
3	Dallas Mavericks	374	117	−33.6
4	Houston Rockets	369	125	35.5
5	Chicago Bulls	368	123	36.8
6	Detroit Pistons	363	121	23.0
7	Phoenix Suns	356	111	20.1
8	Philadelphia 76ers	342	107	7.2
9	Boston Celtics	334	104	25.4
10	Sacramento Kings	330	118	0.6
11	San Antonio Spurs	324	108	26.7
12	Indiana Pacers	311	104	2.6
13	Cleveland Cavaliers	298	93	21.9
14	Toronto Raptors	297	100	5.4
15	New Jersey Nets	296	93	−7.4
16	Minnesota Timberwolves	291	97	−20.0
17	Miami Heat	279	93	18.6
18	Washington Wizards	273	94	21.5
19	Denver Nuggets	268	89	25.2
20	Utah Jazz	257	88	27.5
21	Portland Trail Blazers	247	88	−47.0
22	Memphis Grizzlies	238	75	−4.1
23	Atlanta Hawks	232	83	4.7
24	Golden State Warriors	228	76	8.1
25	New Orleans Hornets	225	80	17.1
26	Los Angeles Clippers	224	77	22.4
27	Orlando Magic	218	78	12.2
28	Seattle SuperSonics	205	73	0.5
29	Milwaukee Bucks	199	77	4.8

Note: Revenues and operating income are for 2003–04 season.
[a]Value of team based on current arena deal (unless new arena is pending) without deduction for debt (other than arena debt).
[b]Earnings before interest, taxes, depreciation and amortization.

SOURCE: Adapted from "NBA Team Valuations," in *Forbes Special Report: The Business of Basketball*, December 8, 2004, http://www.forbes.com/2004/12/08/04nbaland.html (accessed September 22, 2005)

the 2004–05 season with a payroll totaling $115 million, while the Atlanta Hawks paid their players $20 million total. Table 4.7 shows the history of the NBA salary cap since 1984.

Beginning in the late 1980s, it became increasingly common for top college players to leave school before graduating and enter the NBA draft. By the mid-1990s the best high school players were foregoing college altogether and moving straight into the professional ranks. The NBA has long sought to discourage players from making the jump from high school to the pros. Toward that end, in 1995 the league enacted a salary limit for rookies, in the hopes of making the move less enticing (*2005 ESPN Sports Almanac*).

In June of 2005, as another labor dispute seemed possible, the league and the players union reached a new collective bargaining agreement. The agreement's key provisions included: a new rule preventing players from entering the NBA straight out of high school; increased drug testing; a 3% increase in the salary cap; and a reduction in the maximum length of free

TABLE 4.7

NBA salary cap history, 1984–2006

NBA season	NBA salary cap
1984–85	$3.6 million
1985–86	$4.233 million
1986–87	$4.945 million
1987–88	$6.164 million
1988–89	$7.232 million
1989–90	$9.802 million
1990–91	$11.871 million
1991–92	$12.5 million
1992–93	$14.0 million
1993–94	$15.175 million
1994–95	$15.964 million
1995–96	$23.0 million
1996–97	$24.363 million
1997–98	$26.9 million
1998–99	$30.0 million
1999–2000	$34.0 million
2000–01	$35.5 million
2001–02	$42.5 million
2002–03	$40.271 million
2003–04	$43.84 million
2004–05	$43.87 million
2005–06	$49.5 million

SOURCE: "NBA Salary Cap," in *NBA Salaries*, InsideHoops.com, August 9, 2005, http://www.insidehoops.com/nba-salary-cap.shtml (accessed September 22, 2005)

agent contracts from seven to six years (Liz Mullen and John Lombardo, "The NBA's New Labor Deal: What It Means, Who It Impacts," *Sports Business Journal*, June 27–July 3, 2005).

MINIMUM AGE. Among the issues addressed in the NBA's contract, the minimum age requirement generated the most public attention. This provision requires that a player be at least nineteen years old and be out of high school for at least one year. Proponents of age restrictions argue that allowing teens in the NBA does them a disservice, and that they are much better off playing college basketball—even if it is just for a year—or playing in the NBA Developmental League than they are sitting on the end of an NBA team's bench rarely seeing significant playing time. They also say the NBA's skill level can become diluted with players who have not yet mastered the fundamentals of the game. NBA Commissioner David Stern has been the most vocal advocate of age limits, arguing that the presence of NBA recruiters in high school gyms has an overall negative influence on young players; that teens lack the maturity to handle the rigors of NBA life without getting into trouble; and that too many young urban Americans are unrealistically looking to basketball as a pathway out of poverty.

Opponents of the minimum age point out that practicing every day against the best players in the world is not such a bad way to learn the game and wonder what young men can gain from waiting just one extra year before entering the professional league. NBA union director Billy Hunter also questions the possible racial motiva-

tions behind the move toward age limits: "I'm still strongly philosophically opposed to it, and I can't understand why people think one [an age limit] is needed except for the fact that the NBA is viewed as a predominantly black sport. You don't see that outcry in other sports, and the arguments that have been in support of an age limit have been defeated" (Chris Sheridan, "Hunter Still Opposed to Raising NBA Age Limit," *USA Today*, May 12, 2005). Many players also oppose the age limit, including Indiana Pacers forward Jermaine O'Neal, who said, "As a black guy, you kind of think [race is] the reason why it's coming up. . . . You don't hear about it in baseball or hockey. To say you have to be twenty, twenty-one to get in the league, it's unconstitutional. If I can go to the U.S. Army and fight the war at eighteen why can't you play basketball for forty-eight minutes?" (ESPN.com News Service, April 13, 2005).

RACE AND THE NBA. The debate over teens in the NBA and its possible relation to race is related to the broader issue of public image. Because it is dominated by young African-American males, the NBA struggles with the image the league projects to a predominantly white American public. Some basketball executives, particularly NBA Commissioner David Stern, have expressed concern about the message sent by the appearance and behavior of certain players. The arrests of high-profile players on sexual assault, drug, and weapons charges have not helped matters. According to Jeff Benedict, author of *Out of Bounds: Inside the NBA's Culture of Rape, Violence, and Crime* (New York: HarperCollins, 2004), a startling 40% of NBA players have police records, although, not surprisingly, the NBA disputes this claim. Interestingly, it is not the younger players who are getting in trouble the most. Michael McCann, a sports law expert and assistant professor at the Mississippi College School of Law, analyzed arrests of NBA players from 1995 to 2004 and found that 57.1% of the NBA players arrested actually went to college for four years. Another 17.9% of the arrested players went to college for three years. Only 4.8% of those arrested did not go to college at all ("Illegal Defense: The Irrational Economics of Banning High School Players from the NBA Draft," *Virginia Sports and Entertainment Law Journal*, vol. 3, 2004).

Nonetheless, the question of public image persists. As one way of addressing the image problem, Stern announced in October 2005 a new dress code that would apply to all players when they are participating in NBA-related activities, including arriving at and leaving games, participating in interviews, and making promotional appearances. The new rules ban sleeveless shirts, shorts, T-shirts, chains or medallions worn over the clothes, sunglasses while indoors, and headphones (except on a team bus or plane or in the locker room). The code also required players to wear a sport coat when on the bench but not in uniform. Reactions to the code among players were at best mixed. Some players applauded the league's effort to clean up the game's image. Others were outraged. San Antonio Spurs superstar Tim Duncan, a player often touted by the league as a model citizen, described the dress code as "basically retarded" ("Spurs Superstar Tim Duncan Is Known to Be Understated and Shy—But Not about the NBA's New Dress Code," FoxSports.com, October 20, 2005). Stephen Jackson of the Indiana Pacers openly accused the league of targeting black players. Jackson was particularly critical of the ban on wearing chains, noting that chains are associated with hip-hop culture and are a common fashion choice among young black men ("Pacers' Jackson: Dress Code Is 'Racist': Forward Wears Jewelry to Protest Rules, Which He Says Attacks Culture," MSNBC.com, October 20, 2005). Jason Richardson of the Golden State Warriors was widely quoted by the Associated Press: "Hey, a guy could come in with baggy jeans, a do-rag and have a Ph.D., and a person who comes in with a suit could be a three-time felon. So, it's not what you wear, it's how you present yourself."

WOMEN'S NATIONAL BASKETBALL ASSOCIATION (WNBA)

The WNBA started play in June 1997 following the celebrated gold medal run of the U.S. women's basketball team in the 1996 Olympics. There had been other professional women's basketball leagues before, but the WNBA was launched with the full support of the NBA, making it much more viable than other upstart leagues. At its inception the WNBA already had television deals in place with the NBC, ESPN, and Lifetime networks.

In its first season the WNBA had eight teams. By 1999 four more teams had joined the league. That year, players and the league signed the first collective bargaining agreement in the history of women's professional sports. Four more teams were added in 2000. Following the 2002 season, the league's ownership structure was changed. Prior to that, the NBA owned all the teams in the WNBA. In 2002, however, the NBA sold the women's teams either to their NBA counterparts in the same city or to outside parties. As a result of this restructuring, two teams moved to other cities and two teams folded. Another team dropped out after the 2003 season.

With the addition of the Chicago Sky to the Eastern Conference, there were seven teams in each of the WNBA's two conferences in 2005. Each team plays a thirty-four-game regular season schedule, with the four top teams in each conference competing in the playoffs. The first and second rounds of the playoffs are best-of-three series. The WNBA Finals are best of five. The WNBA season starts in the summer, when the NBA season ends.

While the WNBA has gained in popularity, it has not been a big financial success. As of 2005 the league had not yet turned a profit in any year. Average attendance at WNBA games is only about half that of NBA games. Player salaries are much lower as well. According to the WNBA league office, the maximum salary for a WNBA player was $90,000 in 2004; that figure was less than one-fourth the minimum salary for an NBA rookie.

NATIONAL HOCKEY LEAGUE (NHL)

While professional hockey has a long and storied history in the United States, it is currently at a crossroads. Its popularity in the United States is declining, while other sports such as soccer and auto racing are eagerly courting disenchanted hockey fans. The cancellation of the 2004–05 NHL season due to a bitter labor dispute certainly did not help matters. That said, hockey is still big business. According to Plunkett Research, league-wide revenue in the NHL is about $2 billion, less than half that of the NFL or MLB, and more than a billion dollars less than the NBA, which has the same number of teams and the same number of games in a season as the NHL. NHL players earn an average annual salary of $1.81 million. Street & Smith's *SportsBusiness Journal* estimates that sales of merchandise licensed by the NHL and member teams generate about $900 million annually, the lowest among the major sports. The values and most recent revenue figures for NHL teams, as compiled by *Forbes*, are shown in Table 4.8.

Structure of the NHL

The NHL is divided into the Eastern and the Western Conferences. Each conference consists of three divisions, containing five teams. The Eastern Conference is split into the Northeast, Atlantic, and Southeast Divisions. The divisions that make up the Western Conference are the Northwest, Central, and Pacific. (See Table 4.9.) NHL teams play an eighty-two-game regular season (same as the NBA), split evenly between home and away games. Prior to the lockout of 2004–05, each team played all the others at least once during the season, but that is no longer the case. Teams now play ten games against opponents outside of their own conference, and forty games against teams in a different division within their own conference.

At the conclusion of the regular season, the champion of each division plus the five teams in each conference with the next best records compete in the Stanley Cup Playoffs. The structure is similar to that of the NBA: a single-elimination tournament consisting of four rounds of best-of-seven series, culminating in the Stanley Cup Finals, usually played in the late spring.

TABLE 4.8

Hockey team values and revenue, 2004

Rank	Team	Current value[a] ($million)	Revenues ($million)	Operating income[b] ($million)
1	New York Rangers	282	118	−3.3
2	Toronto Maple Leafs	280	117	14.1
3	Philadelphia Flyers	264	106	−4.1
4	Dallas Stars	259	103	−0.3
5	Detroit Red Wings	248	97	−16.4
6	Colorado Avalanche	246	99	−1.1
7	Boston Bruins	236	95	2.3
8	Montreal Canadiens	195	90	7.5
9	Los Angeles Kings	193	80	−5.3
10	Chicago Blackhawks	178	71	9.4
11	Minnesota Wild	163	71	11.5
12	New York Islanders	160	64	−9.5
13	Tampa Bay Lightning	150	88	8.6
14	San Jose Sharks	149	74	1.3
15	Vancouver Canucks	148	74	1.3
16	St Louis Blues	140	66	−28.8
17	Columbus Blue Jackets	139	66	0.9
18	Phoenix Coyotes	136	57	−7.8
19	Ottawa Senators	125	70	−5.0
20	New Jersey Devils	124	61	−13.9
21	Florida Panthers	121	60	−3.7
22	Calgary Flames	116	70	2.3
23	Washington Capitals	115	61	−14.7
24	Nashville Predators	111	57	6.2
25	Mighty Ducks of Anaheim	108	54	−22.4
26	Atlanta Thrashers	106	59	0.9
27	Edmonton Oilers	104	55	3.3
28	Buffalo Sabres	103	51	−10.5
29	Pittsburgh Penguins	101	52	−0.6
30	Carolina Hurricanes	100	52	−18.2

Note: Revenues and operating income are for 2003–04 season.
[a]Value of team based on current arena deal (unless new arena is pending) without deduction for debt (other than arena debt).
[b]Earnings before interest, taxes, depreciation and amortization.

SOURCE: Adapted from "NHL Team Valuations," in *Forbes Special Report: The Business of Hockey*, November 10, 2004, http://www.forbes.com/2004/11/10/04nhland.html (accessed September 22, 2005)

TABLE 4.9

National Hockey League teams and divisions

Eastern Conference	Western Conference
Atlantic Division	**Central Division**
New Jersey Devils	Chicago Blackhawks
New York Islanders	Columbus Blue Jackets
New York Rangers	Detroit Red Wings
Philadelphia Flyers	Nashville Predators
Pittsburgh Penguins	St. Louis Blues
Northeast Division	**Northwest Division**
Boston Bruins	Calgary Flames
Buffalo Sabres	Colorado Avalanche
Ottawa Senators	Edmonton Oilers
Montreal Canadiens	Minnesota Wild
Toronto Maple Leafs	Vancouver Canucks
Southeast Division	**Pacific Division**
Atlanta Thrashers	Anaheim Mighty Ducks
Carolina Hurricanes	Dallas Stars
Florida Panthers	Los Angeles Kings
Tampa Bay Lightning	Phoenix Coyotes
Washington Capitals	San Jose Sharks

SOURCE: Created by Information Plus using data from the National Hockey League, http://www.nhl.com

An Import from the North: History of the NHL

While hockey in North America started in Canada, the first professional version of the game was launched in the United States. In 1904 the International Pro Hockey League was founded in the iron mining areas of Michigan's Upper Peninsula. That league lasted only a few years, but in 1910 a new league, the National Hockey Association (NHA), arose. The Pacific Coast League (PCL) was founded soon after the NHA. It was arranged that the champions of the two leagues would play a championship series, the winner gaining possession of the coveted Stanley Cup, a trophy named for Lord Stanley of Preston, the former English Governor General of Canada.

World War I put a temporary halt to the fledgling sport, but when the war ended professional hockey reorganized itself as the National Hockey League. At first the NHL was strictly a Canadian affair. The league initially consisted of five teams: the Montreal Canadiens, Montreal Wanderers, Ottawa Senators, Quebec Bulldogs, and Toronto Arenas (later renamed the Maple Leafs). The first game took place on December 19, 1917. The NHL expanded into the United States in the 1920s, adding the Boston Bruins in 1924; the New York Americans and Pittsburgh Pirates in 1925; and the New York Rangers, Chicago Blackhawks, and Detroit Cougars (which later became the Red Wings) in 1926. By the end of the 1930–31 season, there were ten teams in the NHL. The Depression and World War II took their toll on the league, however, and by its twenty-fifth birthday the NHL was reduced to six teams. Those six teams—the Canadiens, Maple Leafs, Red Wings, Bruins, Rangers, and Blackhawks—are commonly referred to, not very accurately, as the "Original Six" of the NHL.

The NHL did not expand again until 1967, when six new teams were added, forming their own division. Two other franchises came on board three years later. In 1972 a new rival league, the World Hockey Association (WHA), was formed. In response, the NHL accelerated its own plans for expansion, adding four new teams over the next three years. This double-barreled expansion of professional hockey in North America diluted the pool of available players, however, and the quality of play suffered as a result. The WHA folded in 1979, and four of its teams joined the NHL. The league continued to expand over the next two decades, as league officials sought to follow demographic trends in the United States. The NHL reached its current total of thirty teams in 2000. Unfortunately, the league's southward and westward expansion has not been entirely successful, as interest is weak in warm-weather regions. While many Canadian towns have lost their teams to U.S. cities, and suffered economically as a result, a large percentage of Canadians remain diehard hockey fans. According to Canadian

Broadcast Corporation (CBC) data, the television show *Hockey Night in Canada* is consistently the highest-rated Canadian-produced television program on Canadian television. In the United States, though, hockey is in danger of losing its "major sport" status.

A Season on Ice: Labor Issues in the NHL

In its long history the NHL has been interrupted only three times by labor strife. The first, a 1992 strike by the NHL Players Association (NHLPA), lasted only ten days, short enough for all missed games to be made up. A lockout at the start of the 1994–95 season was more disruptive. It lasted three months and resulted in the cancellation of thirty-six games, nearly half of the regular season.

With the 1995 deal moving toward its 2004 expiration date, negotiations between players and owners turned bitter. Unlike the 1994 lockout, which came at a time when the NHL was enjoying strong fan support and rising popularity, interest in the league had been waning for several years by 2004. As in other major sports, one of the biggest points of contention was proposed limits on the amount teams could spend on player salaries. The league proposed what it called "cost certainty," which the players' union argued was just a fancy term for a salary cap. The union rejected the idea, and instead proposed a luxury tax. The owners, not surprisingly, were opposed. The two sides failed to reach an agreement, and the entire 2004–05 NHL season, from preseason training through the Stanley Cup Finals, was cancelled—the first time a major sport had lost a whole season to labor unrest.

In the summer of 2005 the NHLPA and the league finally agreed to the terms of a new collective bargaining agreement. The deal, which runs through the 2010–11 season, gives players 54% to 57% of league-wide revenues, depending on the total. The agreement includes a salary cap that tops out at about $39 million and enhanced revenue sharing to help the smaller market teams remain competitive. It does not include a luxury tax.

Naturally, hockey fans across North America were greatly disappointed by the loss of an entire season. In response, the NHL took measures to try to lure fans—both those who had wandered away from the sport prior to the lockout and those who lost interest directly because of it—back. These measures included a handful of rule changes designed to speed up the pace of the game and increase scoring.

A bigger challenge to the NHL remains the task of making hockey popular in parts of the United States that do not have longstanding hockey traditions. The expansion that the league undertook in the last two decades of the twentieth century was focused primarily in the Southern and Southwestern regions of the United States, the very parts of the country experiencing rapid population growth. While this expansion strategy made sense at the time, it has not produced the expected new generation of hockey fans in those regions to date.

MAJOR LEAGUE SOCCER (MLS)

Major League Soccer (MLS), the premier professional soccer league in the United States, was launched on April 6, 1996. MLS has a unique ownership and operating structure that is unlike those of other major U.S. sports leagues. While the other leagues are confederations of independent franchise owners, MLS has a "single-entity" structure, which allows investors to own a share of the league as well as individual teams.

As of the 2005 season MLS consisted of twelve teams divided into two conferences, Eastern and Western. (See Table 4.10.) Teams compete through a season that runs from April 2 through the MLS Cup championship on November 13. Each team plays thirty-two regular season games: four games against each opponent within their division, and two against non-conference opponents. The MLS Cup Playoffs begin in mid-October, culminating in the crowning of a new MLS Cup champion.

Plans to start up Major League Soccer were first announced in December 1993. Twenty-two cities submitted bids to secure teams, of which ten were selected. A player draft was conducted in February 1996. The league's first game took place a few months later. A full stadium of 31,683 spectators and a national ESPN viewing audience watched San Jose United defeat D.C. United.

Two additional teams were added in 1998. The following year, the Columbus Crew built the first major league stadium ever constructed specifically for soccer in the United States. The Crew ended up leading the league in attendance for the year. In 2002 the league was forced to cut two teams for financial reasons, returning MLS to its original ten-team size. Two new teams were added in 2005, bringing the league to twelve teams once again.

Major League Soccer is far more ethnically diverse than any of the traditional four major sports in the United States. MLS rosters during the 2005 preseason included players from thirty-one countries, representing all six international soccer Confederations. MLS has also played a huge role in preparing American players for greater impact on the international soccer scene.

Attempts to establish a women's professional soccer league in the United States have not met with great success. The Women's United Soccer Association (WUSA), the first women's professional outdoor league to be sanctioned by U.S. Soccer, was launched in 2001.

TABLE 4.10

Major League Soccer teams and divisions

Eastern Conference	Western Conference
Chicago Fire	Club Deportivo Chivas USA
Columbus Crew	Colorado Rapids
DC United	FC Dallas
Kansas City Wizards	Los Angeles Galaxy
MetroStars	Real Salt Lake
New England Revolution	San Jose Earthquakes

SOURCE: Created by Information Plus using data from Major League Soccer, http://www.mlsnet.com

It featured stars from the popular 2000 U.S. Olympic team, including Mia Hamm, Brandi Chastain, and Julie Foudy. In the face of financial struggles, the WUSA suspended operations in September 2003. Going into 2005, a new nonprofit organization, the Women's Soccer Initiative, Inc., was established with the goal of reviving women's professional soccer in the United States.

DIVERSITY IN THE MAJOR SPORTS

Diversity has long been an issue in major league sports in the United States. Major League Baseball was all white until Jackie Robinson crossed the color line in 1947. Over the next few decades, the number of prominent black ballplayers grew, and baseball took on the appearance of an inclusive sport (at least on the field; managerial jobs for African-Americans have always been scarce). However, the trend has reversed itself. Major League Baseball teams once again have few African-Americans on their rosters, although the number of Hispanic players has increased dramatically. Of the 1,187 players on MLB rosters as of publication of the league's 2005 spring-training media guide, 141 were born in the Dominican Republic, seventy-eight in Venezuela, thirty-nine in Puerto Rico, twenty-one in Mexico, ten in Cuba, and seven in Panama. The percentage of foreign-born players has been climbing for several years, from 19% on opening day in 1997 to 27% in 2004, according to Adam Rubin of the *New York Daily News* ("Fighting a Los Cause," February 26, 2005).

In fact, concerns about diversity in professional sports extend beyond the playing field. Coaching and management opportunities have traditionally been limited for minorities, but even that trend may be shifting. Rubin reports that as of 2005 the New York Mets had one of the most diverse management and coaching staffs in Major League Baseball, with the only Hispanic general manager in the league and New York's first African-American manager, along with three minorities on the coaching staff.

A study from the University of Central Florida's Institute for Diversity and Ethics in Sport ("2004 Racial and Gender Report Card," June 2005) examined the front office, support staff, playing, and coaching opportunities for women and minorities in professional football, basketball, baseball, and soccer, along with colleges. The "Race and Gender Report Card" gave top marks to the NBA and lowest marks to the NFL, noting that while about three-quarters of the players in each of those leagues are minorities, the NBA has three African-American presidents and CEOs, giving it an edge over the other leagues. For gender diversity, only the WNBA received an *A* grade on the UCF report card, which is not surprising since it was the only professional sport analyzed that has female players.

THE STADIUM SCRAMBLE

Since the early 1990s, there has been an unprecedented boom in the construction of new stadiums for America's sports teams. The main reason is that team owners believe that they can make a lot more money selling luxury boxes, which older stadiums lack, to wealthy corporate customers than they can by selling cheaper seats to the masses. A luxury box can sell for upwards of $200,000 a season. Table 4.11 shows the typical cost of a luxury box at venues that host each of the major sports. An additional incentive is that the revenue from sales of these luxury boxes is exempt from the revenue-sharing formulas of both MLB and the NFL, meaning teams get to keep all the money generated by luxury boxes.

Owners have been further encouraged by the success of their peers in obtaining public funding for the construction of their new stadiums. A number of team owners have succeeded in securing public dollars for their new stadiums by threatening to leave town if the taxpayers did not foot the bill. Owners usually argue that a new stadium will generate additional tax revenue, as fans flock to the new facility and, so they claim, spend vast sums of money at nearby businesses. The National Taxpayers Union ("Public Funding of Sports Stadiums: Ballpark Boondoggle," February 28, 2001) reports that taxpayers around the United States spent more than $7.5 billion on stadium construction between 1990 and 2001. Consumer advocate and former presidential candidate Ralph Nader has claimed that the economic benefits of taxpayer-subsidized stadium construction are negligible ("Stadium Subsidies Scalp the Public," *Boston Globe*, March 27, 2000). Citing research that indicated no positive economic impact over the course of thirty years from twenty-seven out of thirty existing taxpayer-funded stadiums, Nader also pointed to polls showing that the public is against public funding for stadiums by about a two-to-one margin.

Nevertheless, team owners have met with great success in selling their proposed public-financed stadium plans to lawmakers. Matthew Tully, in "Smaller NFL

TABLE 4.11

Major sport luxury suite prices, 2005

Sport/league	Qty	Averages	
		Low	High
Major League Baseball	77	$89,997	$177,661
National Football League	142	$59,600	$183,850
National Basketball Association	88	$128,017	$231,203
National Hockey League	94	$109,534	$212,100

SOURCE: "Luxury Suites," in *Revenues from Sports Venues*, http://www
.sportsvenues.com/info.htm#Suites (accessed September 22, 2005)

Markets Pay More for New Stadiums" (*Indianapolis Star*, April 30, 2005) reported that "a review of financing plans for the NFL's ten most recently constructed stadiums found taxpayers in the five larger markets paid about 45% of the bill." Taxpayers in smaller markets, which have less leverage in their negotiations with team owners, paid more than 80% of the cost of building their teams' new stadiums. One team, the NFL's Tennessee Titans, received a free ride altogether; taxpayers covered the entire cost of building their new stadium.

Another source of revenue from stadiums and arenas comes from the sale of naming rights. Where in the past most stadiums had straightforward names like Tiger Stadium or the Houston Astrodome, today an increasing number of facilities bear the name of a corporate sponsor that has paid millions of dollars for the privilege. The following comprise a few examples, as indicated by Revenues from Sports Venues, a company that specializes in directories and other publications about the sports venue industry (http://www.sportsvenues.com/pdf/names.pdf):

- Comerica Park in Detroit, home of the Tigers ($66 million for thirty years)

- San Francisco's 3Com Park, where the San Francisco Giants play baseball ($4 million for five years)

- American Airlines Center in Dallas, home of both basketball's Mavericks and hockey's Stars ($195 million for thirty years)

Sometimes these deals backfire, as in 2002 when the Houston Astros had to buy their way out of a thirty-year, $100 million deal in order to get Enron's name off of the team's stadium.

CHAPTER 5
OTHER PROFESSIONAL SPORTS

As important as professional team sports are in the United States, America's sports obsession extends well beyond them. Not every sports enthusiast is engrossed by the hoopla of *Monday Night Football* or the high-flying acrobatics of the NBA. Some fans prefer the quiet beauty of a perfect putt or the battle of wills that takes place across the Centre Court net at Wimbledon. Others are attracted to the blunt truth of boxing or the raw speed of NASCAR. The following discussion considers several sports that fall below the top tier of American sports in terms of audience or revenue but are nevertheless important components of the nation's professional sports landscape.

GOLF

Professional golf in the United States is coordinated by the Professional Golfers' Association of America (PGA), a nonprofit organization that promotes the sport while enhancing golf's professional standards. There are currently about 28,000 PGA professionals in the United States, both men and women. However, most of these members are primarily golf instructors; only a small fraction compete in high-profile tournaments (http://www.pga.com/home/pgaofamerica/).

The PGA of America traces its roots to 1916, when a group of golf professionals and serious amateurs in the New York area got together at a luncheon sponsored by department store magnate Rodman Wanamaker. The point of the meeting was to discuss forming a national organization to promote golf and elevate the occupation of golf professional. The meeting led to the organization of the first PGA Championship tournament, which was played later that year. The PGA Championship has grown to become one of professional golf's four "major" championships, along with the British Open, the Masters, and the U.S. Open. Together, these four tournaments make up the unofficial "Grand Slam" of golf. (See Table 5.1.) In addition to the PGA Championship, the PGA sponsors

three other top golf events: the Senior PGA Championship; the Ryder Cup, which every two years pits a team of top American golfers against counterparts from Europe; and the PGA Grand Slam of Golf, an annual event in which the winners of the four major championships compete head to head. In addition to the above championships, the PGA also conducts about forty tournaments for PGA Professionals, as well as the Buick Scramble, the world's biggest amateur tournament. The Scramble draws over 100,000 participants each year.

However, while professional golfers in the United States are members of the PGA, most of the actual golf they play is under the auspices of other organizations. Professional golf worldwide is organized into several regional "tours," each of which usually holds a series of tournaments over the course of a season. There at least twenty of these tours around the world, each run by a national or regional PGA, or by an independent tour organization. Each tour has members who may compete in as many of its events as they want. Joining a tour usually requires that a golfer achieve some specified level of success, often by performing well in a qualifying tournament. A player can be a member of multiple tours.

The world's top tour by far, in terms of money and prestige, is the PGA Tour, which since 1968 has been a completely separate organizational entity from the PGA of America. In 2005 the PGA Tour had forty-eight official events offering more than $250 million in total prize money. The PGA Tour organization also runs two other tours: the Champions Tour for golfers over age fifty; and the Nationwide Tour, a sort of minor league of professional golf.

History of the PGA

The first U.S. Open took place in 1895 in Newport, Rhode Island. Ten professionals and one amateur competed in the event. The Western Open made its debut in

TABLE 5.1

Golf Grand Slam events

Event	Location	Scheduled time
The Masters	Augusta, Georgia	April
U.S. Open	Location varies	June
British Open	Location varies	July
PGA Championship	Location varies	August

SOURCE: Created by Information Plus

Chicago, Illinois, four years later. Tournaments were initiated throughout the country at about this time, though there was no coordination or continuity among them. English players dominated the competition in U.S. tournaments. As interest in golf continued to grow, American players improved. Enthusiasm for the sport began to increase quickly after John McDermott became the first American-born player to win the U.S. Open in 1911. By the 1920s professional golf had spread to the West Coast and southward to Florida, and the prize money was becoming substantial.

The PGA Tour was formally launched in late 1968, when the Tournament Players Division of the PGA broke away from the parent organization and hired its own commissioner (http://www.golfweb.com/info/company/pgatour_history). The Tour grew explosively during the 1970s and 1980s, with its total annual revenue increasing from $3.9 million in 1974 to $229 million in 1993.

Champions Tour

The Champions Tour, run by the PGA Tour organization, hosts thirty events each year in the United States and Canada for golfers at least fifty years old. The Tour grew out of a highly successful 1978 event called the Legends of Golf, which featured two-member teams composed of some of the game's best-known former champions. Following up on the success of the Legends event, the Senior PGA Tour was established in 1980, with two tournaments and $250,000 in prize money. The Senior Tour proved remarkably popular, as fans flocked to golf courses and tuned in on television to see such legendary competitors as Arnold Palmer and Sam Snead in action. While their playing skills may have diminished somewhat from the level of their prime playing years, the former champions proved popular with golf lovers across the country. At the start of the 2003 season, the Senior Tour changed its name to the Champions Tour. By 2005 Champions Tour prize money had reached about $50 million.

Most Champions Tour tournaments are played over three rounds (fifty-four holes) rather than the customary four rounds (seventy-two holes) typical of PGA tournaments. The five "majors" of the senior circuit are exceptions; they are played over four rounds. The major tournaments of the Champions Tour are the Senior PGA Championship, the Senior Players Championship, the Senior British Open, the U.S. Senior Open, and The Tradition.

Nationwide Tour

The Nationwide Tour is the developmental tour for the PGA Tour. Its players are professionals who have missed the criteria to get into the main tour by failing to score well enough in the PGA Tour's qualifying tournament, known as Qualifying School; or who have made it into the main tour but failed to win enough money to stay there. The Nationwide Tour gets its name from the company that bought the naming rights in 2003, the Nationwide Mutual Insurance Company of Columbus, Ohio. It was called the Nike Tour and the Buy.com Tour before that. When the tour was first launched in its original form in 1990, it was known as the Ben Hogan Tour; however, naming a tour after a prominent player is not as lucrative as naming it for a corporation.

In 1990 there were thirty events in the tour, and the typical prize money for a tournament was about $100,000. The Nationwide Tour consisted of thirty-two events in 2005. Two of them were in Canada, and one each in Australia, New Zealand, and Panama. The rest were in the United Sates. Prize money for Nationwide Tour events is typically about one-tenth that of a PGA Tour tournament, ranging from about $450,000 to $750,000.

The Nationwide Tour has proven to be an excellent feeder system for the PGA Tour. According to the PGA Tour Web site, Nationwide Tour alumni have won 150 PGA Tour titles, including ten major championships, as of 2005. A number of top players, including Ernie Els, Jim Furyk, David Duval, David Toms, and John Daly, played the Nationwide circuit before achieving success on the PGA Tour (http://www.pgatour.com/info/company/nationwidetour_history).

Other Men's Tours

As noted above, the PGA Tour is merely the biggest and richest of the world's many professional golf tours. There are many others around the world, some of which—like the Nationwide Tour—prepare players for entry into the PGA Tour. In 1996 the International Federation of PGA Tours was formed by golf's five chief governing bodies around the world. As of 2005 the International Federation had six members: the PGA Tour (United States), the Asian Tour, the Japan Golf Tour, the PGA European Tour, the PGA Tour of Australasia, and the Sunshine Tour (Southern Africa). Together, these tours sanction the Official World Golf Rankings.

The PGA European Tour, headquartered in England, is the premier professional golf tour in Europe, and is second only to the PGA Tour in money and international prestige (http://www.europeantour.com/). The European tour was established by the British PGA, but in 1984 it became a separate entity, just as the PGA Tour became independent from the PGA in America in 1968. In 2005 prize money on the European Tour totaled about $150 million, approximately 60% of the money awarded by the PGA Tour. Most of the top players on the European Tour, including Ernie Els, Retief Goosen, Sergio Garcia, and Padraig Harrington, are also members of the PGA Tour and do quite well there. Like the PGA Tour, the European Tour has a developmental tour, called the Challenge Tour, and a senior tour, called the European Seniors Tour.

The Japan Golf Tour is the third biggest professional men's tour (not counting senior tours) in terms of prize money available. However, prize money in the Japanese Tour has not kept pace with the growth of money in the PGA and European Tours in recent years.

Performance in all of the above tours—the six International Federation members, plus the Nationwide and Challenge Tours—earns Official World Golf Ranking points. The Canadian Tour also counts toward Official World Rankings. Other regional tours worth noting are the Tour de las Americas, which is seeking to be included in World Ranking calculations; the Indian Golf Tour; and the Hooters NGA Tour, which is the third-tier U.S.–based professional tour, below the Nationwide Tour, in money and prestige.

Women's Tours

Women's professional golf, like men's golf, is organized into several regional tours. The top tour for female professional golfers is the Ladies Professional Golf Association (LPGA), which operates the LPGA Tour. Unlike the PGA Tour, the LPGA Tour and the LPGA are not distinct organizations. Both of these terms generally refer to the LPGA that is based in the United States. Internationally, there are other regional LPGAs and tours, including the LPGA of Japan, the LPGA of Korea, the Australian Ladies Professional Golf tour (ALPG), and the Ladies European Tour.

The LPGA, founded in 1950 by a group of thirteen golfers, is the oldest continuing women's professional sports organization in the United States. It features the best female golfers from all over the world. The 2005 LPGA Tour consisted of thirty-four events offering total prize money of over $45 million (http://www.lpga.com/content_1.aspx?mid=0&pid=52). Most LPGA Tour events take place in the United States. In 2005 there were also two events in Mexico and one in Canada. In addition, two events were co-sanctioned with the Ladies European Tour, and one with the LPGA of Korea Tour. Four LPGA tournaments are considered the tour's

"majors": the Kraft Nabisco Championship; McDonald's U.S. LPGA Championship Presented by Coca-Cola; the U.S. Women's Open; and the Weetabix Women's British Open (held jointly with the Ladies European Tour).

In addition to the main tour, the LPGA also coordinates a developmental tour called the Futures Tour. The Futures Tour began in Florida in 1981 as the "Tampa Bay Mini Tour" but is now a national tour that functions as a feeder system for the LPGA, filling the same role as the Nationwide Tour does for the men. As of 2005 the Futures Tour featured an eighteen-tournament national schedule and a total purse of nearly $1.25 million (http://www.futurestour.com/AboutUs.html).

In 2001 the LPGA created the Women's Senior Golf Tour (WSGT) for players over age forty-five. As of 2005 the WSGT sponsored only a handful of events per season, but interest was growing and prospects for the future were bright.

TENNIS

Men's professional tennis is coordinated by the Association of Tennis Professionals (ATP), which organizes the ATP Tour (the principal worldwide tennis tour), and the International Tennis Federation, which coordinates international play including the Davis Cup and the Grand Slam tournaments. (See Table 5.2.) The ATP was originally formed in 1972 as a sort of trade union to protect the interests of male professional tennis players. The organization assumed its role as chief coordinating body of the pro tour in 1990. The ATP Tour consisted of sixty-four tournaments in thirty-one countries in 2005. The most important batch of tournaments are those that make up tennis' Grand Slam. They are the Australian Open, French Open, U.S. Open, and Wimbledon. Only two men have ever won the Grand Slam of tennis: Don Budge in 1938, and Rod Laver in both 1962 and 1969. Total prize money for Wimbledon in 2005 was over $18 million. The U.S. Open offered a slightly higher payday, at $19.4 million, according to the U.S. Open Series Web site (http://www.usopenseries.com/home/default.sps). The ATP also operates the Challenger Series, a second-tier professional circuit in which many top players have started their professional careers. The ITF also runs two other circuits that represent a level of professional play below the Challenger Series. They are the Satellite tournaments and the Futures Tour.

Women's Professional Tennis

Women's professional tennis is coordinated by the Women's Tennis Association (WTA, which is to the women's game what the ATP is to the men's game). The WTA runs the premier professional women's tour, which in 2005 became known as the Sony Ericsson WTA Tour. In 2005 the Sony Ericsson Tour involved more than

TABLE 5.2

Tennis Grand Slam events

Event	Location	Scheduled time
Australian Open	Melbourne	Last fortnight of January
French Open	Paris	May/June
Wimbledon	Wimbledon, England	June/July
U.S. Open	Flushing Meadows, Queens, New York	August/September

SOURCE: Created by Information Plus

1,000 players representing seventy-one nations, competing for $57.8 million in prize money at sixty-three events in thirty-three countries. Women also compete in the same four Grand Slam events, governed by the ITF, as do the men.

The WTA was born in 1973, initially, like the ATP, as a professional organization to protect the interests of the players. The Tour itself, which started out as the Virginia Slims Tour, was originally formed out of protest at the disparity between the prize money for men and women. At the dawn of the "open" era (1968), when professionals were first allowed into the big-name tournaments, the male singles winner sometimes received as much as ten times what the female champion was paid. Other sponsors came and went over the years, including Colgate, Avon, Toyota, and Kraft General Foods. By 1980 more than 250 women were playing professionally all over the world in a Tour consisting of forty-seven global events, offering a total $7.2 million in prize money. The Tour remained under the governance of the Women's Tennis Council, an umbrella agency run by representatives from the ITF, the tournament promoters, and the players, into the 1990s. The WTA Tour in its current form was created in 1995 through the merger of the WTA Players Association and the Women's Tennis Council. A series of sponsors have funded the Tour over the years, the most recent being Sony Ericcson in 2006.

History of Tennis

Lawn tennis was invented in 1873 in Wales by an Englishman, Major Walter C. Wingfield. It is based on the older sport of *Real tennis* (French for Royal tennis), which was itself based on other games involving hitting a ball with a racket or the hand that date back to ancient Egypt. The game gained popularity quickly across Great Britain, and the first world tennis championship was held just four years later at the All England Croquet Club at Wimbledon. This tournament evolved into the famous Wimbledon Championships, which remain the most prestigious tennis titles to this day. A women's championship was added at Wimbledon in 1884. Over the next several years, tennis spread across many parts of the British Empire, becoming especially popular in Australia.

Tennis arrived in the United States early on in this process. A tennis court was set up in Staten Island, New York, in about 1874. The first National Championship in the United States—for men only—was held in 1881 in Newport, Rhode Island. A women's championship was added six years later. The National Championship moved to Forest Hills, New York, in 1915, where it remained under various names for more than sixty years. Now known as the U.S. Open, the event moved to the National Tennis Center in Flushing, New York, in 1978.

Professionalization of Tennis

As tennis spread around the British empire early in the twentieth century, national federations were formed in countries where the sport caught on. These federations eventually joined forces to form the International Tennis Federation (ITF), which was the worldwide sanctioning authority for tennis. International competitions between national teams soon arose, the most important being the Davis Cup tournament, founded in 1900, and the Wightman Cup, an annual competition between women's teams from England and the United States, founded in 1923.

As most sports turned professional in the first half of the century, however, tennis remained primarily an amateur endeavor, largely a pastime for wealthy country club members. By the late 1920s it became economically feasible for a top player to make a decent living on the professional tour, but it meant giving up the sport's most prestigious, amateur-only events, like those at Wimbledon and Forest Hills. The move toward professionalism accelerated after Bill Tilden, the best player of his time and a winner of seven U.S. singles championships and three Wimbledon titles as an amateur, turned pro in 1931. More and more top players trickled into the professional ranks over the next few decades, though the pro tour was not glamorous and the money was mediocre. The ITF fought hard all along against the professionalization of tennis. In 1968 the All England Lawn Tennis and Croquet Club decided to open Wimbledon to professional players, thus ushering in the "open" era of tennis in which professional players are allowed to compete in the sport's biggest tournaments.

Around this time, women players became frustrated at the gender disparity in tennis prize money. Women winning a tournament often received a mere fraction of what the men's champion in the same tournament took home. In 1971 a women-only professional tour was formed to address these inequities. This new Virginia Slims Tour was an instant hit. It made Billie Jean King the first woman athlete in any sport to earn more than $100,000 in a single year.

AUTO RACING

There are several different top-level auto racing circuits in the United States, in which different kinds of cars race. The two most popular types of race cars are stock cars and open-wheeled racers. From the outside, stock cars essentially look like the regular cars that populate the highways of America, only covered with corporate logos. Stock car racing is dominated by the National Association for Stock Car Auto Racing (NASCAR). Open-wheel cars are single-seat vehicles with special aerodynamic features that allow them to travel at speeds well over two hundred miles per hour without flying off the track. Open-wheel racing is currently in a state of civil war between its two chief circuits, the Indy Racing League (IRL) and the Champ Car Series. Another open-wheel circuit, Formula One Grand Prix, is dominant in Europe.

NASCAR

The largest sanctioning body of motor sports in the United States is the National Association for Stock Car Auto Racing (NASCAR). NASCAR sanctions a number of racing series, the largest among them being the NEXTEL Cup, the Busch Series, and the Craftsman Truck Series. In all, NASCAR sanctions more than 1,500 races a year at over one hundred different tracks in thirty-eight states, Mexico, and Canada. A November 2005 Reuters article indicated that NASCAR's fan base had grown to seventy-five million over the past ten years, an increase of 19% over that span (Nicole Maestri, "NASCAR Rolling Out New Games to Attract Young Fans," November 9, 2005). The article quoted Blake Davidson, managing director of licensed products for NASCAR, as saying that NASCAR expected $2.1 billion worth of NASCAR licensed products to be sold in 2005. Once a regional obsession in the southeastern part of the country, NASCAR has exploded into a nationwide phenomenon, rivaling baseball for the number two spot behind football for the hearts and viewing hours of American sports fans.

Stock car racing evolved out of bootlegging in the rural South. Alcohol runners would modify their cars to make them faster and more maneuverable. It was natural for these drivers to start racing their souped-up autos against each other.

NASCAR was founded in 1948 by William France, Sr. and Ed Otto as a way to organize, standardize, and promote racing of unmodified, or "stock," cars for entertainment. The first NASCAR "Strictly Stock" race took place at North Carolina's Charlotte Speedway in June 1949. Over time, modifications were allowed into the sport, and by the mid-1960s, only the bodies of the cars looked "stock"; the innards were specially built for speed.

NASCAR's rapid growth began in the 1970s, when R. J. Reynolds Tobacco Company began to sponsor racing as a way to promote their products after they had been banned from TV advertising. The top series, formerly known as the Grand National Series, became the "Winston Cup." At about this time, television networks began covering stock car racing on occasion. CBS's broadcast of the 1979 Daytona 500 was the first time a stock car race had been aired nationwide from start to finish.

In 2004 Nextel assumed sponsorship of the series formerly known as the Winston Cup. The Nextel Cup remains the most prominent and lucrative NASCAR racing series. That year, NASCAR established a new ten-race playoff system called the "Chase for the Cup," in which the top ten drivers (according to NASCAR's point system) after twenty-six races compete for the series championship.

Open-Wheeled Cars

The two major open-wheel series, Indy Racing League (IRL) and Champ Car, have been struggling in the mid-2000s, as fans by the million have flocked to stock car racing. The reasons for this are complex, but it is reasonable to attribute the situation in part to the acrimonious relationship between the IRL and Champ Car. Neither has done well financially in recent years, although the success of rookie Danica Patrick breathed some life into IRL in 2005.

Indy Racing League

The Indy Racing League is the top circuit for single-seat, open-wheel racecars specially designed for high-speed racing on oval tracks. The IRLO was formed in 1994 by a group of drivers breaking away from CART (now known as the Champ Car Series; see below), which had coordinated Indy car racing since breaking away from the United States Auto Club (USAC) in 1979. IRL consists of two series: the IndyCar Series, which is virtually synonymous with IRL, and the Menards Infiniti Pro Series, which functions as a development series for drivers aspiring to join the IndyCar circuit.

Before 1979 the term "IndyCar" was used generically to refer to cars racing in USAC events. By the 1980s IndyCar was a term commonly used to refer to CART, which by that time was the preeminent sanctioning body for open-wheel racing in the United States. The name IndyCar became the subject of fierce legal battles in the 1990s. The Indianapolis Motor Speedway, home of the Indy 500, trademarked the name in 1992 and licensed it to CART, which in turn renamed its championship the IndyCar World Series. Two years later, Tony George, president of the speedway, started his own racing series called the Indy Racing League (IRL). In 1996 CART sued in order to protect its right to continue using the IndyCar name. The speedway countered with its own suit. The two groups eventually reached a settlement in which CART agreed to stop using the IndyCar name after the 1996 season, and the IRL could start using it after the

2002 season. IRL's premier series has been called the IRL IndyCar Series since the beginning of the 2003 season. The 2006 IndyCar Series features fourteen races over twenty-five weeks.

Champ Car

The United States Automobile Club (USAC) was formed in 1956 to take over coordination of the national driving championship from the American Automobile Association (AAA), which had launched the championship in 1909. USAC controlled the championship until 1979, when a group of car owners formed an organization called Championship Auto Racing Teams (CART) that they hoped would give them power in negotiations with USAC over media contracts, race purses, promotion, and other issues. The two entities immediately clashed, and CART soon separated from USAC to establish its own racing series. Most of the top teams defected from USAC, and CART quickly became the dominant open-wheel racing circuit. USAC held its last National Championship in 1979, before reluctantly handing the reins over to CART.

IRL's split from CART threw open-wheel racing into a tailspin from which it has not yet recovered entirely. The rivalry may have helped pave the way for NASCAR's rise, as both competing organizations struggled for control over the sport's available pot of money. Fans grew restless. CART declared bankruptcy during the 2003 off-season, and its stock plummeted to $0.25 a share. CART's assets were liquidated and put up for sale. A group of CART car owners bought the company and opened the 2004 season under the new name Champ Car. As of 2005 Champ Car runs both the Champ Car World Series and the Toyota Atlantic Championship, which functions as a developmental circuit for drivers trying to get into Champ Car. The Champ Car series included thirteen races in 2005, which took place between April and November.

BOXING

Boxing is unique among professional sports in that there is no nationwide commission that oversees it, no regular schedules, no seasons, and few universal rules. Every set of matches (called a "card") is set up separately, usually by one of a handful of top-level boxing promoters. Each state has its own boxing commission with its own set of rules. Some state boxing commissions regulate the sport more rigorously than others, and the different governing organizations establish their own regulations. For example, variations exist regarding whether a boxer who has been knocked down can be "saved by the bell"; whether a referee or a ringside physician has the authority to stop a match; and whether a match should automatically be stopped if a fighter is knocked down three times within one round.

Boxing matches in the United States consist of a maximum of twelve three-minute rounds with one minute of rest between rounds. Opponents in a fight must belong to the same weight class, with competitors being weighed before the fight in an attempt to assure that neither holds an unfair weight advantage. The three judges at ringside score the fight according to a "ten-point must" system; that is, each judge must award ten points to the winner of the round and fewer points to the loser of the round. Matches end in one of five ways:

- *Knockout* (KO)—one fighter is unable to return to his feet within ten seconds of a knockdown
- *Technical knockout* (TKO)—a decision is made to stop the fight because one fighter clearly is losing
- *Decision*—the fight ends without a knockout or technical knockout and is won based on the scoring of the three judges at ringside
- *Draw*—the fight ends without a knockout or technical knockout, and the scorecards award each fighter the same number of points
- *Disqualification*—the fight is stopped due to a rule infraction on the part of one of the fighters

Unlike other professional sports, boxing does not use a playoff series or point system to name a champion. In fact, there is not necessarily even a consensus about who is champion of any given weight class. Different champions are recognized by several competing boxing organizations. The most prominent boxing organizations are the World Boxing Association (WBA), the World Boxing Council (WBC), the World Boxing Organization (WBO), and the International Boxing Federation (IBF). A fighter may be recognized as champion in his weight class by more than one of these organizations at a time, or each may have a different champion at any given time. Some of the biggest boxing matches are "unification" bouts between champions recognized by two different sanctioning organizations, the winner walking away with both titles.

Because boxing competitions are often international in nature, it is very difficult to gauge the size of the boxing industry in the United States. In a 2001 article, author Jack Newfield estimated professional boxing to be a $500-million-a-year business ("The Shame of Boxing," *Nation*, November 12, 2001). Much of the money comes from cable television, where championship fights are usually broadcast on a pay-per-view basis.

Boxing has a long history of both glamour and corruption. It has inspired such famous writers as Norman Mailer, Albert Camus, Ernest Hemingway, and Joyce Carol Oates, and such landmark films as *Body and Soul*, *The Champ*, *Raging Bull*, *Requiem for a Heavyweight*, *On the Waterfront*, and, of course, the *Rocky* series.

However, because the scoring system is complex and because the overall rankings often appear somewhat arbitrary, the sport has long been a tempting target for organized crime and others seeking illicit financial gain. Even today, bribery is thought to be rampant. Mysterious judging decisions and bizarre rankings are not at all rare. Boxing's reputation also suffers because of the sheer brutality of the sport. Fighters have sometimes died or suffered disabling brain trauma as a result of a particularly violent bout. In the article cited above, in fact, Newfield noted quite a few cases of fixed fights, rigged rankings, cronyism, and instances of money being prioritized over safety.

World Boxing Association (WBA)

The WBA was the first sanctioning body of professional boxing. It was formed as the National Boxing Association (NBA) in 1921. The first NBA-sanctioned match was a heavyweight championship fight between Jack Dempsey and Georges Carpentier. Brilliant and colorful champions such as Joe Louis carried the WBA through the World War II era. The dawn of television boosted the popularity of professional boxing in the 1950s. The sport's globalization during this period led the organization to change its name to the World Boxing Association in 1962.

World Boxing Council (WBC)

The WBC was formed in 1963 by representatives of eleven countries (United States, Mexico, Venezuela, Panama, Peru, Brazil, Japan, Argentina, Spain, Great Britain, and the Philippines) and Puerto Rico. Its purpose, according to WBC founders, was to improve the standards of professional boxing, including the safety of fighters. Among the WBC's innovations was the 1983 shortening of world championship fights from fifteen to twelve rounds, a move adopted by the other sanctioning organizations later. In 2003 the WBC filed for bankruptcy in an attempt to avoid paying $30 million in damages from a lawsuit over questionable handling of title fight eligibility. The following year, the lawsuit was settled for a lesser amount, allowing the WBC to avoid having to disband and liquidate its assets.

International Boxing Federation (IBF)

The IBF was formed in 1983 by a group of WBA representatives upset with political machinations within that agency. Its creation was spearheaded by Bob Lee, president of a smaller regional organization called the United States Boxing Association (USBA). The new group was originally called IBF-USBA. In its first year of operation, the IBF remained fairly obscure. In 1984, however, the IBF decided to recognize as champions a number of high-profile fighters who were already established as other organizations' title holders, including Larry Holmes and Marvin Hagler. When Holmes opted to relinquish his WBC title in order to accept the IBF's, it instantly gave the IBF the credibility it had previously lacked. The IBF's reputation took a major hit in 1999, when IBF president Lee was convicted on racketeering and other charges. It nevertheless remains one of professional boxing's major sanctioning bodies.

World Boxing Organization (WBO)

The WBO was formed in 1988 by a group of Puerto Rican and Dominican businessmen disenchanted with what they perceived as illegitimate rules and rating systems within the WBA. The WBO's first championship fight was a Junior Welterweight championship match between Héctor "Macho" Camacho and Ray "Boom Boom" Mancini. The WBO fairly quickly achieved a level of legitimacy comparable to that of the WBA, WBC, and IBF, largely thanks to its recognition as champions of many of the sport's best-known competitors. The WBO has also tended at times to provide more opportunities for non-U.S.-based fighters than the other organizations. While the WBO was formed out of protest against allegedly corrupt practices, it has certainly exhibited its share of inexplicable decisions that raise questions about the organization's integrity. A particularly embarrassing example took place in 2001, when the WBO twice moved fighter Darrin Morris up in its super-middleweight rankings, despite the fact that he had fought only once in the past three years, and, more important, was dead.

CHAPTER 6
COLLEGE AND HIGH SCHOOL SPORTS

College athletics function as a minor, or preparatory, league for some professional sports, particularly football and basketball, but there is nothing minor about Americans' passion for them or about the sums of money intercollegiate sports generate. Just as college sports serve as a feeder system for professional leagues, high schools fill the same role for colleges, and schools often compete for the services of elite teenage athletes. For the most part, high school and college athletes participate in sports for their own rewards. They understand that the chances of striking it rich as a professional athlete are remote. Table 6.1 shows a high school athlete's chances of playing at a higher level. However, so abundant is the money that flows through the sports industry—an industry of which intercollegiate sports are an integral part—that its influence can be felt even in America's high schools.

COLLEGE SPORTS

In contrast to professional sports, where turning a profit is the motivating force behind most decisions, college sports must reconcile commercial interests, educational priorities, and a jumble of other influences ranging from alumni pride to institutional prestige. While it may make high-minded university officials uncomfortable to admit it, college sports have become big business in the United States.

The most important governing organization of college sports in the United States is the National Collegiate Athletic Association (NCAA), though there are other governing bodies as well.

National Collegiate Athletic Association (NCAA)

The NCAA is a voluntary association whose members comprise 1,250 institutions, conferences, organizations, and individuals; 1,024 of them are active member schools (http://www2.ncaa.org/about_ncaa/membership/). The NCAA's main purpose, according to its constitution, is to "maintain

intercollegiate athletics as an integral part of the educational program and the athlete as an integral part of the study body and, by so doing, retain a clear line of demarcation between intercollegiate athletics and professional sports." In other words, college sports are supposed to be strictly amateur, and are supposed to fulfill an educational role.

Organizationally, the NCAA's structure consists of more than 125 committees, which, since a new governance structure was adopted in 1997, have enjoyed a fair amount of autonomy. Several of these committees are association-wide, including the Executive Committee and committees having to do with ethics, women's opportunities, and minority opportunities. The rest are specific to one of the NCAA's three divisions—Divisions I, II, and III—which classify the schools by the number of sports they sponsor and other factors. NCAA member schools and organizations vote on the rules they will have to follow. It is then up to the NCAA National Office staff of about three hundred to implement and enforce the rules and bylaws dictated by the members.

The NCAA's divisions are based on such factors as the number of sports sponsored, attendance at the school's sporting events, and financial support to athletes. Division I is further divided into Divisions I-A, I-AA, and I-AAA. Intercollegiate sports under the auspices of the NCAA are also divided into conferences, which function like the leagues and divisions in professional sports. The most prominent conferences, often referred to collectively as the Big Six, are shown in Table 6.2. The colleges in these conferences sponsor many sports, have big athletic budgets, and draw a lot of fans. Table 6.3 summarizes the number of schools sponsoring each sport across each of the divisions.

History of the NCAA

Up until the middle of the nineteenth century, there was no governing body that oversaw intercollegiate athletics. In fact, it was typically students rather than

TABLE 6.1

Estimated probability of competing in athletics beyond high school

Student-athletes	Men's basketball	Women's basketball	Football	Baseball	Men's hockey	Men's soccer
High school student-athletes	549,500	456,900	983,600	455,300	29,900	321,400
High school senior student-athletes	157,000	130,500	281,000	130,100	8,500	91,800
NCAA* student-athletes	15,700	14,400	56,500	25,700	3,700	18,200
NCAA freshman roster positions	4,500	4,100	16,200	7,300	1,100	5,200
NCAA senior student-athletes	3,500	3,200	12,600	5,700	800	4,100
NCAA student-athletes drafted	44	32	250	600	33	76
Percent high school to NCAA	2.9	3.1	5.8	5.6	12.9	5.7
Percent NCAA to professional	1.3	1.0	2.0	10.5	4.1	1.9
Percent high school to professional	0.03	0.02	0.09	0.5	0.4	0.08

Note: These percentages are based on estimated data and should be considered approximations of the actual percentages.

*NCAA=National Collegiate Athletic Association

SOURCE: "Estimated Probability of Competing in Athletics Beyond the High School Interscholastic Level," National Collegiate Athletic Association, 2004, http://www.ncaa.org/research/prob_of_competing/ (accessed September 22, 2005)

faculty or administrators who ran the programs. Even so, there was already a fair amount of commercialization and illicit professionalism in college sports. For example, James Hogan, captain of the Yale football team in 1904, was compensated with, among other things, a suite of rooms in the dorm, free University Club meals, profits from the sale of programs, and a ten-day vacation to Cuba. However, what finally led administrators to the conclusion that formal oversight was necessary was the sheer brutality of college sports, particularly football. According to *The Business of Sports*, edited by Scott R. Rosner and Kenneth L. Shropshire (Sudbury, MA: Jones and Bartlett, 2004), there were at least eighteen deaths and over one hundred major injuries in intercollegiate football in the year 1905 alone. In response to the growing violence of college football, President Theodore Roosevelt convened a White House conference of representatives from Harvard, Princeton, and Yale to review the rules of the game. When the deaths and serious injuries continued, New York University Chancellor Henry MacCracken called for a national gathering of representatives from the major football schools. In early December 1905 representatives of thirteen schools, including West Point, Columbia, and the University of Kansas, met with MacCracken and formed a Rules Committee. This group held another meeting on December 28, attended by representatives of more than sixty college football programs, during which the Intercollegiate Athletic Association (IAA) was formed. The IAA was a national organization with sixty-two founding members, including schools in Minnesota, Nebraska, New Hampshire, New York, Ohio, Pennsylvania, and Texas. The IAA became the NCAA in 1910.

Initially, the NCAA did not really govern college sports. Its chief role was simply to make rules to keep the sports safe and fair. It also served as a forum for discussion of any other issues that happened to arise in the world of intercollegiate athletics, such as the formation of conferences and the transition of oversight responsibilities from students to faculty. In 1921 the NCAA organized its first national championship, the National Collegiate Track and Field Championships. More championships in other sports followed, as did an increasingly complex bureaucracy featuring additional rules committees.

By the 1920s college athletics were firmly entrenched both as an integral part of college life and a subject of intense public interest. Along with that interest came creeping commercialism. In 1929 the esteemed Carnegie Foundation for the Advancement of Education issued a major report on college sports, which stated that:

> [A] change of values is needed in a field that is sodden with the commercial and the material and the vested interests that these forces have created. Commercialism in college athletics must be diminished and college sport must rise to a point where it is esteemed primarily and sincerely for the opportunities it affords to mature youth.

In response to the Carnegie report, token attempts were made to reduce commercial influences on college sports, but the trend continued. A dramatic increase in access to higher education following World War II further accelerated both interest in and commercialization of college athletics. A series of gambling scandals and questionable recruiting incidents finally moved the NCAA to act. In 1948 the NCAA adopted the "Sanity Code," which established guidelines for recruiting and limited financial aid. In addition, the code set academic standards for players and defined the status of college athletes as amateurs, that is, those "to whom athletics is an avocation." The NCAA also created a Constitutional Compliance Committee to enforce the Sanity Code and investigate possible violations. The Sanity Code did not have much of an impact and was repealed in 1951. The Constitutional Compliance Committee was replaced by the Committee on Infractions, which was given broader authority to sanction institutions that broke the rules. The

TABLE 6.2

NCAA "Big 6" conferences

ACC (Atlantic Coast Conference)

Boston College (2005)
Clemson University (1953)
Duke University (1953)
Florida State University (1991)
Georgia Tech (1978)
University of Maryland (1953)
University of Miami (2004)
University of North Carolina (1953)
North Carolina State University (1953)
University of Virginia (1953)
Virginia Tech (2004)
Wake Forest University (1953)

Big East

Boston College (scheduled to leave
in 2005)
University of Connecticut (UConn)
Georgetown University (Plays Division
I-AA football in the Patriot League)
University of Notre Dame (Plays Division
I-A football as an Independent)
University of Pittsburgh
Providence College (Does not
play football)
Rutgers University
St. John's University (Does not
play football)
Seton Hall University (Does not
play football)
Syracuse University
Temple University (football-only
member; scheduled for expulsion in
2005)
Villanova University (Plays Division I-AA
football in the Atlantic Ten
Conference)
West Virginia University

Big Ten

University of Illinois at Urbana-
Champaign (joined 1895)
University of Minnesota, Twin Cities
(joined 1895)
Northwestern University (joined 1895)
Purdue University (joined 1895)
University of Wisconsin-Madison
(joined 1895)
Indiana University, Bloomington
(joined 1899)
University of Iowa (joined 1899)
The Ohio State University at Columbus
(joined 1912)

University of Michigan (joined 1895,
left 1908, rejoined 1917)
Michigan State University (joined 1950,
began play 1953)
Pennsylvania State University (joined
1990, began play 1993)

Big 12

North Division

University of Colorado
Iowa State University
University of Kansas
Kansas State University
University of Missouri
University of Nebraska

South Division

Baylor University
University of Oklahoma
Oklahoma State University
University of Texas
Texas A&M University
Texas Tech University

Pac-10 (Pacific-10)

University of Arizona
Arizona State University
University of California, Berkeley (Cal)
University of California, Los Angeles
(UCLA)
University of Oregon
Oregon State University
University of Southern California (USC)
Stanford University
University of Washington
Washington State University

SEC (Southeastern Conference)

East Division

University of Florida (1932)
University of Georgia (1932)
University of Kentucky (1932)
University of South Carolina (1991)
University of Tennessee (1932)
Vanderbilt University (1932)

West Division

University of Alabama (1932)
University of Arkansas (1991)
Auburn University (1932)
Louisiana State University (1932)
University of Mississippi (Ole Miss) (1932)

SOURCE: Created by Information Plus using data from the NCAA, http://www
.ncaa.org

NCAA also hired its first full-time executive director, Walter Byers, that year. A national headquarters was established in Kansas City, Missouri, the following year. The 1950s also brought the first lucrative television broadcast contracts, which provided the NCAA with the revenue it needed to become more active. Its capacity to enforce rules expanded throughout the 1950s and 1960s. Nevertheless, the influence of money on college sports continued to grow. In 1956 the NCAA moved to regulate athletic scholarships, but the eight schools of the Ivy League—Brown, Columbia, Cornell, Dartmouth, Harvard, Penn, Princeton, and Yale—refused to comply.

In 1973 the NCAA divided its membership into three divisions in order to group schools by their competitive firepower. Three years later, the NCAA acquired the authority to penalize colleges directly for violating rules, opening itself up to criticisms of unfair enforcement practices. In 1978, in response to the rapid growth in the number of football programs relative to other sports, Division I members voted to break the division solely for football purposes into two subdivisions, I-A and I-AA.

In the 1970s and 1980s major football colleges began to see that they could make more money from broadcast revenue by negotiating their own deals. A group of schools, led by the University of Georgia and Oklahoma University, began to challenge the NCAA's monopoly on negotiation of lucrative TV contracts. In 1984 the U.S. Supreme Court ruled in *NCAA v. Board of Regents of the University of Oklahoma, et al.* (468, U.S. 85) that the NCAA had violated antitrust laws. This ruling allowed colleges to start negotiating broadcast deals directly. Meanwhile, the relationship between sports and academics remained a matter of intense debate, as reports of student-athletes ignoring the first half of that role proliferated. In 1986 the NCAA implemented Proposition 48, later modified by Proposition 16 (1995), which set down minimum academic standards for athletes entering college. Among the requirements, student-athletes needed to maintain a 2.0 grade point average (GPA) in academic courses and have an SAT score of 1010 or a combined ACT score of 86.

SCANDALS AND SANCTIONS IN NCAA SPORTS PROGRAMS. More than a century after James Hogan's royal treatment at Yale, payments and other special perks for student athletes remain prevalent in college sports, in spite of the NCAA's enforcement efforts. There have been several cases of institutions and their boosters making illicit payments to players. In the early 1980s Southern Methodist University (SMU) was a football powerhouse. Its ability to attract top football players was enhanced by a highly organized system of player payments in blatant violation of NCAA rules. According to Chris DuFresne in "Life after Death" (*Newsday*, December 28, 2005), the payoff system, which had been in place for decades, began to unravel in November 1986, when SMU linebacker David Stanley admitted to reporters that he had accepted $25,000 from boosters. Within days another player, Albert Reese, told the *Dallas Morning News* that he had been living in a rent-free apartment provided by a booster. After an investigation that turned up widespread corruption and cover-ups that went as high as the Texas governor's office, the NCAA hit the university with what became known in college sports as the "death penalty." The sanctions included cancellation of SMU's entire 1987 football season, and restriction of the following season to eight games.

TABLE 6.3

NCAA sports sponsorship, by sport and division, 2005

	Men's				Women's				Mixed			
	I	II	III	Total	I	II	III	Total	I	II	III	Total
Baseball	285	230	359	874								
Basketball	327	281	394	1,002	325	279	425	1,029				
Bowling					29	15	2	46				
Cross country	302	223	348	873	322	253	377	952				
Fencing	20	3	12	35	25	4	14	43	1			1
Field hockey					77	26	155	258				
Football	235	150	231	616								
(I-A 117)												
(I-AA 118)												
Golf	289	200	270	759	228	109	145	482				
Gymnastics	17	0	2	19	64	7	15	86				
Ice hockey	58	7	68	133	29	2	43	74				
Lacrosse	56	30	130	216	80	33	153	266				
Rifle	7	1	4	12	11	0	1	12	18	1	7	26
Rowing					86	16	42	144				
Skiing	14	8	14	36	16	9	14	39				
Soccer	198	160	381	739	301	208	406	915				
Softball					265	257	396	918				
Swimming	141	50	191	382	188	67	235	490				
Tennis	265	168	313	746	311	214	360	885				
Track, indoor	243	112	218	573	291	115	226	632				
Track, outdoor	261	150	248	659	296	158	257	711				
Volleyball	22	17	41	80	312	265	411	988				
Water polo	21	9	16	46	31	11	19	61				
Wrestling	85	39	99	223								
Emerging sports for women												
Archery					3	0	0	3				
Badminton					1	0	3	4				
Equestrian					13	4	N/A	17				
Rugby					1	1	2	4				
Squash					8	0	19	27				
Synchronized swimming					4	1	3	8				
Team handball					0	0	0	0				

Note: These totals include sponsorship by provisional members.

SOURCE: "Sports Sponsorship Summary," National Collegiate Athletic Association, March 1, 2005, http://www1.ncaa.org/membership/membership_svcs/sponssummary (accessed September 22, 2005)

The NCAA has not wielded the death penalty again since then. Moreover, its threat has not halted these practices on the part of boosters elsewhere. A recent high-profile case involved NBA star Chris Webber. On July 14, 2003, Webber pleaded guilty to criminal contempt related to charges that he had received tens of thousands of dollars from booster Ed Martin while a member of the University of Michigan basketball team in 1994. Martin pleaded guilty to money laundering in May 2002. Webber's sentence, a fine of $100,000, was announced in August 2005.

Special treatment of student athletes does not always involve money. Sometimes it comes in the form of academic breaks. In 1998 Texas Tech was penalized by the NCAA for, among other things, allowing a star running back to play despite maintaining a 0.0 grade point average. According to David Lagesse in *U.S. News and World Report* ("Troubleshooting," March 18, 2002), nine Texas Tech sports departments were sanctioned after the resulting investigation, and the football team's ban from postseason bowl games cost the school an estimated $1.7 million. In March of the following year, a University of Minnesota employee told the *St. Paul Pioneer Press* that she had completed course work for at least twenty members of the school's basketball program. Four top sports officials at Minnesota lost their jobs in the resulting scandal.

College Sports Participation

The NCAA's *1981–82—2003–04 Sports Sponsorship and Participation Report* contains detailed information on participation across the full range of college sports. The *Participation Report*, published in December 2004, provides compelling evidence of the impact of Title IX (see below for an explanation of Title IX): Of the nearly 17,000 championship sport teams sponsored by NCAA member schools, 52.8% were women's teams in 2003–04 (http://www.ncaa.org/library/research/participation_rates/1982-2003/olympic_sports_supplement.pdf).

As of 2003–04, there were more than 375,000 student-athletes participating in championship sports at NCAA schools, according to the *Participation Report*. While

TABLE 6.4

NCAA participation in women's sports, 2003–04

	Division I		Division II		Division III		Overall	
	Teams	Athletes	Teams	Athletes	Teams	Athletes	Teams	Athletes
Championship sports								
Basketball	325	4,778	276	3,851	421	5,967	1,022	14,596
Bowling	26	218	14	117	2	23	42	358
Cross country	322	5,215	251	2,730	369	4,733	942	12,678
Fencing*	26	415	3	33	15	205	44	653
Field hockey	76	1,695	26	607	153	3,128	255	5,430
Golf	224	1,929	102	691	151	1,008	477	3,628
Gymnastics	64	1,047	7	100	15	233	86	1,380
Ice hockey	30	690	2	48	40	862	72	1,600
Lacrosse	77	1,995	32	674	149	2,876	258	5,545
Rifle*	29	163	2	4	8	38	39	205
Rowing	85	4,945	16	497	42	1,363	143	6,805
Skiing*	16	227	9	73	17	157	42	457
Soccer	296	7,522	203	4,467	396	8,448	895	20,437
Softball	265	5,056	254	4,448	389	6,575	908	16,079
Swimming/diving	187	4,833	69	1,258	232	4,448	488	10,539
Tennis	312	2,934	210	1,798	358	3,716	880	8,448
Track, indoor	289	10,033	109	2,904	219	5,128	617	18,065
Track, outdoor	294	10,208	156	3,740	251	5,710	701	19,658
Volleyball	312	4,368	260	3,369	406	5,573	978	13,310
Water polo	30	660	10	189	19	277	59	1,126
Championship sports subtotal	3,285	68,931	2,011	31,598	3,652	60,468	8,948	160,997
Emerging sports								
Archery	3	46	0	N/A	0	N/A	3	46
Badminton	0	N/A	0	N/A	3	33	3	33
Equestrian	13	574	5	120	23	426	41	1,120
Rugby	1	25	0	N/A	1	38	2	63
Squash	8	125	0	N/A	19	264	27	389
Synchronized swimming	4	67	1	7	3	30	8	104
Team handball	0	N/A	0	N/A	0	N/A	0	N/A
Emerging sports subtotal	29	837	6	127	49	791	84	1,755
Total	**3,314**	**69,768**	**2,017**	**31,725**	**3,701**	**61,259**	**9,032**	**162,752**

*Coed championship sport.
Notes:
• Participation totals are adjusted to reflect all institutions sponsoring each sport.
• Provisional members are included in these numbers.
• Coed sport teams from the sports sponsorship database were added to both the men's AND women's team data. The following sports had coed teams: a) cross country, b) equestrian, c) fencing, d) golf, e) rifle, f) swimming & diving, g) indoor track & field and h) outdoor track & field.
• The total row contains data from the emerging sports subtotal row added to the championship sports subtotal row.
• N/A=not applicable.

SOURCE: Adapted from "2003–04 Participation Study—Women's Sports," in *1981–82—2003–04 Sports Sponsorship and Participation Report*, National Collegiate Athletic Association, 2004, http://www.ncaa.org/library/research/participation_rates/1982-2004/1982_2004_participation_rates.pdf (accessed September 22, 2005)

women's teams outnumber men's teams as noted above, there are still more men than women actually playing on those teams. The average NCAA institution had about 366 student-athletes in 2003–04, 209 of them men and 157 women. The gap has been closing since the 1980s, however. Compared to 1981–82, the average NCAA school had fifty-eight more female student-athletes in 2003–04, while the number of male student-athletes had actually decreased by seventeen.

Table 6.4 shows overall participation in women's sports at NCAA schools in 2003–04. According to the *Participation Report*, 10,208 women participated on the NCAA's 294 Division I outdoor track and field teams that year. Nearly as many participated during the indoor track season. (These are essentially the same group of athletes; a few schools offer only outdoor track and field.) The NCAA's 296 women's Division I soccer teams had 7,522 total participants in 2003–04. Including all sports, both championship and "emerging," 69,768 women participated in Division I sports that year. Another 31,725 women played at the Division II level; Division III had 61,259 female athletes.

Table 6.5 shows participation in men's collegiate sports in 2003–04. According to the *Participation Report*, 86,826 student-athletes participated on the NCAA's 2,924 Division I men's teams that year. The sport with the greatest number of Division I teams was basketball, with 327. However, basketball squads are relatively small, averaging 15.3 members per school in Division I. Therefore several other sports actually have

TABLE 6.5

NCAA participation in men's sports, 2003–04

	Division I		Division II		Division III		Overall	
	Teams	Athletes	Teams	Athletes	Teams	Athletes	Teams	Athletes
Championship sports								
Baseball	286	9,749	227	7,269	351	10,244	864	27,262
Basketball	327	4,995	278	4,259	389	6,774	994	16,028
Cross country	306	4,291	224	2,556	341	4,426	871	11,273
Fencing*	21	356	3	43	13	211	37	610
Football	238	25,363	151	14,206	228	20,411	617	59,980
I-A	117	13,711	N/A	N/A	N/A	N/A	N/A	N/A
I-AA	121	11,652	N/A	N/A	N/A	N/A	N/A	N/A
Golf	290	3,039	196	1,989	272	2,710	758	7,738
Gymnastics	17	289	1	9	2	28	20	326
Ice hockey	58	1,626	7	205	68	1,951	133	3,782
Lacrosse	54	2,301	29	876	128	3,926	211	7,103
Rifle*	22	118	3	13	10	61	35	192
Skiing	14	206	8	92	17	169	39	467
Soccer	199	5,301	157	3,781	373	9,430	729	18,512
Swimming/diving	143	3,484	53	858	191	2,991	387	7,333
Tennis	269	2,632	166	1,443	309	3,144	744	7,219
Track, indoor	246	8,823	108	3,188	209	6,146	563	18,157
Track, outdoor	264	9,672	151	4,306	242	6,891	657	20,869
Volleyball	23	432	15	226	43	537	81	1,195
Water polo	21	478	9	137	16	250	46	865
Wrestling	86	2,557	39	1,070	98	2,316	223	5,943
Championship sports subtotal	2,884	85,712	1,825	46,526	3,300	82,616	8,009	214,854
Non-championship sports								
Archery	1	8	0	N/A	0	N/A	1	8
Badminton	0	N/A	0	N/A	0	N/A	0	N/A
Bowling	0	N/A	1	25	0	N/A	1	25
Equestrian	0	N/A	0	N/A	4	49	4	49
Rowing	22	873	6	105	27	780	55	1,758
Rugby	0	N/A	0	N/A	2	31	2	31
Sailing	9	99	1	6	16	154	26	259
Squash	8	134	0	N/A	15	191	23	325
Non-championship sports subtotal	40	1,114	8	136	64	1,205	112	2,455
Total	**2,924**	**86,826**	**1,833**	**46,662**	**3,364**	**83,821**	**8,121**	**217,309**

*Coed championship sport.
Notes:
- Participation totals are adjusted to reflect all institutions sponsoring each sport.
- Provisional members are included in these numbers.
- Coed sport teams from the sports sponsorship database were added to both the men's AND women's team data. The following sports had coed teams: a) cross country, b) equestrian, c) fencing, d) golf, e) rifle, f) swimming & diving, g) indoor track & field and h) outdoor track & field.
- The total row contains data from the emerging sports subtotal row added to the championship sports subtotal row.
- N/A=not applicable.

SOURCE: Adapted from "2003–04 Participation Study—Men's Sports," in *1981–82—2003–04 Sports Sponsorship and Participation Report*, National Collegiate Athletic Association, 2004, http://www.ncaa.org/library/research/participation_rates/1982-2004/1982_2004_participation_rates.pdf (accessed September 22, 2005)

more participants. Over 25,000 men played football at either the Division I-A or I-AA level in 2003–04, according to the *Participation Report*. Baseball was second, with 9,749 participants, followed closely by outdoor track and field with 9,672. Division II sports included 46,662 men participants in 2003–04; Division III had 83,821. Football had the most participants at both of those levels as well.

Table 6.6 puts college sports participation in historical perspective. In 1981–82, there were 231,445 athletes competing in NCAA championship sports, all divisions; 167,055 of them were men. By 1994–95, the total number of athletes had grown to 294,212.

About twice as much of that growth was on the women's side as on the men's. The total had grown to 375,851 by 2003–04. However, it is important to note a change in the way the total is calculated: "provisional" NCAA members were included in the count beginning in 1995–96. In addition, the numbers for 1995–96 and 1996–97 were adjusted to comply with the Equity in Athletics Disclosure Act, making it difficult to compare current participation numbers with data from before 1995. Table 6.7 and Table 6.8 show total participation numbers for 2003–04, on a sport-by-sport basis, for women and men respectively.

Table 6.9 shows the number of sports sponsored by NCAA member schools over the same period. There

TABLE 6.6

Overall NCAA championship sports participation, 1981–82—2003–04

Year	Men	Percent change men	Women	Percent change women	Total
1981–82	167,055	N/A	64,390	N/A	231,445
1982–83	176,822	5.85	78,027	21.18	254,849
1983–84	186,008	5.20	82,452	5.67	268,460
1984–85	197,446	6.15	89,072	8.03	286,518
1985–86	196,437	−0.51	92,192	3.50	288,629
1986–87	187,561	−4.52	89,640	−2.77	277,201
1987–88	176,396	−5.95	88,266	−1.53	264,662
1988–89	178,521	1.20	90,180	2.17	268,701
1989–90	175,539	−1.67	88,206	−2.19	263,745
1990–91	182,836	4.16	92,473	4.84	275,309
1991–92	183,675	0.46	94,922	2.65	278,597
1992–93	184,732	0.58	97,978	3.22	282,710
1993–94	186,939	1.19	102,994	5.12	289,933
1994–95	186,607	−0.18	107,605	4.48	294,212
1995–96*	206,385	10.60	125,250	16.40	331,635
1996–97*	199,391	−3.39	129,289	3.22	328,680
1997–98*	200,030	0.32	133,445	3.21	333,475
1998–99*	207,685	3.83	145,873	9.31	353,558
1999–00*	208,481	0.38	146,617	0.51	355,098
2000–01*	214,186	2.74	155,698	6.19	369,884
2001–02*	209,890	−2.01	153,601	−1.35	363,491
2002–03*	214,464	2.18	158,469	3.17	372,933
2003–04*	214,854	0.18	160,997	1.60	375,851

Note: N/A=not applicable
*Provisional members are included in these numbers.

SOURCE: Adapted from "NCAA Championship Sports Participation, Divisions I, II and III Overall, 1981–82—2003–04," in *1981–82—2003–04 Sports Sponsorship and Participation Report*, National Collegiate Athletic Association, 2004, http://www.ncaa.org/library/research/participation_rates/1982-2004/1982_2004_participation_rates.pdf (accessed September 22, 2005)

were just over 11,000 teams in NCAA championship sports in 1981–82. By 1994–95 there were 13,799. Much more of that growth was in women's sports than in men's. The number of women's teams surpassed the men's total in 1996–97 and has remained higher since then. The total number of teams was nearly 17,000 in 2003–04, according to the NCAA *Participation Report*, though the same caveat pertaining to comparisons of older and newer participation data apply.

Table 6.10 vividly illustrates the trend in the number of sports offered per school since the early 1980s. While the overall average number of teams per college, across all Divisions, has increased slightly during that period, the gender balance has shifted. According to the *Participation Report*, the number of men's sports teams per school has declined, while the number of women's teams has grown. This trend is apparent in each Division. A similar trend holds with regard to the average number of student-athletes per college, as shown in Table 6.11, though in this case men have continued to outnumber women in terms of average per institution.

Women's Sports and Gender Equity

The NCAA assembled a considerable amount of data on women's participation in college sports in comparison to men in its *2002–03 NCAA Gender-Equity Report* (September 2004). This report indicated no substantial

gains for women athletes from the previous year in most categories. The proportion of all athletic money that was spent on women's sports remained unchanged. One exception, according to the report, was scholarship disbursements; spending on scholarships for women's teams outpaced the men's teams in 2002–03. Figure 6.1 graphically illustrates what has happened to the gender gap since 1991 at the Division I-AA level. The graphic shows women gaining on men in terms of the number of athletes per institution. In terms of average expenses, however, the gender gap has not narrowed significantly in Division I-AA since 1997, though spending on women's sports jumped dramatically between 1995–96 and 1997–98. (See Figure 6.2.) Considerable progress has been made in equalizing scholarship spending, as shown in Figure 6.3, though on average women's scholarships still lagged behind men's as of 2002–03 in Division I-AA.

Linda Jean Carpenter and R. Vivian Acosta, both professors emerita at Brooklyn College of the City University of New York, published a report that examined the status of women's college athletics over the twenty-seven-year period between 1977 and 2004. The report, *Women in Intercollegiate Sport: A Longitudinal, National Study*, was sponsored by both Brooklyn College and Smith College's Project on Women and Social Change. Carpenter and Acosta found that nationwide, college women have more athletic teams available to

TABLE 6.7

Total number of female college athletes, by sport, 2003–04

Sport	Female athletes[a]
Archery	46
Badminton	33
Basketball	14,596
Bowling	358
Cross country	12,678
Equestrian	1,120
Fencing	653
Field hockey	5,430
Golf	3,628
Gymnastics	1,380
Ice hockey	1,600
Lacrosse	5,545
Rifle[b]	205
Rowing	6,805
Rugby	63
Skiing	457
Soccer	20,437
Softball	16,079
Squash	389
Synchronized swimming	104
Swimming/diving	10,539
Team handball	0
Tennis	8,448
Track, indoor	18,065
Track, outdoor	19,658
Volleyball	13,310
Water polo	1,126

[a]Provisional members are included in these numbers.
[b]Prior to the 1995–96 academic year, women's rifle data were included with the men's rifle data. Rifle is a co-ed championship sport.

SOURCE: Adapted from "NCAA Sports Participation 1981–82—2003–04, Divisions I, II and III Overall Number of Female Student Athletes," in *1981–82—2003–04 Sports Sponsorship and Participation Report*, National Collegiate Athletic Association, 2004, http://www.ncaa.org/library/research/participation_rates/1982-2004/1982_2004_participation_rates.pdf (accessed September 22, 2005)

TABLE 6.8

Total number of male college athletes, by sport, 2003–04

Sport	Male athletes[a]
Archery	8
Badminton	0
Baseball	27,262
Basketball	16,028
Bowling	25
Cross country	11,273
Equestrian	49
Fencing	610
Football	59,980
Golf	7,738
Gymnastics	326
Ice hockey	3,782
Lacrosse	7,103
Rifle[b]	192
Rowing	1,758
Rugby	31
Sailing	259
Skiing	467
Soccer	18,512
Squash	325
Swimming/diving	7,333
Tennis	7,219
Track, indoor	18,157
Track, outdoor	20,869
Volleyball	1,195
Water polo	865
Wrestling	5,943

[a]Provisional members are included in these numbers.
[b]Prior to the 1995–96 academic year, women's rifle data were included with the men's rifle data. Rifle is a co-ed championship sport.

SOURCE: Adapted from "NCAA Sports Participation 1981–82—2003–04, Divisions I, II and III Overall Number of Male Student Athletes," in *1981–82—2003–04 Sports Sponsorship and Participation Report*, National Collegiate Athletic Association, 2004, http://www.ncaa.org/library/research/participation_rates/1982–2004/1982_2004_participation_rates.p df (accessed September 22, 2005)

them than ever before. Since 1978, the mandatory compliance date for Title IX, the number of women's athletic teams per school rose from 5.61 to 8.32 in 2004 (a slight decrease from a high of 8.34 in 2002). For Division I, the figure was 9.26 per school; Division II schools averaged 6.90. In 2004 there were a total of 8,402 varsity women's intercollegiate teams in the NCAA. That means there are nearly half as many teams today as there were female college *athletes* in 1968 (16,000, according to Carpenter and Acosta).

The sport most frequently found in women's intercollegiate athletic programs, according to Carpenter and Acosta, was basketball, which was offered by 98.3% of NCAA schools in 2004. (See Table 6.12.) Basketball has been the most popular sport throughout the period covered in the study. It ranked number one in 1977, when it was offered at 90.4% of colleges (http://webpages.charter.net/womeninsport). The only other women's sport offered at more than 90% of colleges in 2004 was volleyball, which was available at 94.6% of NCAA schools. Like basketball, volleyball has maintained its ranking since 1977, when it was offered at 80.1% of schools. Cross-country, soccer, softball, and tennis followed in

the 2004 rankings, each available at more than 80% of schools. Of those, only softball was among the top five in 1977.

Title IX

No piece of legislation has had a greater impact on gender equity in sports participation than Title IX of the Education Amendments of 1972 of the Civil Rights Act of 1964, usually referred to simply as Title IX. In 1971 the gender disparity in sports participation was overwhelming. According to the Women's Sports Foundation (http://www.womenssportsfoundation.org/cgi-bin/iowa/index.html), about 300,000 girls were participating in interscholastic sports programs that year, compared to 3.5 million boys. Title IX was based on the notion that unequal federal funding between genders was an illegal form of discrimination. Title IX requires institutions receiving federal funding—including both secondary schools and colleges—to provide resources equally to male and female students. In practice, this has meant that schools must attempt to maintain equal facilities, equal coaching staffs, and a gender ratio among athletes similar to the ratio among the student body as a whole. Critics of

TABLE 6.9

Overall NCAA championship sports teams, 1981–82—2003–04

Year	Men	Women	Total
1981–82	6,746	4,279	11,025
1982–83	6,807	4,915	11,722
1983–84	6,807	5,053	11,860
1984–85	6,826	5,217	12,043
1985–86	6,787	5,504	12,291
1986–87	6,715	5,570	12,285
1987–88	6,721	5,635	12,356
1988–89	6,644	5,661	12,305
1989–90	6,628	5,708	12,336
1990–91	6,824	5,870	12,694
1991–92	6,940	6,032	12,972
1992–93	7,026	6,173	13,199
1993–94	7,127	6,430	13,557
1994–95	7,172	6,627	13,799
1995–96*	7,857	7,447	15,304
1996–97*	7,608	7,618	15,226
1997–98*	7,602	7,765	15,367
1998–99*	7,838	8,201	16,039
1999–00*	7,803	8,271	16,074
2000–01*	7,737	8,312	16,049
2001–02*	8,037	8,792	16,829
2002–03*	8,002	8,831	16,833
2003–04*	8,009	8,948	16,957

Note: N/A=Not applicable.
*Provisional members are included in these numbers.

SOURCE: Adapted from "NCAA Championship Sports Sponsorship, Divisions I, II and III Overall, 1981–82—2003–04," in *1981–82—2003–04 Sports Sponsorship and Participation Report*, National Collegiate Athletic Association, 2004, http://www.ncaa.org/library/research/participation_rates/ 1982-2004/1982_2004_participation_rates.pdf (accessed September 22, 2005)

Title IX have been dismayed by the fact that compliance has sometimes meant cuts in men's sports programs, but the biggest impact has been an explosion in the prevalence and popularity of women's sports. In 2002 President George W. Bush officially renamed Title IX the Patsy T. Mink Equal Opportunity in Education Act, after the legislation's author, a congresswoman from Hawaii. However, it is still generally referred to as Title IX.

The Women's Sports Foundation has noted that there is both good news and bad news regarding gender equity in high school and college sports in the Title IX era. According to the Foundation, female high school sports participation increased by 875% between 1972, when Title IX went into effect, and 2005. Female college sports participation increased by 437% during that period. On the other hand, the Foundation pointed out that female high school athletes received 1.17 million (41%) fewer opportunities to participate in athletics than their male peers. Female college athletes received 54,557 (34%) fewer opportunities. According to the Foundation, women athletes in college receive only 37% of sports operating dollars, 45% of athletic scholarship dollars, and 33% of recruitment spending. In high school, while girls represent 47.3% of all students, they get only 41.5% of the opportunities to participate in school athletics. The Foundation also pointed out that based on NCAA data from 2003–04, female college athletes receive only 43%

of all college sports participation opportunities, even though they make up about 57% of the total student body.

Women Coaches in College

One ironic consequence of the increase in the number of women's sports offered in college is a decrease in the percentage of teams that are coached by women. In 1972, the year Title IX was enacted, women coached over 90% of women's college sports teams. By 1978, the year compliance with Title IX became mandatory, that percentage had dropped to 58.2%. (See Table 6.13.) Acosta and Carpenter suggest in *Women in Intercollegiate Sport* that this drop was due to the rapid increase in the number of women's sports teams, which was not accompanied by a comparable growth in the number of qualified female coaches. However, the percentage has continued to fall since 1978, and in 2004 stood at 44.1%, very close to the all-time low registered in both 2002 and 2003. Acosta and Carpenter argue that this decline in women's representation in college coaching is due in part to discrimination and differences in the way male and female coaches are recruited. The percentage varies substantially from sport to sport. More than 60% of women's college basketball teams had female coaches in 2004 according to *Women in Intercollegiate Sport*, and 59.5% of volleyball coaches were female. Among the rest of the top five sports, only softball, at 64.8%, had more female than male coaches. Men dominated the coaching ranks of women's cross country (22% women) and soccer (30.1%). Other prominent women's sports in which women outnumbered men among coaches in 2004 were field hockey (96.6%) and lacrosse (86.2%). Table 6.14 shows percentage comparisons of female coaches by sport in 1977 and 2004. Overall in 2004, the percentage of female coaches was higher in Division I than in Division II, 44.9% to 39.4%. Division III had the highest percentage: 46% of its women's sports teams had female coaches in 2004.

Acosta and Carpenter noted that the percentage of female coaches is higher among schools at which the athletic director is also a woman. However, only 18.5% of NCAA schools had female athletic directors. In Division I women comprised 8.7% of athletic directors in 2004; in Division II women held 16.9% of the athletic director positions that year; and in Division III, 27.5% of athletic directors were women.

College Sports and Ethnicity

In addition to gender, the NCAA carefully monitors racial balances in sports participation and hiring. Data the NCAA has collected in this area was reported in the *1999–2000—2003–04 NCAA Student-Athlete Ethnicity Report*, published in January 2005. According to the report, the percentage of African-American male student-athletes increased from 16.3% in 1999–2000 to 18.1% in

TABLE 6.10

Average number of teams per college, 1981–82—2003–04

Year	Division I			Division II			Division III			Overall		
	Men's	Women's	Overall	Men's	Women's	Overall	Men's	Women's	Overall	Men's	Women's	Overall
1981–82	10.3	7.3	17.5	7.9	5.5	13.4	8.8	6.0	14.8	9.1	6.4	15.5
1982–83	10.2	6.9	17.1	7.4	5.7	13.1	8.3	6.2	14.6	8.8	6.3	15.1
1983–84	10.2	7.1	17.3	7.5	5.9	13.4	8.2	6.3	14.6	8.7	6.5	15.3
1984–85	10.2	7.3	17.4	7.5	6.1	13.6	8.2	6.6	14.8	8.7	6.7	15.5
1985–86	10.1	7.7	17.9	7.3	6.3	13.6	8.2	6.8	15.0	8.7	7.0	15.7
1986–87	9.7	7.8	17.5	7.1	6.2	13.3	8.4	7.0	15.4	8.6	7.1	15.7
1987–88	9.6	7.8	17.4	7.1	6.2	13.3	8.4	7.1	15.6	8.6	7.2	15.7
1988–89	9.4	7.7	17.2	6.9	6.1	13.0	8.3	7.2	15.4	8.4	7.1	15.5
1989–90	9.4	7.8	17.2	6.9	6.2	13.1	8.2	7.2	15.4	8.3	7.2	15.5
1990–91	9.5	7.8	17.3	6.8	6.0	12.8	8.3	7.2	15.4	8.3	7.1	15.4
1991–92	9.6	8.1	17.6	6.7	5.9	12.6	8.2	7.2	15.4	8.3	7.2	15.5
1992–93	9.5	8.2	17.7	6.7	5.9	12.6	8.1	7.3	15.3	8.2	7.2	15.4
1993–94	9.6	8.4	18.0	6.5	5.9	12.4	7.9	7.4	15.3	8.1	7.3	15.4
1994–95	9.5	8.5	18.0	6.1	5.6	11.7	7.3	7.0	14.3	7.7	7.1	14.8
1995–96*	9.6	9.0	18.6	6.5	6.1	12.5	7.8	7.7	15.5	8.0	7.6	15.6
1996–97*	9.4	9.1	18.5	6.3	6.1	12.4	7.6	7.8	15.5	7.8	7.7	15.5
1997–98*	9.3	9.3	18.7	6.4	6.4	12.8	7.7	8.0	15.7	7.8	8.0	15.8
1998–99*	9.4	9.6	19.0	6.3	6.5	12.8	7.6	8.1	15.7	7.8	8.1	15.9
1999–00*	9.1	9.7	18.8	6.1	6.4	12.4	7.5	8.2	15.7	7.8	8.1	15.7
2000–01*	9.2	10.0	19.2	6.4	6.8	13.2	7.9	8.5	16.4	7.9	8.5	16.3
2001–02*	9.2	10.1	19.2	6.5	7.0	13.4	7.9	8.6	16.5	7.9	8.6	16.5
2002–03*	9.0	10.1	19.1	6.4	7.1	13.5	7.9	8.7	16.6	7.9	8.7	16.5
2003–04*	8.9	10.1	19.1	6.5	7.2	13.7	7.8	8.6	16.4	7.8	8.7	16.5

*Provisional members are included in these numbers.

SOURCE: "NCAA Sports Sponsorship, 1981–82—2003–04, Average Number of Teams Per Institution," in *1981–82—2003–04 Sports Sponsorship and Participation Report*, National Collegiate Athletic Association, 2004, http://www.ncaa.org/library/research/participation_rates/1982-2004/1982_2004_participation_rates.pdf (accessed September 22, 2005)

TABLE 6.11

Average number of student-athletes per college, 1981–82—2003–04

Year	Division I			Division II			Division III			Overall		
	Men's	Women's	Overall	Men's	Women's	Overall	Men's	Women's	Overall	Men's	Women's	Overall
1981–82	273.5	114.8	388.3	185.8	81.6	267.4	206.5	94.7	301.1	225.8	98.7	324.5
1982–83	293.3	120.3	413.6	180.2	78.1	258.3	202.8	100.3	303.1	228.7	101.6	330.3
1983–84	301.8	120.3	422.0	194.1	91.2	285.3	213.8	107.5	321.3	239.9	107.9	347.8
1984–85	318.2	127.2	445.4	203.6	97.8	301.4	227.1	116.6	343.7	254.2	115.9	370.1
1985–86	315.2	133.0	448.2	199.5	103.8	303.3	227.0	118.3	345.3	251.9	120.1	372.0
1986–87	290.8	128.7	419.5	186.7	95.3	282.0	224.2	114.0	338.2	239.9	115.0	354.9
1987–88	275.6	125.9	401.5	177.1	94.3	271.4	207.5	112.5	320.0	225.7	113.3	338.9
1988–89	277.9	127.8	405.7	172.2	92.7	264.9	208.2	114.7	322.9	225.2	114.3	339.4
1989–90	275.8	126.0	401.7	168.4	90.1	258.5	202.2	110.5	312.7	220.9	111.2	332.1
1990–91	277.7	128.3	405.9	171.2	87.3	258.6	206.3	113.2	319.4	222.9	112.1	335.0
1991–92	278.7	132.9	411.6	168.6	87.6	256.2	200.1	114.2	314.3	219.7	113.9	333.5
1992–93	277.5	137.8	415.3	164.5	86.2	250.7	197.2	115.4	312.7	216.5	115.6	332.1
1993–94	286.5	147.4	433.8	159.1	85.8	244.9	186.2	116.1	302.3	212.6	118.3	330.9
1994–95	278.8	153.1	431.8	146.6	81.3	227.9	173.7	112.4	286.0	199.7	116.7	316.4
1995–96*	284.9	169.4	454.3	157.3	90.7	248.0	189.5	129.2	318.7	209.4	130.3	339.7
1996–97*	276.8	172.3	449.1	154.3	90.6	244.9	185.0	129.7	314.7	204.4	131.5	335.9
1997–98*	277.7	180.4	458.1	157.4	96.6	254.0	186.6	132.4	319.0	206.8	137.2	344.0
1998–99*	274.1	194.1	468.3	160.0	103.0	263.0	185.6	136.7	322.3	205.0	144.4	349.4
1999–00*	267.3	195.6	463.0	152.5	99.4	251.9	188.9	136.8	325.7	202.7	144.3	346.9
2000–01*	272.3	203.2	473.6	159.4	107.6	266.4	195.5	143.6	338.5	209.0	151.8	359.8
2001–02*	263.9	203.2	467.2	156.6	104.6	261.2	192.4	140.6	333.1	204.8	150.1	354.9
2002–03*	266.1	210.0	476.1	163.4	108.9	272.2	197.9	144.5	342.4	210.0	155.5	365.6
2003–04*	265.5	213.4	478.9	165.5	112.5	278.0	194.9	142.5	337.4	209.2	156.6	365.8

*Provisional members are included in these numbers.

SOURCE: "NCAA Sports Participation 1981–82—2003–04, Average Number of Student-Athletes Per Institution," in *1981–82—2003–04 Sports Sponsorship and Participation Report*, National Collegiate Athletic Association, 2004, http://www.ncaa.org/library/research/participation_rates/1982-2004/1982_2004_participation_rates.pdf (accessed September 22, 2005)

FIGURE 6.1   FIGURE 6.2

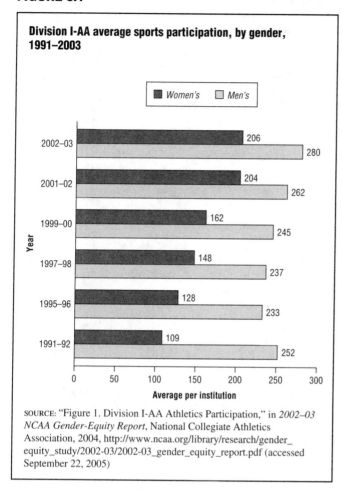

Division I-AA average sports participation, by gender, 1991–2003

SOURCE: "Figure 1. Division I-AA Athletics Participation," in *2002–03 NCAA Gender-Equity Report*, National Collegiate Athletics Association, 2004, http://www.ncaa.org/library/research/gender_equity_study/2002-03/2002-03_gender_equity_report.pdf (accessed September 22, 2005)

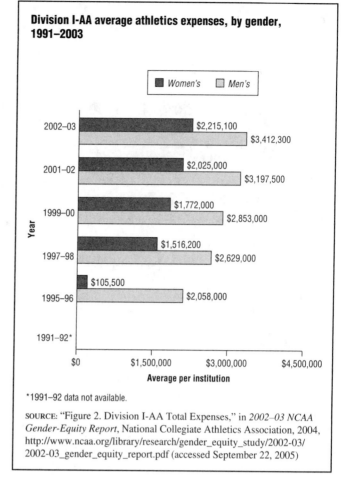

Division I-AA average athletics expenses, by gender, 1991–2003

*1991–92 data not available.

SOURCE: "Figure 2. Division I-AA Total Expenses," in *2002–03 NCAA Gender-Equity Report*, National Collegiate Athletics Association, 2004, http://www.ncaa.org/library/research/gender_equity_study/2002-03/2002-03_gender_equity_report.pdf (accessed September 22, 2005)

2003–04. During that same period, the percentage of African-American female athletes increased from 9.4% to 10.6%.

Table 6.15 breaks down sports participation percentages (all divisions combined) by ethnicity and sport. According to the *Ethnicity Report*, the overall ethnic balance across all divisions has remained fairly stable over the last several years, among both male and female athletes. This stability is represented visually in Figure 6.4 and Figure 6.5, which trace the ethnicity percentages of student-athletes between 1999 and 2004. Table 6.16, however, shows that there have indeed been small increases in participation, in both genders, among African-American, Hispanic, and non-resident alien athletes. The only ethnic category that did not show a significant increase was Native American/Alaskan.

Spending on College Sports

According to an analysis of NCAA and U.S. Department of Education data published in *USA Today* in February 2004, spending on Division I sports increased at more than twice the rate overall average university spending did between 1995 and 2001 (MaryJo Sylwester and Tom Witosky, "Athletic Spending Grows as Academic Funds Dry Up," February 18, 2004). Spending on athletics, adjusted for inflation, grew an average of about 25% during that period, while university spending increased only 10% on average. According to Sylwester and Witosky, part of the disparity was due to increases in basic costs, such as scholarships and travel; however, a bigger factor was simply the desire by schools to have winning teams, which translate into higher attendance at sports events, better television ratings, and increased alumni support.

Revenue generated by university sports does not typically cover the costs of running the programs. According to Sylwester and Witosky in *USA Today*, only about forty schools had self-sustaining athletic departments. Most departments were therefore reliant on the school for financial support. About 60% of Division I schools used student fees, usually ranging from $50 to $1,000 a year for full-time students, to help fund their athletic department.

The trend toward university-subsidized sports appears to be accelerating, leading to growing tensions between athletics and academics on the campuses of many top schools. The debate has gotten fiercer as substantial cuts

FIGURE 6.3

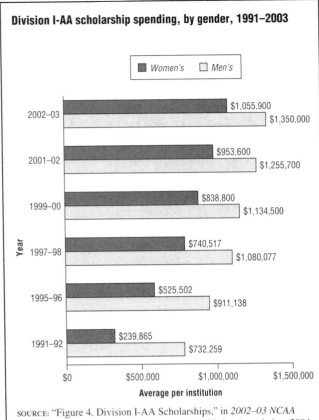

Division I-AA scholarship spending, by gender, 1991–2003

■ Women's   □ Men's

Year	Women's	Men's
2002–03	$1,055,900	$1,350,000
2001–02	$953,600	$1,255,700
1999–00	$838,800	$1,134,500
1997–98	$740,517	$1,080,077
1995–96	$525,502	$911,138
1991–92	$239,865	$732,259

Average per institution

SOURCE: "Figure 4. Division I-AA Scholarships," in *2002–03 NCAA Gender-Equity Report*, National Collegiate Athletics Association, 2004, http://www.ncaa.org/library/research/gender_equity_study/2002-03/2002-03_gender_equity_report.pdf (accessed September 22, 2005)

TABLE 6.12

Most popular intercollegiate women's sports, 2004

Rank in 2004	Percent of schools offering
1. Basketball	98.3
2. Volleyball	94.6
3. Cross country	88.8
4. Soccer	88.6
5. Softball	86.4
6. Tennis	85.2
7. Track & field	67.4
8. Golf	48.7
9. Swimming	48.7
10. Lacrosse	28.5
11. Field hockey	28.2
12. Crew/rowing	14.0
13. Gymnastics	11.0
14. Ice hockey	8.8
15. Water polo	6.5
16. Skiing	5.8
17. Fencing	4.6
18. Squash	3.8
19. Riding/equestrian	3.6
20. Bowling	3.3
21. Sailing	3.2
22. Riflery	2.8
23. Synchro swim	0.5
24. Badminton	0.3
25. Archery	0.2

SOURCE: R. Vivan Acosta and Linda Jean Carpenter, "Most Popular Sports in 2004 (Most Frequently Found Sports in Women's Intercollegiate Programs)," in *Women in Intercollegiate Sport: A Longitudinal, National Study—Twenty Seven Year Update, 1977–2004*, Acosta/Carpenter, 2004, http://www.webpages.charter.net/womeninsport (accessed September 22, 2005)

in higher education funding by state governments has led many schools to eliminate jobs, downsize academic programs, increase class sizes, and raise tuition. Criticism of this system is often led by faculty members. Terry Meyers, an English professor at the College of William & Mary, pointing out that the student fee that supports athletics is not itemized on the tuition bill students and their parents receive, is quoted by Sylwester and Witosky in *USA Today* as saying, "... if parents and students knew they were paying $916 per year to essentially support football and men's and women's basketball, they would be startled." Athletic directors respond that sports play a legitimate role in the college experience, and yield financial rewards of their own.

The NCAA actively rebuts the argument that college sports have become "big business." In "Is College Sports Big Business?" (*NCAA News Online*, August 29, 2005, http://www2.ncaa.org/), the NCAA asserted that the money that flows through college athletic programs pales in comparison to the dollars that professional sports and the corporate world overall generate. In the article NCAA director Myles Brand places the blame on the media for creating the impression that college sports are all about money. Brand argues, for example, that media coverage of college sports love to mention the NCAA's

$6.2 billion television contract, but rarely mention the fact that the $6.2 billion is spread over eleven years. He points out that it would take Nike, with 2004 revenue of $12.2 billion, only about two weeks to bring in the $470 million in revenue that the NCAA generated over the entire 2003–04 fiscal year.

The NCAA publishes an analysis of revenue from and spending on athletic programs, the most recent available edition being the *2002–03 NCAA Revenues and Expenses of Divisions I and II Intercollegiate Athletics Programs Report*, published in February 2005. According to the NCAA revenues and expenses report, the average Division I-A athletic program had total revenues of $6.9 million ($6.7 million of it from men's sports) and expenses of $7 million ($6.2 million on the men's side) in 1985. By 2003 average sports revenue for Division I-A schools had more than quadrupled to $29.4 million, $18.6 million of that total coming from men's sports. These schools were also typically operating in the black in 2003; average expenses were $27.2 million, $2.2 million less than average revenue. Figure 6.6 displays these trends visually.

Table 6.17 shows average Division I-A revenue and expenses by sport for 2003. Football and basketball account for a huge share of both the spending and revenue in college sports, and both produce sizeable net

TABLE 6.13

TABLE 6.14

Percentage of female coaches in women's intercollegiate sports, 1972–2004

2004	**44.1%**
2003	44.0%
2002	44.0%
2001	44.7%
2000	45.6%
1999	46.3%
1998	47.4%
1997	47.4%
1996	47.7%
1995	48.3%
1994	49.4%
1993	48.1%
1992	48.3%
1991	47.7%
1990	47.3%
1989	47.7%
1988	48.3%
1987	48.8%
1986	50.6%
1985	50.7%
1984	53.8%
1983	56.2%
1982	52.4%
1981	54.6%
1980	54.2%
1979	56.1%
1978	58.2%
1972	90.0%+

SOURCE: R. Vivan Acosta and Linda Jean Carpenter, "Percentage of Female Coaches All Division, All Sports 2004," in *Women in Intercollegiate Sport: A Longitudinal, National Study—Twenty Seven Year Update, 1977–2004,* Acosta/Carpenter, 2004, http://www.webpages.charter.net/womeninsport (accessed September 22, 2005)

Percentage of female coaches, by sport, 1977 and 2004

	2004	1977
Archery	0.0%	83.4%
Badminton	50.0%	75.0%
Basketball	60.7%	79.4%
Bowling	33.3%	42.9%
Crew/rowing	41.6%	11.9%
Cross country	22.0%	35.2%
Fencing	10.3%	51.7%
Field hockey	96.6%	99.1%
Golf	41.7%	54.6%
Gymnastics	38.6%	69.7%
Ice hockey	28.6%	37.5%
Lacrosse	86.2%	90.7%
Riding	82.6%	75.0%
Riflery	16.7%	17.4%
Sailing	5.0%	7.1%
Skiing	21.6%	22.7%
Soccer	30.1%	29.4%
Softball	64.8%	83.5%
Squash	12.5%	71.4%
Swim/diving	25.6%	53.6%
Synchronized swim	100.0%	85.0%
Tennis	34.6%	72.9%
Track & field	19.7%	52.3%
Volleyball	59.5%	86.6%
Water polo	22.0%	—

SOURCE: R. Vivan Acosta and Linda Jean Carpenter, "Percentage of Female Coaches All Divisions, 1977 and 2004," in *Women in Intercollegiate Sport: A Longitudinal, National Study–Twenty Seven Year Update, 1977—2004,* Acosta/Carpenter, 2004, http://www.webpages.charter.net/womeninsport (accessed September 22, 2005)

financial gains. Figure 6.7 shows the trends in football and basketball spending and revenue from 1985 to 2003 in Division I-A. As the graphic indicates, the amount of surplus revenue these sports generated grew substantially over that time span. Average football revenue at Division I-A schools grew from $3.7 million in 1985 to $13 million in 2003, while expenses only increased from $2.4 million to $7.1 million. Men's and women's basketball showed similar trends during that period. The only other men's sport to typically turn a profit in 2003 was ice hockey, which brought in an average of $1.5 million and cost only $1.2 million. No women's sport generated nearly as much in revenue as was spent on it.

Table 6.18 details where Division I-A schools' athletics revenue came from in 2003, according to the NCAA's revenue and expense report. Ticket sales were the biggest source, accounting for a little over one-quarter of revenue on average. This is consistent with the paragraph above, since football and basketball are the sports that the most people buy tickets to watch.

In "Big Money in College Sports Flows to the Few" (*Chronicle of Higher Learning,* October 2004), Welch Suggs makes the case that NCAA revenue is distributed unfairly, with the lion's share of the dollars going to a

select handful of elite universities. The article, for example, compares two athletic conferences: the Big Ten, a collection of large state universities located across the Midwest; and the Northeast Conference (NEC), whose members are small private colleges in the mid-Atlantic region. The Big Ten took in $117 million in 2002–03, including revenue from football bowl games and television contracts. Of that total, $110 million went to its member schools, and the remainder was spent on administrative costs and championships. The Big Ten was one of only two conferences to bring in over $100 million. The NEC, in contrast, reported revenue of just $1.2 million in 2001–02 (which Suggs notes was only about two-and-a-half times NCAA president Myles Brand's annual salary). All of the money was spent on administration and championships; none went to its members. According to the article, the disparity goes beyond dollars and cents. The NCAA's governance structure also favors members of the big conferences, giving them more seats on key committees and more say in how resources are distributed. The big schools that benefit from this disparity, according to Suggs, counter that the current distribution system is fair because it is the members of the prominent conferences that are responsible for the lucrative television contracts that provide most of the NCAA's revenue. In other words, CBS is not paying millions of dollars for the right to broadcast Quinnipac University vs. Central Connecticut State.

TABLE 6.15

College athletes and ethnicity, 2003–04

Sport	American Indian/Alaskan Native Men	American Indian/Alaskan Native Women	Asian/Pacific Islander Men	Asian/Pacific Islander Women	Black, non-Hispanic Men	Black, non-Hispanic Women	Hispanic Men	Hispanic Women	Nonresident alien Men	Nonresident alien Women	Other Men	Other Women	White, non-Hispanic Men	White, non-Hispanic Women
Archery	0.0	0.0	0.0	13.0	0.0	0.0	0.0	4.3	0.0	0.0	0.0	2.2	0.0	80.4
Badminton	0.6	0.0	0.9	21.2	4.5	9.1	4.8	0.0	0.8	0.0	2.0	27.3	86.7	42.4
Baseball	0.4	N/A	0.6	N/A	4.5	N/A	4.8	N/A	3.0	N/A	0.0	N/A	86.7	N/A
Basketball	0.4	0.5	0.0	1.1	42.0	27.0	2.4	2.7	3.0	2.5	2.6	1.9	49.6	64.2
Bowling	0.0	0.0	0.0	0.6	0.0	66.8	0.0	1.7	0.0	2.8	0.0	0.6	0.0	27.7
Cross country	0.4	0.4	1.3	1.3	9.2	9.8	4.5	4.7	2.7	2.1	0.0	2.3	79.3	79.4
Equestrian	0.0	0.4	3.3	0.9	3.3	0.6	0.0	6.2	0.0	0.4	11.3	5.6	93.3	85.9
Fencing	0.3	0.2	12.7	13.8	4.9	4.8	3.8	6.0	16	2.2	N/A	11.2	64.4	61.8
Field hockey	N/A	0.5	N/A	1.5	N/A	1.2	N/A	1.0	N/A	1.3	N/A	3.1	N/A	91.4
Football	0.4	N/A	1.2	N/A	33.3	N/A	2.6	N/A	0.4	N/A	1.9	N/A	61.4	N/A
Golf	0.5	0.2	1.7	3.6	2.1	3.2	1.5	2.4	5.3	6.8	1.8	1.7	81.6	82.1
Gymnastics	0.6	0.0	5.5	4.1	4.6	3.1	2.8	2.0	2.8	2.6	2.1	4.4	79.6	83.6
Ice hockey	0.2	0.6	0.5	2.1	0.6	0.3	0.9	0.4	15.3	16.4	2.9	4.3	91.9	75.9
Lacrosse	0.4	0.2	0.6	1.6	1.9	1.9	1.0	1.4	0.7	0.3	1.4	3.6	82.1	90.9
Rifle	0.0	1.0	6.3	2.9	3.2	1.9	3.2	3.9	0.5	1.0	4.7	1.9		87.4
Rowing		0.6		3.7		1.9		4.0		2.3		6.0		81.6
Rugby														N/A
Sailing		N/A		N/A		0.0		N/A		5.8		N/A		
Skiing	0.4	0.6	0.6	0.9	0.2	0.0	0.0	0.2	5.3		1.1	4.9	92.4	87.6
Soccer	0.2	0.2	1.7	1.8	5.9	3.4	6.4	3.4	5.9	2.2	2.9	2.1	77.0	86.8
Softball	N/A	0.5	N/A	1.4	N/A	6.3	N/A	4.5	N/A	0.8	N/A	1.7	N/A	84.7
Squash		0.3		7.5		0.0		0.8		5.1		15.7		70.7
Swimming/diving	0.2	0.2	2.4	2.4	1.5	1.2	2.6	2.0	4.3	6.7	3.3	3.1	85.7	88.1
Synchronized swimming	N/A	1.0	N/A	5.8	N/A	1.0	N/A	1.9	N/A	0.0	N/A	0.0	N/A	83.7
Team handball	N/A	0.0	N/A	0.0	N/A	0.0	N/A	0.0	N/A	10.5	N/A	0.0	N/A	0.0
Tennis	0.2	0.2	5.4	4.8	5.3	5.6	3.9	3.6	15.6	2.6	4.3	3.6	65.2	71.7
Track, indoor	0.3	0.3	1.2	1.3	20.3	20.5	3.1	2.8	2.4	2.5	2.8	2.7	69.9	69.8
Track, outdoor	0.3	0.3	1.4	1.4	21.1	20.8	3.7	3.3	2.3	2.8	2.8	2.7	68.5	69.0
Volleyball	0.3	0.3	5.3	2.1	6.4	8.9	12.7	3.5	3.4	1.4	5.1	1.9	66.8	80.4
Water polo	0.8	0.4	4.4	4.3	0.7	0.6	5.5	4.8	5.8	1.4	9.9	7.6	72.8	78.9
Wrestling	0.6	N/A	1.5	N/A	5.9	N/A	5.6	N/A	0.3	N/A	3.1	N/A	83.0	N/A
All sports	0.4	0.3	1.4	2.0	18.1	10.6	3.5	3.2	2.7	2.9	2.5	2.8	71.4	78.2

Notes: N/A=not applicable.
Empty cells indicate the data are unavailable.

SOURCE: "2003–04 Student-Athlete Ethnicity Percentages for Divisions I, II and III Overall," in *1999–00—2003–04 NCAA Student-Athlete Ethnicity Report*, National Collegiate Athletic Association, January 2005, http://www.ncaa.org/library/research/ethnicity_report/2003–04/2003–04_ethnicity_report.pdf (accessed September 22, 2005)

FIGURE 6.4

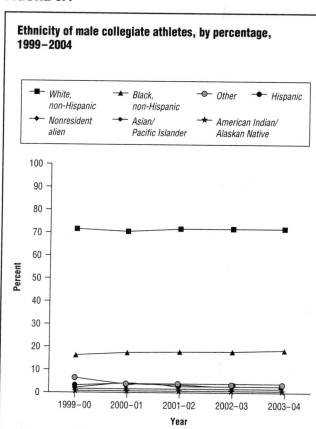

Ethnicity of male collegiate athletes, by percentage, 1999–2004

SOURCE: "Male Student-Athlete Ethnicity Percentages for Divisions I, II and III Overall," in *1999–00—2003–04 NCAA Student-Athlete Ethnicity Report*, National Collegiate Athletic Association, January 2005, http://www.ncaa.org/library/research/ethnicity_report/2003-04/2003-04_ethnicity_report.pdf (accessed September 22, 2005)

FIGURE 6.5

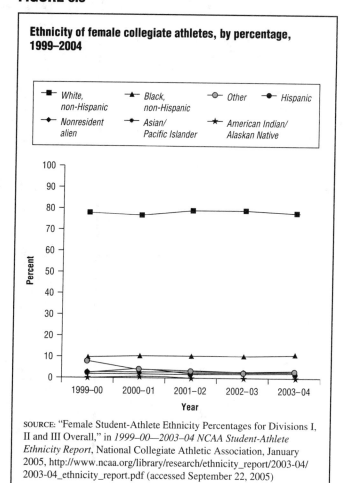

Ethnicity of female collegiate athletes, by percentage, 1999–2004

SOURCE: "Female Student-Athlete Ethnicity Percentages for Divisions I, II and III Overall," in *1999–00—2003–04 NCAA Student-Athlete Ethnicity Report*, National Collegiate Athletic Association, January 2005, http://www.ncaa.org/library/research/ethnicity_report/2003-04/2003-04_ethnicity_report.pdf (accessed September 22, 2005)

Academic Eligibility

Incoming student-athletes must meet a set of academic standards in order to participate in NCAA-sanctioned sports programs. These standards vary according to the division in which a school competes. According to the NCAA's *Guide for the College-Bound Student-Athlete* (http://www2.ncaa.org/media_and_events/ncaa_publications/general_interest/index.html), Division I academic eligibility rules through 2007 require that the student:

- graduate from high school

- complete fourteen core courses: four years of English; two of math; two of science; one extra year of one of the above; two years of social science; and three extra core courses from any of the above, or foreign language, nondoctrinal religion, or philosophy

- achieve a minimum required grade point average in core courses

- achieve a combined SAT or ACT score that matches the student's grade point average on a special NCAA chart

These requirements are scheduled to change beginning in 2008. The new requirements will include an additional year of math and an additional year of any of the above extra courses. The requirements for Divisions II and III (also slated to change in 2008) are similar to those of Division I, though less stringent.

The *Guide for the College-Bound Student-Athlete* also outlines the rules for recruiting high school athletes, which vary somewhat by sport as well as by division. These recruiting rules are summarized in Table 6.19 and include regulations pertaining to phone contact, campus visits, and other forms of communication between coaches and prospective college athletes.

HIGH SCHOOL SPORTS

Participation

According to the U.S. Census Bureau in *Statistical Abstract of the United States: 2004–2005*, 57.6% of U.S. high school students played on a sports team in 2003. The percentage was higher among boys than girls, 64% to 51%. Among boys, participation was highest in eleventh grade, while the greatest percentage of girls played on sports teams in ninth grade. Nearly 61% of white students played on a sports team. Minorities played sports in lesser

TABLE 6.16

NCAA sports participation by ethnicity, 1999–2004

Year	American Indian/ Alaskan Native		Asian/ Pacific Islander		Black, non-Hispanic		Hispanic		Nonresident alien		Other		White, non-Hispanic	
	Men	Women	Men	Women	Men	Women	Men	Women	Men	Women	Men	Women	Men	Women
1999–00*	0.3	0.3	1.2	1.5	16.3	9.4	3.0	2.4	1.8	1.5	6.0	6.8	71.6	78.1
2000–01*	0.3	0.4	1.3	1.7	17.2	10.2	3.3	2.7	4.1	4.5	3.3	3.7	70.4	77.0
2001–02*	0.3	0.3	1.4	1.7	17.7	10.4	3.5	2.8	2.5	2.4	3.1	3.2	71.6	79.1
2002–03*	0.3	0.3	1.4	1.9	17.9	10.5	3.5	3.0	2.6	2.6	2.7	2.9	71.6	78.9
2003–04*	0.4	0.3	1.4	2.0	18.1	10.6	3.5	3.2	2.7	2.9	2.5	2.8	71.4	78.2

*Provisional members are included in these numbers.

Note: N/A=not applicable.

SOURCE: Adapted from "Student-Athlete Ethnicity Percentages for Divisions I, II and III Overall," in *1999–00—2003–04 NCAA Student–Athlete Ethnicity Report*, National Collegiate Athletic Association, January 2005, http://www.ncaa.org/library/research/ethnicity_report/2003–04/2003–04_ethnicity_report.pdf (accessed September 22, 2005)

FIGURE 6.6

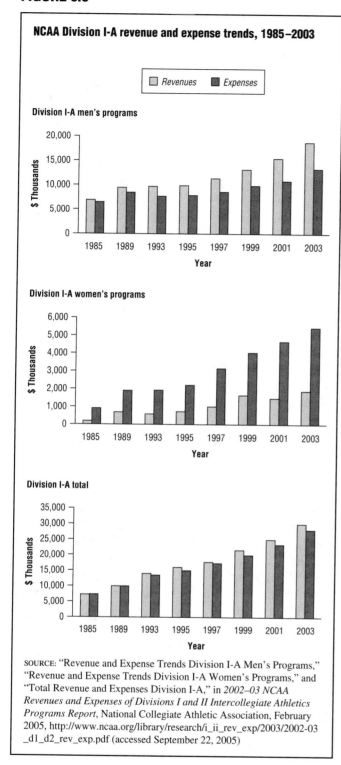

NCAA Division I-A revenue and expense trends, 1985–2003

Division I-A men's programs

Division I-A women's programs

Division I-A total

SOURCE: "Revenue and Expense Trends Division I-A Men's Programs," "Revenue and Expense Trends Division I-A Women's Programs," and "Total Revenue and Expenses Division I-A," in *2002–03 NCAA Revenues and Expenses of Divisions I and II Intercollegiate Athletics Programs Report*, National Collegiate Athletic Association, February 2005, http://www.ncaa.org/library/research/i_ii_rev_exp/2003/2002-03 _d1_d2_rev_exp.pdf (accessed September 22, 2005)

this NFHS data, as reported in the *Statistical Abstract*, for 1972 through 2003. While complete data from the 2004–05 survey was not yet available as of November 2005, NFHS had released a number of key statistics for that year.

In 2004–05, the number of participants in high school sports increased for the sixteenth straight year, reaching 7.02 million based on figures supplied by the fifty state high school athletic associations (plus the District of Columbia) that are members of NFHS. This was an increase of 115,157 over the previous year. According to the survey, nearly 53% of high school students participated in school sports in 2004–05.

At 2.9 million, participation among girls reached an all-time high in 2004–05. The total for boys, 4.11 million, was the second highest in the survey's history, trailing only the 4.37 million who participated in 1977–78.

Football has long been the most popular high school sport among boys. According to the NFHS survey, more than one million boys participated in football in 2004–05. Boys' basketball, in second place at 545,497, had about half as many participants as football. Track and field (516,703), baseball (459,717), and soccer (354,587) were the third, fourth, and fifth most popular boys' sports respectively. In addition to having the most participants, football also added the most participants (12,812) over the previous year. Other boys' sports that gained a significant number of participants in 2004–05 were track and field (11,902), swimming and diving (7,192), and lacrosse (6,557).

Among high school girls, basketball was the most popular sport, with 456,543 participants, followed by outdoor track and field (428,198), volleyball (386,022), fast pitch softball (364,759), and soccer (316,104). Track and field gained the most participants (9,212) among high school girls in 2004–05, according to the NFHS survey. Soccer had the second largest gain, with 7,072.

On a percentage-increase basis, the NFHS survey suggests that bowling and lacrosse are emerging high school sports among both boys and girls. Boys' bowling jumped 14% in number of participants, from 17,654 in 2003–04 to 20,534 in 2004–05; lacrosse was close behind, climbing 11%, from 53,436 to 59,993. Bowling and lacrosse were also the fastest growing sports among girls. Bowling participation grew by 13% among high school girls, and lacrosse 10%. In terms of the number of schools offering a sport, snowboarding showed the fastest growth between 2003–04 and 2004–05—85% for boys and 89% for girls.

The state with the largest number of high school athletes in 2004–05, according to the NFHS survey, was Texas, with 740,052. Other leading states included California (678,019), New York (350,349), Michigan (311,814), Illinois (310,791), and Ohio (310,585).

proportions: 53.2% of non-Hispanic African-American students and 49.5% of Hispanic students played on sports teams. However, at 67.5%, African-American males were the subgroup with the highest rate of sports team participation. (See Table 6.20.)

Since 1971 the National Federation of State High School Associations (NFHS) has compiled data on sports participation from its member associations. Table 6.21 summarizes

TABLE 6.17

Division I-A revenue and expenses, by sport, 2003

[Dollar amounts in thousands]

Sport	Men's programs			Women's programs		
	Revenues	Expenses	Number of respondents	Revenues	Expenses	Number of respondents
Baseball	367	760	102	N/A	N/A	N/A
Basketball	4,252	2,227	116	506	1,279	115
Fencing	39	133	8	50	165	10
Field hockey	N/A	N/A	N/A	166	535	24
Football	12,969	7,046	115	N/A	N/A	N/A
Golf	102	251	107	80	263	94
Gymnastics	110	331	17	163	593	46
Ice hockey	1,522	1,169	12	104	923	4
Lacrosse	270	664	14	176	545	18
Rifle	9	43	10	20	68	14
Rowing	264	472	9	206	682	39
Skiing	52	205	5	50	227	5
Soccer	130	454	57	156	531	111
Softball	N/A	N/A	N/A	151	545	93
Squash	20	80	1	0	0	0
Swimming	120	418	65	132	492	86
Synchronized swimming	N/A	N/A	N/A	55	289	3
Tennis	83	285	91	90	317	110
Track & field/cross country	121	496	108	157	623	114
Volleyball	221	416	9	181	597	113
Water polo	102	287	7	68	312	12
Wrestling	164	460	42	N/A	N/A	N/A

Note: N/A=not applicable.

SOURCE: "Table 3.29. Total Revenues and Expenses by Sport, Division I-A, Fiscal Year 2003," in *2002–03 NCAA Revenues and Expenses of Divisions I and II Intercollegiate Athletics Programs Report*, National Collegiate Athletic Association, February 2005, http://www.ncaa.org/library/research/i_ii_rev_exp/2003/2002-03_d1_d2_rev_exp.pdf (accessed September 22, 2005)

SGMA International, the industry association of sporting goods manufacturers, publishes an annual report on participation in team sports, drawing from several data sources including the NFHS. SGMA compared high school sports participation in 2003–04 with participation in 1990–91. Based on SGMA's analysis, football's dominance among boys appears quite stable. In 2003–04, 1.06 million boys played on 14,779 high school football teams. This represented a 12% increase over the 941,423 boys who played on the 13,900 teams that were active in the 1990–91 school year. It was also nearly twice as many boys as played basketball. In 2003–04, there were 17,389 boys' high school basketball teams with 544,811 members. At 6%, basketball's rate of growth over the previous decade was slower than that of football. Track and field was the third most popular boys' high school sport in 2003–04, and one of the fastest growing over the previous decade. A total of 504,801 boys participated in track and field that year, compared with 401,350 in 1990–91. Even faster growing was soccer, which grew 53% between 1990–91 and 2003–04, from 228,330 players to 349,785. (See Table 6.22.)

Table 6.23 shows the most popular girls' high school sports, based on SGMA data. Every one of the eight most popular girls' sports showed substantial growth between 1990–91 and 2003–04. Basketball remained the most popular. A total of 457,986 girls played on 17,061 high school basketball teams in 2003–04, though basketball's 18% growth since 1990–91 was the smallest increase among the top sports. Track and field was second most popular, with 415,322 participants in 2003–04, followed by volleyball with 396,322. The girls' sport with the largest percentage increase in participants between 1990–91 and 2003–04 was soccer, which experienced a 154% increase in participation. Other fast-growing sports were softball (65%), swimming/diving (64%), and cross country (53%).

Data from *Monitoring the Future*, an ongoing nationwide study of youth behavior and attitudes funded by the National Institute on Drug Abuse and conducted by the Institute for Social Research at the University of Michigan, suggest that the percentage of middle and high school students participating in school sports has generally declined over the past decade, though girls' participation has held fairly steady. A greater percentage of boys than girls have participated in school sports throughout that span. The national advocacy group Child Trends analyzed data on school sports participation from *Monitoring the Future* over several years, and their findings are summarized in Table 6.24. Child Trends' analysis showed that participation in athletics among tenth-grade boys decreased from 69% to 63% between

FIGURE 6.7

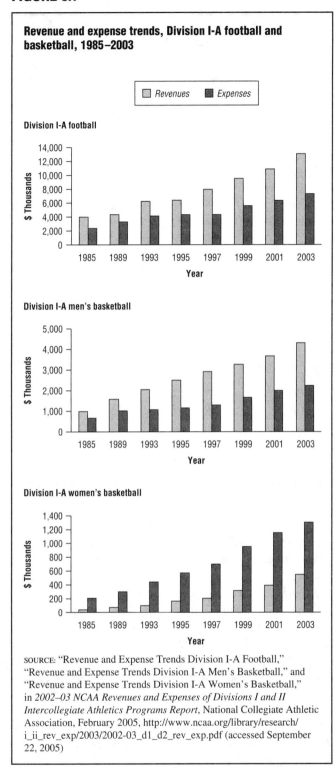

Revenue and expense trends, Division I-A football and basketball, 1985–2003

Division I-A football

Division I-A men's basketball

Division I-A women's basketball

SOURCE: "Revenue and Expense Trends Division I-A Football," "Revenue and Expense Trends Division I-A Men's Basketball," and "Revenue and Expense Trends Division I-A Women's Basketball," in *2002–03 NCAA Revenues and Expenses of Divisions I and II Intercollegiate Athletics Programs Report*, National Collegiate Athletic Association, February 2005, http://www.ncaa.org/library/research/i_ii_rev_exp/2003/2002-03_d1_d2_rev_exp.pdf (accessed September 22, 2005)

girls declined from seventeen percentage points in 1991 to six points in 2003. The gap declined from eighteen percentage points to eleven points for twelfth graders during that time span. (See Figure 6.8.)

Child Trends also found a correlation between parents' education and students' participation in school athletics. (See Figure 6.9.) Youth whose parents were better educated were more likely to participate than their peers whose parents had fewer years of education. In 2003, 74% of tenth graders with a parent who had attended graduate school participated in school sports, while participation among students whose parents did not finish high school was only 44%. Similarly, high school students who plan to attend college are more likely (56% of twelfth-graders) to participate in school athletics than students without college aspirations (41% of twelfth-graders).

Benefits of High School Sports Participation

The National Center for Education Statistics (NCES) published a report in 2005 that analyzed the status of high school athletes eight years after their senior year (*Statistics in Brief*, September 2005, http://nces.ed.gov/pubs2005/2005303.pdf). The report was part of the National Education Longitudinal Study of 1988, which tracked a large sample of students who were seniors in 1992. This report examined their educational achievement, employment success, and health status as of 2000. NCES found that elite (for this study defined as those who were "team captains or most valuable players") and varsity level athletes were more likely than nonathletes to have received some postsecondary education and more likely to have earned a bachelor's degree. They also found that elite athletes were more likely than nonathletes to be employed, and employed full time, in 2000. Elite and varsity athletes had higher incomes on average than those who did not participate in high school sports. In addition, NCES found that high school athletes were more likely than nonathletes to participate in fitness activities and group sports eight years after their senior year. Elite and varsity athletes were less likely to be daily smokers than their nonathletic peers. The only negative impact the report noted was that elite and varsity athletes were more likely than nonathletes to binge drink (that is, these survey respondents reported having five or more alcoholic drinks on at least one occasion during the two weeks prior to the survey).

Money and High School Athletics

The perceived corruption of college sports by money appears to have seeped down to the high school level. A series of *New York Times* articles by Duff Wilson and Pete Thamel in November and December 2005, including "The Quick Fix" (November 27) and "NCAA Calls for Investigation into Correspondence School" (December 2), reported on a Florida high school that was functioning as

1990–91 and 2003–04, while participation among tenth-grade girls increased from 52% to 57%. The pattern was similar among twelfth graders. Among boys, participation shrank from 65% to 59%, while girls' participation rose slightly, from 47% to 48%. (See Table 6.24.) Child Trends found that since 1991, the gender gap in high school sports participation has decreased substantially. Among tenth graders, the difference between boys and

TABLE 6.18

Sources of revenue, NCAA Division I-A, 2003

[Dollar amounts in thousands]

Category	Public	Percent of total	Private	Percent of total	Total division	Percent of total
Ticket sales						
Public/faculty/staff	7,686	26	6,298	20	7,495	26
Students	384	1	202	1	359	1
Total ticket sales	**8,070**	**28**	**6,500**	**20**	**7,854**	**27**
Postseason compensation						
Bowl games	613	2	1,180	4	691	2
Tournaments	183	1	358	1	207	1
Total postseason	**796**	**3**	**1,538**	**5**	**898**	**3**
NCAA and conference distributions	2,723	9	2,126	7	2,641	9
Student activity fees	2,038	7	703	2	1,854	6
Guarantees and options	978	3	1,455	5	1,043	3
Cash contributions from alumni and others	5,301	18	5,081	16	5,271	18
Direct government support	482	2	2	0	416	1
Institutional support	2,239	8	7,968	25	3,029	10
Other						
Concessions	576	2	401	1	552	2
Radio/television	2,061	7	2,473	8	2,118	7
Program sales/advertising	111	0	155	0	117	0
Signage/sponsorship	1,259	4	1,262	4	1,259	4
Sports camps	294	1	101	0	268	1
Miscellaneous	2,110	7	2,013	6	2,096	7
Total other	**6,411**	**22**	**6,405**	**20**	**6,410**	**22**
Total	**29,038**	**100**	**31,778**	**100**	**29,416**	**100**

Notes: Total public institutions reporting=97. Total private institutions reporting=17.

SOURCE: "Table 3.27. Sources of Total Revenues—Public, Private, Total Division, Division I-A, Fiscal Year 2003," in *2002–03 NCAA Revenues and Expenses of Divisions I and II Intercollegiate Athletics Programs Report*, National Collegiate Athletic Association, February 2005, http://www.ncaa.org/library/research/i_ii_rev_exp/2003/2002-03_d1_d2_rev_exp.pdf (accessed September 22, 2005)

a de facto diploma mill for elite athletes whose poor school performance threatened their chances to play at top-level universities. The school, University High School in Miami, had no accreditation from the state, offered no classes for students to attend, and provided no real instruction. Students "attended" University High via correspondence courses, which essentially consisted of a series of open-book tests. The *Times* identified twenty-eight athletes who raised their sagging grade point averages, often just enough to qualify for intercollegiate athletics, by enrolling in University High. Fourteen of them had already committed to attend NCAA Division I schools. Students paid about $400 to boost their grades in this way.

The vast sums of money involved in college sports have also led to extremely aggressive recruiting practices. According to an August 6, 2004, *Washington Post* article, "NCAA Cracks Down on Recruiting Practices," high-profile recruiting scandals at two major colleges, the University of Colorado and the University of Miami, led to the creation of a special NCAA task force. The

work of the task force culminated in new rules, approved by the NCAA Division I Board of Directors in August 2004, aimed at eliminating what NCAA President Brand has called a "culture of entitlement." Prior to that time, colleges were wooing prospects with high-priced meals and stays in luxury hotels, often transporting them to campus in expensive chartered planes and limousines. The *Post* article also mentioned widely reported earlier charges that colleges were plying top high-school athletes with sex and alcohol. It specifically referred to the case of Willie Williams of Miami, Florida, a top 2004 prospect who kept a diary of his recruiting visits for the *Miami Herald*. Williams wrote about a visit to Florida State University, during which he ate four lobster tails and stayed in a hotel suite with a Jacuzzi. The revised rules prohibit schools from employing any of these practices, requiring that prospects be transported from airports in standard vehicles and fed "standard meals similar to those offered on campus." They also require schools to establish policies explicitly forbidding illegal actions during recruiting, such as underage drinking and sex for hire.

TABLE 6.19

Summary of NCAA Division I recruiting rules, 2004–05

Recruiting method	Men's basketball	Women's basketball	Football	Other sports
Sophomore year				
Recruiting materials	• You may start to receive at end of year.	• You may receive brochures for camps and questionnaires.	• You may receive brochures for camps and questionnaires.	• You may receive brochures for camps and questionnaires.
Telephone calls	• College may accept collect calls from you at end of year. • College coach cannot call you.	• You may make calls to coach at your expense only. • College coach cannot call you.	• You may make calls to coach at your expense only. • College coach cannot call you.	• You may make calls to coach at your expense only. • College coach cannot call you. • Ice hockey—if you are an international prospect, a college coach may call you once in July after sophomore year.
Off-campus contact	• None allowed.	• None allowed.	• None allowed.	• None allowed.
Official visit	• None allowed.	• None allowed.	• None allowed.	• None allowed.
Unofficial visit	• Allowed.	• Allowed.	• Allowed.	• Allowed.
Junior year				
Recruiting materials	• Allowed.	• You may begin receiving September 1 of junior year.	• You may begin receiving September 1 of junior year.	• You may begin receiving September 1 of junior year.
Telephone calls College coaches may call you	• Once during March of your junior year. • Once between June 21 and June 30 after your junior year. • Three times in July after your junior year.	• Once during March of your junior year. • Once between June 21 and June 30 after your junior year. • Three times in July after your junior year.	• Once during May of your junior year.	• Once during May of your junior year. • Once per week starting July 1 after your junior year.
Off-campus contact	• Once per week beginning August 1. • Allowed, once only during April on your high-school campus. • Allowed starting July 1 after your junior year.	• Once per week beginning August 1. • Allowed, once only during April on your high-school campus. • Allowed starting July 1 after your junior year.	• None allowed.	• Allowed, once only during April on your high-school campus. • Allowed starting July 1 after your junior year. • For gymnastics—allowed after July 15 following your junior year.
Official visit	• Allowed, beginning January 1 of your junior year, but not during the summer of your junior and senior year.	• None allowed.	• None allowed.	• None allowed.
Unofficial visit	• Allowed.	• Allowed.	• Allowed.	• Allowed.
Senior year				
Recruiting materials	• Allowed.	• Allowed.	• Allowed.	• Allowed.
Telephone calls	• Once per week.	• Once per week.	• Once per week beginning September 1.	• Once per week.
Off-campus contact	• Allowed.	• Allowed.	• Allowed.	• Allowed.
Official visit	• Allowed beginning opening day of classes your senior year.	• Allowed beginning opening day of classes your senior year.	• Allowed beginning opening day of classes your senior year.	• Allowed beginning opening day of classes your senior year.
Unofficial visit	• Allowed.	• Allowed.	• Allowed.	• Allowed.
Evaluation and contacts	• Up to five times during your senior year.	• Up to five times during your senior year.	• Up to six times during your senior year.	• Up to seven times during your senior year.
How often can a coach see me or talk to me off the college's campus?	• A college coach may contact you or your parents/legal guardians not more than three times during your senior year.	• A college coach may contact you or your parents/legal guardians not more than three times during your senior year.	• A college coach may contact you or your parents/legal guardians, (including evaluating you off the college's campus) six times. • One evaluation during September, October and November.	• A college coach may contact you or your parents/legal guardians not more than three times during your senior year.

Note: Information presented here on NCAA recruiting rules is accurate as of Fall 2005; however, the rules are revised periodically. Current information is available on the NCAA website at www.ncaa.org.

SOURCE: "Summary of Recruiting Rules for Each Sport—Division I," in *2004–05 Guide for the College-Bound Student-Athlete*, National Collegiate Athletic Association, 2004, http://www.ncaa.org/library/general/cbsa/2004–05/2004–05_cbsa.pdf (accessed September 22, 2005)

TABLE 6.20

High school students engaged in organized physical activity, by sex, race, and Hispanic origin, 2003

[In percent. For students in grades 9 to 12. Based on the Youth Risk Behavior Survey, a school-based survey.]

Characteristic		Enrolled in physical education class		Played on a sports team
	Total	Attended daily	Exercised 20 minutes or more per class*	
All students	55.7	28.4	80.3	57.6
Male	58.5	30.5	84.5	64.0
Grade 9	70.8	37.7	84.8	65.0
Grade 10	63.0	33.5	83.2	62.0
Grade 11	50.5	26.0	83.7	66.3
Grade 12	44.5	21.4	87.2	62.3
Female	52.8	26.4	75.3	51.0
Grade 9	71.2	38.0	75.7	55.2
Grade 10	58.0	29.1	77.0	53.9
Grade 11	40.8	19.2	71.6	47.8
Grade 12	34.6	15.2	74.9	45.9
White, non-Hispanic	53.7	24.9	81.5	60.8
Male	55.9	26.8	85.8	65.4
Female	51.5	23.1	76.6	55.9
Black, non-Hispanic	56.0	33.0	74.0	53.2
Male	63.1	37.1	80.0	67.5
Female	49.3	29.0	66.7	39.6
Hispanic	58.8	36.7	78.2	49.5
Male	61.4	39.5	82.5	56.2
Female	56.1	34.0	73.5	42.8

*For students enrolled in physical education classes.

SOURCE: "No. 1242. High School Students Engaged in Organized Physical Activity by Sex, Race and Hispanic Origin: 2003," in *Statistical Abstract of the United States: 2004–2005*, U.S. Census Bureau, August 2005, http://www.census.gov/prod/2004pubs/04statab/arts.pdf (accessed September 22, 2005)

TABLE 6.21

Participation in high school athletic programs, by sex, 1972–2003

[Data based on number of state associations reporting and may underrepresent the number of schools with and participants in athletic programs]

Year	Participants*	
	Males	Females
1972–73	3,770,621	817,073
1973–74	4,070,125	1,300,169
1975–76	4,109,021	1,645,039
1977–78	4,367,442	2,083,040
1978–79	3,709,512	1,854,400
1979–80	3,517,829	1,750,264
1980–81	3,503,124	1,853,789
1981–82	3,409,081	1,810,671
1982–83	3,355,558	1,779,972
1983–84	3,303,599	1,747,346
1984–85	3,354,284	1,757,884
1985–86	3,344,275	1,807,121
1986–87	3,364,082	1,836,356
1987–88	3,425,777	1,849,684
1988–89	3,416,844	1,839,352
1989–90	3,398,192	1,858,659
1990–91	3,406,355	1,892,316
1991–92	3,429,853	1,940,801
1992–93	3,416,389	1,997,489
1993–94	3,472,967	2,130,315
1994–95	3,536,359	2,240,461
1995–96	3,634,052	2,367,936
1996–97	3,706,225	2,474,043
1997–98	3,763,120	2,570,333
1998–99	3,832,352	2,652,726
1999–00	3,861,749	2,675,874
2000–01	3,921,069	2,784,154
2001–02	3,960,517	2,806,998
2002–03	3,988,738	2,856,358

*A participant is counted in the number of sports participated in.

SOURCE: Adapted from "No. 1243. Participation in High School Athletic Programs by Sex: 1972 to 2003," in *Statistical Abstract of the United States: 2004–2005*, U.S. Census Bureau, August 2005, http://www.census.gov/prod/2004pubs/04statab/arts.pdf (accessed September 22, 2005)

TABLE 6.22

Most popular high school sports for boys, 1990–91 and 2003–04

[Players; number of teams in ( )]

Sport	1990–91	2003–04
Football	941,423 (13,900)	1,057,660 (14,779)
Basketball	515,644 (16,462)	544,811 (17,389)
Track & field	401,350 (13,905)	504,801 (5,221)
Baseball	419,015 (13,608)	457,146 (14,984)
Soccer	228,380 (6785)	349,785 (10,219)
Wrestling	230,673 (8404)	238,700 (9526)
Cross country	155,375 (10,419)	196,428 (12,649)

SOURCE: Michael Jacobsen, "Most Popular High School Sports—Boys," in *Sporting Goods Dealer*, March–April 2005

TABLE 6.23

Most popular high school sports for girls, 1990–91 and 2003–04

[Players; number of teams in ( )]

	1990–91		2003–04		Percent increase
Basketball	387,802	(15,864)	457,986	(17,061)	+18%
Track & field	320,763	(13,751)	415,322	(15,089)	+29%
Volleyball	300,810	(12,017)	396,322	(14,181)	+32%
Softball	219,464	(8,867)	362,468	(14,181)	+65%
Soccer	121,722	(4,490)	309,032	(9,559)	+154%
Tennis	132,607	(8,580)	181,329	(10,367)	+37%
Cross country	106,514	(9,470)	166,287	(12,235)	+53%
Swimming/diving	88,122	(4,295)	155,565	(6,176)	+64%
Spirit squads		NA	88,443	(3,693)	NA

Note: NA=not available.

SOURCE: Michael Jacobsen, "Most Popular High School Sports—Girls, in *Sporting Goods Dealer*, March–April 2005. Data from SGMA (Sporting Goods Manufacturers Association) International

TABLE 6.24

Participation in school athletics, 1991–2003

	1991	1992	1993	1994	1995	1996	1997	1998	1999	2000	2001	2002	2003
Eighth grade	69.6	67.3	66.6	66.5	68.1	67.4	66.7	68.7	67.7	67.3	69.1	67.2	65.3
Gender													
Male	73.4	71.0	71.1	70.2	72.5	69.8	68.0	71.7	69.0	69.2	70.8	68.3	68.0
Female	66.2	64.0	62.7	63.2	64.3	65.6	65.5	65.8	66.6	65.8	67.5	66.1	62.9
Race													
White	71.1	68.7	70.0	69.8	69.5	70.7	70.1	71.2	70.0	70.2	72.6	71.9	67.5
Black	73.8	68.4	61.8	62.4	69.7	64.5	63.0	64.9	69.5	63.4	67.3	65.9	67.2
Parental education*													
Less than high school	54.3	47.7	49.9	51.0	50.5	53.4	52.3	53.0	55.0	47.5	53.3	55.5	51.3
Completed high school	66.1	63.7	62.5	63.9	64.8	64.2	61.5	63.0	63.3	64.3	64.1	63.0	64.4
Some college	73.3	67.6	69.7	69.5	73.8	69.4	70.5	70.2	69.6	69.8	69.1	66.8	65.0
Completed college	73.6	75.5	72.7	72.3	71.3	75.3	71.6	74.0	74.1	74.0	77.0	72.5	69.7
Graduate school	76.6	76.7	76.3	74.4	74.9	77.7	74.8	76.6	75.4	75.8	78.7	76.9	76.2
College plans													
None or under 4 years	49.9	46.9	47.9	51.0	51.3	50.5	50.2	49.4	46.8	46.8	46.5	49.0	41.4
Complete four years	72.7	70.4	69.0	68.7	70.3	70.0	68.9	70.9	70.2	69.5	71.6	68.7	67.8
Tenth grade	60.2	62.9	62.0	61.8	62.6	61.5	61.7	61.6	62.2	61.5	62.9	61.1	60.2
Gender													
Male	68.7	69.8	68.0	69.2	68.2	65.5	66.0	67.8	68.1	65.5	66.3	64.3	63.4
Female	51.9	56.6	56.5	54.9	57.5	57.7	57.5	56.1	57.4	58.3	60.0	57.8	57.0
Race													
White	61.8	64.6	64.1	64.0	63.6	63.5	63.3	63.6	65.4	63.8	65.2	62.8	62.8
Black	55.7	62.8	59.9	57.2	62.3	56.5	62.5	58.8	57.2	55.7	60.9	64.8	58.5
Parental education*													
Less than high school	44.5	40.1	42.5	42.7	40.9	42.7	44.2	46.7	44.0	45.9	48.3	40.2	44.0
Completed high school	54.4	56.8	58.2	53.2	54.3	53.7	56.3	53.6	54.0	51.7	56.5	54.7	50.9
Some college	59.8	63.6	62.9	62.0	62.6	62.4	60.5	64.7	65.2	61.4	63.0	60.9	61.8
Completed college	67.2	72.6	67.3	70.3	71.8	68.3	68.8	68.1	70.0	69.9	68.9	70.6	66.4
Graduate school	70.9	74.6	75.1	74.0	74.9	73.5	72.7	72.9	71.9	75.9	75.5	72.0	74.4
College plans													
None or under 4 years	38.9	42.7	41.3	39.9	39.9	40.3	42.0	45.5	39.0	39.4	41.1	37.5	40.6
Complete four years	64.6	66.9	66.0	66.5	66.2	65.1	64.8	64.4	66.0	65.0	66.4	64.9	63.1
Twelfth grade	56.2	55.6	55.7	56.3	55.1	55.1	55.5	55.9	54.3	55.0	55.0	54.0	53.3
Gender													
Male	64.9	63.8	65.5	66.1	62.4	62.7	63.4	63.0	62.3	64.2	61.9	60.2	58.9
Female	47.0	48.0	46.2	47.5	48.1	48.0	48.4	48.7	47.3	46.9	48.6	48.7	48.0
Race													
White	57.0	57.3	56.7	57.7	54.9	56.8	56.3	57.7	56.5	57.4	57.5	56.3	55.4
Black	56.2	50.9	52.9	59.7	56.7	53.1	52.9	54.1	50.1	55.4	57.9	48.4	50.5
Parental education*													
Less than high school	41.3	46.7	44.4	41.7	38.7	35.3	37.2	41.3	43.5	33.2	38.0	39.7	42.6
Completed high school	50.3	49.1	52.8	51.2	48.4	50.1	50.2	52.5	49.5	53.5	50.1	47.0	49.1
Some college	60.3	54.9	55.8	57.1	53.2	54.3	55.5	57.4	54.6	56.8	56.1	53.3	51.5
Completed college	61.7	63.8	60.8	61.8	62.2	62.1	60.6	59.1	57.3	58.6	62.1	62.1	57.8
Graduate school	66.4	67.5	66.4	68.4	68.0	64.6	66.7	66.2	65.8	63.0	63.5	62.6	66.7
College plans													
None or under 4 years	42.6	41.0	40.0	44.0	41.2	41.6	39.8	42.2	43.3	42.0	40.7	41.6	40.9
Complete four years	61.5	60.7	60.4	60.0	58.8	59.0	60.3	59.9	57.8	58.4	58.8	57.7	56.2

*Parental education is calculated by the Institute of Social Research as the average of the mother's and father's education. Child Trends has relabeled these results to reflect the education level of the most educated parent. In those circumstances where the gap between mothers' and fathers' education is more than one level, this results in an underestimate of the most educated parent's education level.

SOURCE: "Table 1. Participation in School Athletics, 1991–2003," in Child Trends, *Child Trends DataBank Indicator: Participation in School Athletics* (original data from Child Trends' analysis of Monitoring the Future), http://www.childtrendsdatabank.org/pdf/37_PDF.pdf (accessed September 13, 2005)

FIGURE 6.8

Percentage of students who participated in school athletics, by gender, 1991 and 2003

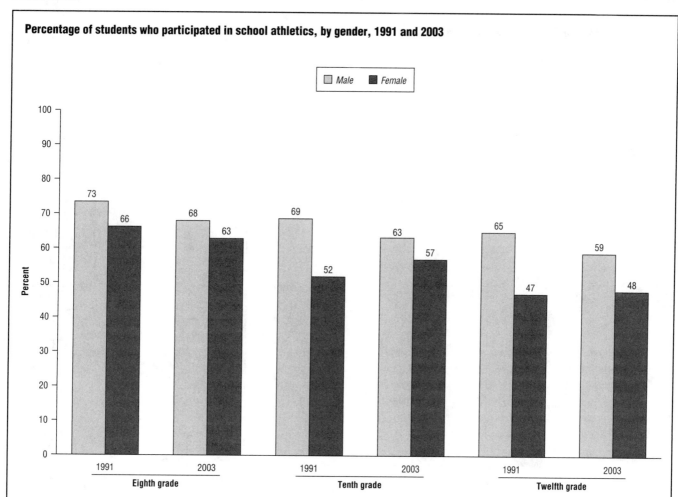

Note: Participation in school athletics includes all students who have participated to any degree in school athletic teams during the school year.

SOURCE: "Figure 1. Percentage of Students in Grades 8, 10, and 12 Who Participate in School Athletics, by Gender, 1991 and 2003," in Child Trends, *Child Trends DataBank Indicator: Participation in School Athletics* (original data from Child Trends' analysis of Monitoring the Future), http://www .childtrendsdatabank.org/pdf/37_PDF.pdf (accessed September 13, 2005)

FIGURE 6.9

Percentage of students who participated in school athletics, by parents' education, 2003

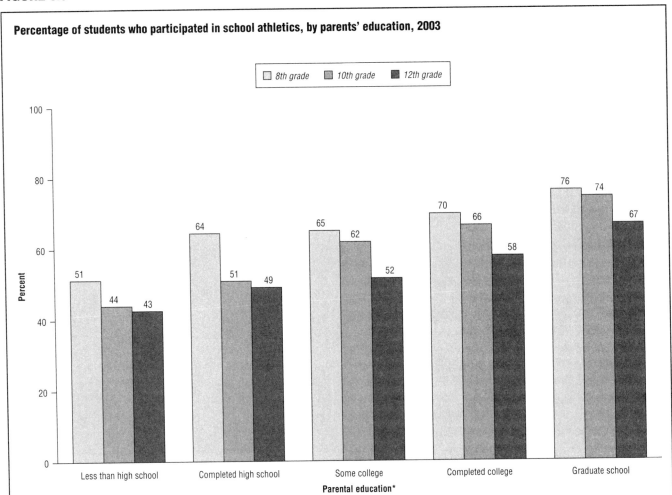

Note: Participation in school athletics includes all students who have participated to any degree in school athletic teams during the school year.
*Parental education is calculated by the Institute of Social Research as the average of the mother's and father's education. Child Trends has relabeled these results to reflect the education level of the most educated parent. In those circumstances where the gap between mother's and father's education is more than one level, this results in an underestimate of the most educated parent's education level.

SOURCE: "Figure 2. Percentage of Students in Grades 8, 10, and 12 Who Participate in School Athletics, by Parent's Education, 2003," in Child Trends, *Child Trends DataBank Indicator: Participation in School Athletics* (original data from Child Trends' analysis of Monitoring the Future), http://www .childtrendsdatabank.org/pdf/37_PDF.pdf (accessed September 13, 2005)

CHAPTER 7
THE OLYMPICS

If professional team sports in the United States epitomize the corporatization of athletics, the Olympic games, at least in theory, exemplify the opposite—global goodwill and celebration that surround the pursuit of athletic excellence for its own sake. That does not, however, diminish the fact that vast sums of money change hands via the Olympics. Nor does it prevent the pursuit of those vast sums, or political grandstanding, from sometimes overshadowing the Olympic ideal.

The XXVIII Olympiad took place over seventeen days in August 2004. These summer Olympics were held in Athens, Greece, the birthplace of Olympic athletic events. According to the International Olympic Committee (IOC), about 11,000 athletes representing 202 countries competed in twenty-eight sports in Athens. Medals were awarded in 301 separate events (http://www.olympic.org/uk/games/past/index_uk.asp?OLGT=1&OLGY=2004). Table 1.5 in Chapter 1 shows the current list of Olympic sports as of the 2004 summer games and 2006 winter games. Based on live attendance at the Olympics, track and field is consistently the most popular Olympic sport, and it generally takes place at the largest venues, according to IOC data. Gymnastics, particularly the women's all-around competition, is second in popularity.

The winter Olympics are much smaller than the summer games. There were 2,400 athletes from seventy-seven countries at the 2002 winter games in Salt Lake City, Utah. They competed in seventy-eight total events in seven sports (http://www.olympic.org/uk/games/past/index_uk.asp?OLGT=2&OLGY=2002).

The International Olympic Committee regularly reviews which sports are to be included in the Olympic games. A number of factors are taken into consideration, most prominently popularity and cost. For example, beach volleyball made its Olympic debut in 1996. Snowboarding was added to the winter games program in 1998. The IOC has also decided to eliminate baseball and softball as of 2012. The Olympic Charter limits the number of sports that can take place at the Olympics; therefore sports must be cut in order to accommodate the addition of new ones. Sports that have come and gone from the lineup over the decades include tug-of-war (1900–20), golf (1900–04), rugby (1900, 1908, 1920–24), and polo (1900, 1908, 1920–24, 1936).

Prior to the 1996 games, the Olympics sometimes included "demonstration sports," the purpose of which was to showcase an emerging or locally popular sport before a global audience. Winners in these sports were not officially recognized as Olympic champions. Some of these sports, such as flatwater canoeing and kayaking, were later added as regular Olympic events at subsequent games. Winter sports that have been demonstrated include speed skiing, curling, and freestyle aerial skiing.

HISTORY OF THE OLYMPICS

The roots of the Olympic games are in ancient Greece. Exactly when the ancient Olympics started is unknown, but the first recorded games took place in the city of Olympia in 776 BC. The games grew in importance over the next few centuries, reaching their peak in the fifth and sixth centuries BC. By that time, they had grown from a single event—a 200-yard foot race called the stadion—to twenty events spread over several days. Like today, the Greek Olympic games were held every four years.

As the Roman Empire rose to power in the region, and subsequently adopted Christianity as its official religion, the Olympic games declined in stature. The games, which had always been a religious as much as an athletic celebration, were eventually outlawed in 393 AD by the emperor Theodosius.

Interest in the Olympics was revived in the mid-nineteenth century when modern archaeologists began to unearth the ruins of ancient Olympia. In 1890 French historian and educator Baron Pierre de Coubertin developed the idea of holding an international competition of young athletes as a way to promote peace and cooperation among nations. He presented his ideas at the Sorbonne University in Paris in 1894, and two years later the first modern Olympic games were held in Athens, Greece.

The inaugural Olympic games of 1896 featured 241 athletes from fourteen countries competing in forty-three events—the largest international sporting event ever held up to that time (http://www.olympic.org/uk/games/past/index_uk.asp?OLGT=1&OLGY=1896). The event was repeated in Paris in 1900, and again in St. Louis, Missouri, in 1904.

Winter Olympics History

By 1908 movement toward establishing a winter version of the Olympics had begun. That year, figure skating was introduced during the summer games in London. A cluster of winter events was scheduled to be added for 1916, but the games were cancelled because of the outbreak of World War I in 1914. When the Olympics resumed in 1920, they included figure skating and ice hockey as medal events. Over the objections of Coubertin and the organizers of an Olympic-style Scandinavian winter competition that had been held periodically since 1901, the IOC approved an eleven-day "International Winter Sports Week," featuring Nordic skiing, speed skating, figure skating, hockey, and bobsledding, in Chamonix, France, in 1924. These games were a success and were retroactively dubbed the first Olympic Winter Games by decision of the 1926 International Olympic Committee Session. The winter games took place during regular Olympic years until 1992. Beginning with the 1994 games in Lillehammer, Norway, the winter games have been held every four years, alternating with the summer games.

Politics and the Olympics

Coubertin's dream of a world made more peaceful through sport did not materialize. Moreover, wars and other political complications crippled the Olympic Movement at several points during the twentieth century. The 1916 games were a casualty of World War I, and World War II claimed two Olympics, 1940 and 1944.

Twice the Olympics have been the scene of violent acts of terrorism. At the 1972 summer games in Munich, West Germany, Palestinian terrorists took eleven members of the Israeli team hostage. An attempt to rescue the hostages was bungled, and as a result all eleven hostages, five terrorists, and a police officer died.

In 1996 two people were killed and 111 injured when a bomb exploded on a crowded Centennial Olympic Park at the summer games in Atlanta, Georgia. The perpetrator, Eric Robert Rudolph—a member of a radical Christian group violently opposed to abortion and homosexuality—was not arrested until 2003. In 2005 he was sentenced to consecutive life sentences without parole for another bombing that killed a police officer.

BOYCOTTS. Even when the Olympics have taken place on schedule, they have sometimes been used to make political statements. Boycotts have been a frequent occurrence. The 1956 games in Melbourne, Australia, were the scene of two different boycotts: by the Netherlands, Spain, and Switzerland in response to the Soviet Union's brutal handling of that year's Hungarian Uprising; and by Egypt, Lebanon, and Iraq in protest of British and French involvement in the Suez Crisis in the Middle East.

Several African nations threatened to boycott the Olympics in 1968, 1972, and 1976, in protest of South African and Rhodesian racial policies. The IOC bowed to this pressure and banned South Africa and Rhodesia from participating in the 1968 and 1972 Olympics. In 1980 and 1984 the two major Cold War powers traded boycotts. The United States and sixty-four other Western nations stayed home from the 1980 Olympics in Moscow in protest of the Soviet invasion of Afghanistan. Four years later, the Soviet Union and fourteen of its allied nations retaliated by boycotting the Los Angeles games of 1984, on the grounds that the American hosts could not guarantee their safety. In 1988 North Korea boycotted the Olympics in South Korea, arguing that the two countries should have been named co-hosts.

SCANDAL. In 1998 information was uncovered revealing that several members of the IOC had accepted gifts from the 2002 Salt Lake City Winter Olympics organizing committee in exchange for their site selection votes. Ten IOC members were forced off of the committee as a result, and in the aftermath of the scandal changes were made in the process for selecting host cities. Questions remain as to whether the reforms have really eliminated the possibility of bribery in the Olympic site selection process. An August 2004 BBC documentary, "Panorama: Buying the Games," used hidden cameras and journalists posing as agents interested in securing the games for London to reveal that the IOC was still ripe for corruption (http://news.bbc.co.uk/1/hi/programmes/panorama/3937425.stm).

STRUCTURE OF THE OLYMPIC MOVEMENT

The Olympics are run by a complex array of organizations known primarily by their initials. At the center of the structure is the International Olympic Committee (IOC), based in Lausanne, Switzerland. The IOC, according to its Web site, is the "supreme authority of the Olympic Movement." Its role is to "promote top-level sport as well as sport for all in accordance with the

Olympic Charter. It ensures the regular celebration of the Olympic games and strongly encourages, by appropriate means, the promotion of women in sport, that of sports ethics and the protection of athletes."

The next layer of Olympic oversight, the International Federations (IFs), coordinates international competition within a particular sport. Track and field, for example, is governed by the International Amateur Athletics Federation. There are currently twenty-eight IFs involved in the summer Olympics and another seven that preside over sports in the winter games. These federations make all the rules that pertain to their sport and run the world championships and other international competitions within their realm (http://www.olympic.org/uk/organisation/if/index_uk.asp). Each country that competes in a sport at the international level has a national governing body (NGB), which coordinates the sport domestically.

International Olympic Committee (IOC)

The IOC was created by the International Athletic Congress of Paris on June 23, 1894, convened by Coubertin, who is generally considered the father of the modern Olympic movement. The original committee in 1894 consisted of fourteen members plus Coubertin (http://www.olympic.org/uk/organisation/ioc/index_uk.asp). Coubertin remained at the helm of the IOC through the 1924 Olympics. The IOC was charged with the control and development of the modern Olympic games. Membership on the IOC is limited to one member from most countries, and two members from the largest and most active member countries, or countries that have hosted the Olympics. Members must speak French or English and be citizens and residents of a country with a recognized National Olympic Committee.

The IOC runs the Olympic Movement according to the terms of the Olympic Charter, most recently amended in September 2004. The Charter outlines the six "Fundamental Principles of Olympism." These principles, as written in the Charter, are:

1. Olympism is a philosophy of life, exalting and combining in a balanced whole the qualities of body, will, and mind. Blending sport with culture and education, Olympism seeks to create a way of life based on the joy of effort, the educational value of good example, and respect for universal fundamental ethical principles.

2. The goal of Olympism is to place sport at the service of the harmonious development of man, with a view to promoting a peaceful society concerned with the preservation of human dignity.

3. The Olympic Movement is the concerted, organised, universal and permanent action, carried out under the supreme authority of the IOC, of all individuals and entities who are inspired by the values of Olympism. It covers the five continents. It reaches its peak with the bringing together of the world's athletes at the great sports festival, the Olympic games. Its symbol is five interlaced rings.

4. The practice of sport is a human right. Every individual must have the possibility of practising sport, without discrimination of any kind and in the Olympic spirit, which requires mutual understanding with a spirit of friendship, solidarity, and fair play. The organisation, administration, and management of sport must be controlled by independent sports organisations.

5. Any form of discrimination with regard to a country or a person on grounds of race, religion, politics, gender, or otherwise is incompatible with belonging to the Olympic Movement.

6. Belonging to the Olympic Movement requires compliance with the Olympic Charter and recognition by the IOC.

The IOC has a maximum of 115 members, who meet at least once a year. During this "Session," the committee elects a President for a term of eight years (renewable for another four), and an Executive Board, whose members serve for four years. The IOC is administered by a Director General, with the assistance of the directors of the IOC's various units, which include International Cooperation; Olympic Games Coordination; Relations with IFs, NOCs, and OCOGs; Finance; Marketing; Legal Affairs; Technology; Control and Coordination of Operations; Communications; and Medical.

United States Olympic Committee (USOC)

In the United States, building a team to represent the nation at the Olympics is the responsibility of the United States Olympic Committee (USOC). The USOC comprises seventy-three member organizations. Thirty-nine of them are "national governing bodies," or NGBs— such as USA Gymnastics and USA Track and Field— each of which supports a particular sport. Other USOC members include community-based and education-based multisport organizations, US Armed Forces sports, and organizations involved in sports for people with disabilities. In addition to the Olympics, the USOC is the driving force for U.S. sports that are part of the Pan-American Games program. The Pan Am Games are an international goodwill sports competition featuring athletes from the Americas; they take place every four years in the year preceding the Olympics. In the United States the NGBs are responsible for selecting the athletes who will represent their country in their sport at the Olympics. In most events this is done at national competitions called Olympic Trials.

In addition to its role in developing the American Olympic team, the USOC is instrumental in American cities' bids to host the winter or summer Olympic games or the Pan Am Games. The USOC may vote on and endorse a particular city's bid to serve as host. All U.S. Olympic Trial site selections also go through the USOC. The USOC gets much of its funding from the IOC; in fact, 25% of the IOC's broadcast revenue ends up with the USOC. Of the money NBC will have spent for televising the Olympics from 2000 to 2008, the USOC will bank $418 million, according to *The Business of Sports* (Scott R. Rosner and Kenneth L. Shropshire, eds., Sudbury, MA: Jones and Bartlett, 2004). The USOC also receives a large share of what the IOC takes in from corporate sponsorships—more than the other 198 NOCs combined, according to Rosner and Shropshire. In addition to these sources, the USOC also earns nearly $200 million per year through its own domestic sponsorships, licensing fees, and other joint ventures.

The USOC was created as a small, informal organization in 1896 by James E. Sullivan, founder of the Amateur Athletic Union. The first elected president of the USOC was A. G. Spalding, a well-known sporting goods manufacturer. The committee became a formal entity, called the American Olympic Association, in 1921. The name was changed twice in the 1940s—to the United States of America Sports Federation in 1940, and to the United States Olympic Association (USOA) in 1945. The USOA received its federal charter as a private nonprofit corporation in 1950. The USOC got its current name in 1961.

In 1978 the USOC acquired its status as the legal coordinating body for the Olympic and Pan Am Games through passage of the Amateur Sports Act. The Act also recognized the authority of the NGBs to oversee development within their own sports. In addition, the Act mandated that 20% membership and voting power within both the USOC and the sport-specific agencies be held by "recent or active" athletes. That year, the USOC moved its headquarters from New York City to Colorado Springs, Colorado.

As of 2005 the USOC operated three training centers, located in Colorado Springs; Lake Placid, New York; and San Diego, California. The USOC also maintains an Olympic Education Center in Marquette, Michigan, where athletes can pursue an academic degree without interrupting their training.

The USOC has struggled financially in recent years, its nonprofit status notwithstanding. Its administrative costs and overhead are quite high, and according to Rosner and Shropshire it provides more than $80 million a year in monetary support to American athletes and NGBs. In addition, unlike most NOCs around the world, the USOC does not receive direct financial support from the government.

THE FLOW OF OLYMPIC MONEY

All of the symbols, images, phrases, and other intellectual property associated with the Olympics belong to the IOC. According to the IOC Web site, the Olympic Movement generates marketing revenue through five major channels: broadcasting, The Olympic Partner (TOP) worldwide sponsorship program, domestic sponsorships, ticketing, and licensing. The IOC manages the first two; the others are managed by the Organizing Committees for the Olympic Games (OCOGs) within the host country, under the IOC's direction. According to the IOC's *2005 Olympic Marketing Fact File* (http://multimedia.olympic.org/pdf/en_report_344.pdf), total marketing revenue for the 2001–04 quadrennium was $4.187 billion, up from $3.770 billion in the previous four-year period and $2.630 billion in 1993–96.

As with the major professional sports in the United States, the biggest financial driver of the Olympics is television, with a startling growth in revenue generated through television broadcasts of the Olympics. For the Olympic cycle running from 2001 to 2004, worldwide broadcast rights netted the IOC $2.230 billion, about half of its total revenue, according to the *Marketing Fact File*. About three-quarters of the total came from the United States, specifically from NBC, which paid $793.5 million to broadcast the 2004 Athens Olympics. European networks contributed another 16%. The rest of the world contributed the remainder. These proportions are not likely to change for the next several years; as of 2005 NBC had a $4.5 billion deal to broadcast the Olympics in the United States through the 2012 games. Broadcast revenue in the previous quadrennium was $1.845 billion; the 1993–96 total was $1.251 billion.

According to the IOC Web site, half of the broadcast rights fees for each Olympics is distributed to the Organizing Committee for the Olympic Games (OCOG) responsible for that particular Olympic games. The OCOG is made up of top officials from the national Olympic Committee of the host nation and other key representatives of the host city and country. The other half of the broadcast revenue goes to the Olympic Movement. Worldwide, 203 million unique viewers watched at least some part of NBC's broadcast of the *2004 Summer Olympic Games*, according to Nielsen Media Research, a new record for Olympic viewing. According to the *Marketing Fact File*, the 2004 summer games were watched for a total of 34.4 billion viewer hours, down slightly from the 36.1 billion during the 2000 summer games. Total viewer hours for the 2002 winter games were 13.1 billion.

A second key revenue source is the IOC's corporate sponsorship program, known officially as The Olympic Partners (TOP) program. Sponsorships accounted for about 40% of the IOC's revenues from 2001 to 2004, according to *The Business of Sports*. The TOP program brought in $1.8 billion during the 2001–04 quadrennium. (The *Marketing Fact File* lists TOP program revenue as $663 million for the quadrennium.) The program is comprised of ten international corporations, which in return for their money are assured exclusive sponsorship in their business category. For example, as long as Coca-Cola remains a TOP sponsor, Pepsi will not be one. As with broadcast rights, the United States dominates the TOP program; eight of the TOP sponsors are U.S.-based.

The IOC received another $380 million, representing 8% of its total revenue, from ticket sales to the events and opening and closing ceremonies of the Olympics during the 2001–04 quadrennial, according to Rosner and Shropshire ($411 million according to the *Marketing Fact File*). The other major revenue source, the sale of licensed merchandise bearing Olympic logos and other trademarks, including Olympic coins and stamps, generated the remaining 2% of the IOC's revenue, or about $100 million (*Marketing Fact File*: $87 million).

About 92% of IOC revenue is subsequently distributed to the other organizations that collectively make up the Olympic Movement, including OCOGs, which as noted above are the committees formed to run the Olympics within the country that has been selected to host the games; National Olympic Committees (NOCs), whose main role within each of the 199 countries in the Olympic family is to field their country's Olympic team; and international federations (IFs), which coordinate and monitor international competition within their specific sport or family of sports. The IOC retains only about 8% of its overall revenue. These funds are used to cover the organization's operating and administrative costs. According to Rosner and Shropshire, the IOC distributed $305 million to the NOCs that fielded Olympic teams in 2002 (winter games) and 2004 (summer games). According to the *Marketing Fact File*, the sum the IOC contributed to the NOCs during the 2001–04 quadrennium was $319.5 million. An additional $85.8 million was distributed to the international federations that coordinated specific winter sports for the 2002 winter games, according to the *Marketing Fact File*. The IFs for the 2000 summer games received $190 million. Figures for distribution to the IFs for the 2004 summer games were not yet available as of the July 2005 publication of the most recent *Marketing Fact File*.

According to the *2005 Marketing Fact File*, the summer and winter OCOGs for each four-year period share about half of the TOP program revenue and in-kind contributions. Before 2004 the IOC contributed 60% of broadcast revenue for each games to the OCOGs; since 2004 it has contributed 40%.

The vast commercial activity that fuels the Olympic flame would seem to conflict with the philosophical groundings of the Olympic Movement, which value the noble spirit of competition above financial matters. The Olympic Charter acknowledges this apparent contradiction, and the IOC has implemented policies designed to address it. No advertising is allowed in the venues where events take place, or on the uniforms of athletes, coaches, or officials. The TOP program is designed to generate the maximum amount of support with a minimum number of corporate sponsors, and images of Olympic events are not allowed to be used for commercial purposes.

SELECTION OF OLYMPIC SITES

One of the IOC's chief responsibilities is to select the cities that will host the Olympics. Olympic site selection is a two-phase procedure. The first phase is called Applicant Cities. Applicant Cities must be proposed to the IOC by their National Olympic Committee. They must then complete a questionnaire that outlines how they plan to carry out the monumental task of hosting the games. The IOC assesses the applications with regard to the cities' ability to organize the games. Criteria include technical capacity, government support, public opinion, general infrastructure, security, venues, accommodations, and transportation. The IOC then accepts a handful of these applicants as Candidate Cities.

In the second phase, Candidate Cities must provide the IOC with a "candidature file." These files are analyzed by the IOC Evaluation Commission, which is made up of IOC members; representatives of the IFs, NOCs, the IOC Athletes' Commission, the International Paralympics Committee; and other experts. The Evaluation Commission also physically inspects the candidate cities. It then issues a report, on whose basis the IOC Executive Board prepares a list of final candidates. This list is submitted to the IOC Session for a vote.

In contrast to the IOC, IFs, NOCs, and NGBS, the Olympic Games Organizing Committees (OCOGs) are temporary agencies. They disband once the games they were created to organize are over. OCOGs are highly dependent on the IOC for their funding, receiving a substantial share of the IOC's revenue from sponsorships and broadcasting. OCOGs also generate revenue of their own. For example, the OCOG that organized the 2002 winter games in Salt Lake City, Utah (SLOC), brought in $575 million in sponsorship revenue, $180 million from ticket sales, and $25 million in sales of licensed merchandise, according to Rosner and Shropshire. While the IOC turns over most of its revenue to other organizations, the OCOGs give only 5% of the revenue they generate to the IOC, and retain the other

95%, most of which is spent on facility rentals and the construction and removal of temporary facilities.

OLYMPIC ATHLETES: PROFESSIONALS OR AMATEURS?

In its early years the Olympics were considered an arena for strictly amateur competition. Professional athletes were not allowed to participate. This led to a number of controversies and disqualifications over the years, the most famous being the disqualification of 1912 Olympic pentathlon and decathlon champion Jim Thorpe, who was stripped of his gold medals when it was discovered that he had played semi-professional baseball.

Over time, the rigid rules regarding professionalism became less practical. Many countries were supporting their athletes financially, allowing them to train full-time and making a mockery of their "amateur" status. This put athletes in other countries at a competitive disadvantage. The regulations prohibiting professional athletes from participating in the Olympics were relaxed in the 1980s, and eliminated entirely in the 1990s. This change allowed, for example, the development of the American basketball "Dream Team," featuring a number of top NBA players, and the participation of National Hockey League players on winter Olympics hockey teams.

DOPING

Almost from the beginning, the use of performance-enhancing substances ("doping") has plagued the Olympics. An early example was Thomas Hicks, winner of the 1904 marathon, who was given strychnine and brandy. Doping methods improved over time, sometimes with disastrous results. Danish cyclist Knut Jensen died after falling from his bicycle during the 1960 games. He was found to have taken amphetamines. The international sports federations and the IOC banned doping in the 1960s, but for most of the time since then officials have lacked the tools to adequately police the use of illicit substances. Until recently, the highest-profile Olympic athlete to be disqualified for doping was Canadian sprinter Ben Johnson, winner of the 100-meter race in 1988. A few years later, it was revealed that East German sports officials had doped female athletes for years without their knowledge. As the problem of doping grew out of control in the 1990s, the international sports community responded by forming the World Anti-Doping Agency (WADA) in 1999. WADA oversees the monitoring and enforcing of doping regulations at the Olympics. The creation of WADA did not, however, solve the problem entirely. Athletes in every Olympic games since its formation have been found to be in violation of anti-doping rules.

OTHER OLYMPIC GAMES
Special Olympics

Special Olympics is a global nonprofit organization that provides opportunities for athletic training and competition for people with developmental disabilities. According to the Special Olympics Web site, the organization was serving more than 1.7 million people as of 2005, with more than two hundred programs in at least 150 countries. Participants may train or compete in any of twenty-six Olympic-style summer and winter sports (http://www.specialolympics.org/Special+Olympics+Public+Website/English/About_Us/default.htm).

The Special Olympics movement began in the summer of 1968, when the First International Special Olympic Games were held at Soldier Field in Chicago, Illinois, home of the National Football League's Chicago Bears. The roots of the Special Olympics go back to 1962, when Eunice Kennedy Shriver, sister of President John F. Kennedy, started a day camp for developmentally disabled children. In June of that year Shriver invited thirty-five boys and girls to Camp Shriver at Timberlawn, her home in Rockville, Maryland. Her idea was that children who were cognitively impaired were capable of accomplishing much more than was generally believed at the time, if they were given opportunities to do so. Building on Camp Shriver, Shriver began to actively promote the notion of involving people with disabilities in physical activities and competition. Through the Kennedy Foundation, she targeted grants to universities, community centers, and recreation departments that created such opportunities. The Foundation helped fund eleven camps similar to Camp Shriver across the country in 1963. By 1969 thirty-two camps serving 10,000 children were being supported by the Foundation (http://www.specialolympics.org/Special+Olympics+Public+Website/English/About_Us/History/default.htm).

In 1967 the Kennedy Foundation worked with the Chicago Park District to organize a citywide track meet for mentally disabled people that was modeled on the Olympics. The first Special Olympics at Soldier Field attracted 1,000 athletes from twenty-six states and Canada, competing in track and field, floor hockey, and aquatics. Special Olympics, Inc., was officially incorporated in December of 1968.

By the Fourth International Special Olympics Summer Games, which took place at Central Michigan University in August of 1975, the number of participants had more than tripled, to 3,200, representing ten countries. Those games were broadcast to a nationwide audience on the television show *CBS Sports Spectacular*. The Special Olympics Winter Games were launched two years later, with about five hundred athletes competing in skating and skiing events at Steamboat Springs, Colorado. In 1988 the IOC formally recognized the Special Olympics, signing an agreement proclaiming its support.

The Tenth Special Olympics World Summer Games, held in Raleigh-Durham and Chapel Hill, North Carolina, attracted 7,000 athletes from 150 countries. The games featured nineteen sports by this time.

According to the Special Olympics' *2004 Global Athlete Participation Report*, published in May 2005, the Special Olympics Movement served 1,738,385 people as of December 2004. That represented an increase of 357,989 from the previous year, a growth rate of 26% (http://www.specialolympics.org/Special+Olympics+Public+ Website/English/About_Us/2004+Athlete+Participation+ Report.htm). For the last few years, the fastest growth in Special Olympics participation has taken place in East Asia, which contributed nearly one-quarter (24%) of participating athletes in 2004, according to the *Report*.

In the United States the Special Olympics also has a formal relationship with the USOC, and has been designated as the National Governing Body/Disabled Sports Organization for athletes with intellectual disabilities. Special Olympics also has relationships, some of them formal, others less so, with the NOCs of many other nations. Special Olympics also has links with the IFs and NGBs that govern individual sports. Competition must be in accordance with the rules of those organizations, except in cases where they conflict with the Special Olympics' own rules; in those instances, Special Olympics rules take precedence.

Paralympics

While the Special Olympics serves people with mental disabilities, athletes with physical disabilities, including mobility limitations, amputees, people with visual disabilities, and those with cerebral palsy, may compete in the Paralympic Games. The concept for the Paralympics grew out of a 1948 event called the Stoke Mandeville Games, a competition for World War II veterans with spinal cord injuries. The first Olympic-style competition for people with physical disabilities took place in 1960 in Rome. These became the Paralympic Games. Winter Paralympic Games were added in 1976.

Unlike the Special Olympics, the Paralympics have always been held in the same year as the Olympic games. Since the 1988 summer games in Seoul, South Korea, and the 1992 winter games in Albertville, France, the Paralympics have been held in the same venues as well. This arrangement has been cemented into place by an agreement reached with the IOC in 2001. Since the 2002 games in Salt Lake City, both the Olympic and Paralympic games have been set up by the same organizing committee as well. Paralympic athletes live in the same Olympic village with the same food and medical facilities as their Olympic counterparts, and the ticketing, technology, and transportation systems are shared. A total of 3,806 athletes competed in the 2004 Paralympic Summer Games in Athens, Greece. These athletes, representing thirty-six countries, competed in 119 different sports at the games (http://www.paralympic.org/release/Main_ Sections_Menu/Paralympic_Games/). As of late 2005, the 2006 Paralympic Winter Games, set for March 2006 in Turin, Italy, were expected to draw about 590 athletes from forty countries, according to the IOC Web site, competing in alpine skiing, ice sledge hockey, Nordic skiing, and wheelchair curling. The International Paralympic Committee (IPC) oversees the Paralympic Games, performing much the same role as the IOC does for the Olympic games. The IPC is made up of 160 National Paralympic Committees and five disability-specific international sports federations, similar to the IFs that oversee specific Olympic sports. The national Paralympics organization for the United States is U.S. Paralympics, which is a division of the USOC.

Deaflympics

In addition to the Special Olympics and the Paralympics, the IOC also sanctions the Deaflympic Games, which have existed since 1924, almost as long as the Olympics themselves. The first Deaflympic Games, organized by the Comité International des Sports des Sourds, (International Committee of Sports for the Deaf), were held in Paris that year. Winter games were added in 1949. From their appearance in 1924 until 1965, they were known as the International Games for the Deaf. They were called the World Games for the Deaf from 1966 through 1999. The current name was adopted in 2000.

According to the Deaflympics Web site, 2,300 deaf athletes from seventy-five countries participated in the Twentieth Summer Games, held in Melbourne, Australia, in January 2005. The Sixteenth Winter Games, scheduled for Salt Lake City in 2007, are expected to host about three hundred athletes from twenty different nations. Athletes must have a hearing loss of at least fifty-five decibels in their better ear in order to qualify for the Deaflympics. Hearing aids, cochlear implants, and other devices that augment hearing are not used during the competition, in order to ensure a level playing field.

CHAPTER 8
SPORTS AND HEALTH

Sport is a preserver of health.

—Hippocrates

The truth of Hippocrates's assertion has been nearly universally accepted for centuries, but only since the twentieth century have researchers worked to quantify the impact of physical activity, or the lack thereof, on physical and mental well-being. In the April 2004 Power-Point presentation *Focus Area 22: Physical Activity and Fitness Progress Review*, the Centers for Disease Control and Prevention (CDC) reported that about 1.16 million, or 48%, of the nation's 2.4 million deaths in 2000 were preventable; and of those preventable deaths, 400,000 were due to poor diet and physical activity, nearly as many as were due to tobacco, the biggest cause of preventable deaths.

Hippocrates may not have appreciated as fully the other side of the sports–health nexus. As sports become bigger business and the pressure to perform becomes increasingly intense, greater attention has fallen in recent years on the potential negative health impact of sports participation, especially on children and youth.

BENEFITS OF PHYSICAL ACTIVITY

The CDC presentation cited above is a progress report on one area of a broader initiative called "Healthy People 2010." It lists several benefits of physical activity and fitness. They are:

- Builds and maintains healthy bones and muscles, controls weight, builds lean muscle, reduces fat, reduces blood pressure, and improves blood glucose control

- Decreases the risk of obesity and chronic diseases (coronary heart disease, high blood pressure, diabetes, colon cancer, and osteoporosis)

- Reduces feelings of depression and anxiety and promotes psychological well-being

- Relates to functional independence of older adults and quality of life of people of all ages

The specific health benefits of sports participation depend on the sport. In the online article "Sampler of Sports Benefits: Something for Everyone" (*Pfizer Journal*), speed walking, jogging, cycling, swimming, and skiing are described as sports that build cardiovascular endurance. Sports that involve gentle bending or stretching, including bowling, golf, and tai chi, are identified as promoting flexibility, which in turn may reduce the risk of injury. Other sports, such as those involving weightlifting or throwing, build strength. One important result of building strong muscles and, especially, bones is that it helps stave off osteoporosis, by increasing the mineral content of bones. Penn State University's *Young Women's Health Study* found in June of 2004 that exercise was more important than taking calcium supplements in promoting strong bones, and that exercise was responsible for between 16% and 22% of the variation in hip bone mineral density in the eighty women studied over ten years.

There is no doubt that participation in sports that provide an aerobic workout, even a mild one, improves cardiovascular health. For example, a study involving 40,000 women reported in the *Journal of the American Medical Association* ("Physical Activity and Coronary Heart Disease in Women Is 'No Pain, No Gain' Passé?" 2001) found that an hour per week of slow walking cut the risk of a heart attack in half. That same year, "Step Aerobics May Raise 'Good' Cholesterol Level" (*Journal of Sports Medicine and Physical Fitness*, December 24, 2001), reported on research at the University of Southern California showing that three to six months of regular exercise could reduce bad cholesterol (low-density lipoprotein, or LDL) by 10% and increase good cholesterol (high-density lipoprotein, or HDS) by 17%.

The prevalence of preventable chronic diseases underscores the importance of being physically active. A 2002 U.S. Department of Health and Human Services (DHHS) document titled *Physical Activity Fundamental to Preventing Disease* noted that engaging in regular physical activity, defined as at least thirty minutes of moderate activity on at least five days per week, or twenty minutes of vigorous physical activity at least three times per week, has been shown conclusively to reduce deaths from many chronic diseases. The publication cites numerous studies to support this, including the 1994 Framingham Heart Study, involving 1,404 women aged fifty to seventy-four who were free of cardiovascular disease. The most active group had a 33% lower death rate than the least active. As of 2002 in the United States, according to the DHHS:

- 12.6 million people had coronary heart disease

- 1.1 million people per year suffered from a heart attack

- Seventeen million people had diabetes; about 90% to 95% of those cases were type 2 diabetes, which is associated with obesity and physical inactivity; approximately sixteen million additional people have "pre diabetes"

- 107,000 people were being newly diagnosed with colon cancer each year

- 300,000 people suffered from hip fractures each year

- Fifty million people had high blood pressure

- Nearly fifty million adults (between the ages of twenty and seventy-four), or 27% of the nation's adult population, were obese; overall more than 108 million adults, or 61% of the adult population, were either obese or overweight. (By 2004, CDC estimates were even higher—123 million overweight or obese adults, or 64% of the total adult population of the United States.)

All of these conditions can be prevented or improved through regular physical activity. *Physical Activity Fundamental to Preventing Disease* also points to the impact of regular physical activity on mental health. The beneficial effect regular physical activity has on symptoms of depression and anxiety in people with affective disorders has been well documented by research. In "Physical Activity Improves Mental Health" (*Physician and Sportsmedicine*, October 2000), author Kevin R. Fontaine summarizes the body of credible research as showing that physical activity causes "moderate" improvement in depression and small improvements in anxiety and panic disorders. Studies conducted on animals, according to DHHS, suggest that exercise can enhance two of the functions—memory and learning—that are hindered by depression by stimulating the growth of new brain cells. There is also evidence that regular exercise may reduce the risk

TABLE 8.1

Time required to burn 150 calories through selected sports and other moderate physical activities[1]

Washing and waxing a car for 45–60 minutes	Less vigorous, more time[2]
Washing windows or floors for 45–60 minutes	
Playing volleyball for 45 minutes	
Playing touch football for 30–45 minutes	
Gardening for 30–45 minutes	
Wheeling self in wheelchair for 30–40 minutes	
Walking 1¾ miles in 35 minutes (20 min/mile)	
Basketball (shooting baskets) for 30 minutes	
Bicycling 5 miles in 30 minutes	
Dancing fast (social) for 30 minutes	
Pushing a stroller 1 miles in 30 minutes	
Raking leaves for 30 minutes	
Walking 2 miles in 30 minutes (15 min/mile)	
Water aerobics for 30 minutes	
Swimming laps for 20 minutes	
Wheelchair basketball for 20 minutes	
Basketball (playing a game) for 15–20 minutes	
Bicycling 4 miles in 15 minutes	
Jumping rope for 15 minutes	
Running 1½ miles in 15 minutes (10 min/mile)	
Shoveling snow for 15 minutes	More vigorous, less time
Stairwalking for 15 minutes	

[1]A moderate amount of physical activity is roughly equivalent to physical activity that uses approximately 150 calories of energy per day, or 1,000 calories per week.
[2]Some activities can be performed at various intensities; the suggested durations correspond to expected intensity of effort.

SOURCE: "Table IV-4. Examples of Moderate Amounts of Activity," in *Clinical Guidelines on the Identification, Evaluation, and Treatment of Overweight and Obesity in Adults, The Evidence Report,* National Heart, Lung, and Blood Institute in cooperation with The National Institute of Diabetes and Digestive and Kidney Diseases, National Institutes of Health, NIH Publication No. 98-4083, September 1998 [Online] http://www.nhlbi.nih.gov/guidelines/obesity/ob_gdlns.htm [accessed January 4, 2006]

of cognitive decline in older adults. Physical activity may even enhance cognitive ability in non-elderly adults. A 2001 study by Kisou Kubota and other researchers at Nihon Fukushi University in Japan found that individuals consistently scored better on tests of intellectual function after starting a running program.

One of the key negative consequences of a sedentary lifestyle is obesity. Sports participation helps control weight by burning calories that would otherwise be stored as fat. The more vigorous the sport and the more frequent the participation, the more calories are burned. "How Many Calories Have You Burned?" (*USA Today*, March 28, 2005), reports that a 154-pound person burns 440 calories playing basketball for an hour, 210 calories in an hour of bowling, 489 calories during an hour of tennis, and 559 calories in an hour of cross-country skiing. Table 8.1 compares the time required to burn 150 calories through a variety of sports and other physical activities. For example, playing a game of basketball for fifteen to twenty minutes burns 150 calories, the same number as playing volleyball for forty-five minutes, playing touch football for thirty to forty-five minutes, or swimming laps for twenty minutes.

Sports Participation and Mental Health

In addition to the obvious physical benefits of sports participation, there appear to be psychological benefits as well. A 2001 survey conducted by researchers at the University of Florida found that athletes have better images of their own bodies than non-athletes. The effect is visible without regard to sport, gender, or level of expertise. The study's lead author, Heather Hausenblas, is quoted in the University's news release as positing that the effect is part of a broader improvement in self-esteem that accompanies sports participation (http://news.ufl.edu/2001/03/07/body-image/). According to Hausenblas's review of more than eighty other studies, athletes are 20% more likely than non-athletes to have positive self-images. Competitive athletes have better body images than casual athletes, and casual athletes have better body images than non-athletes. The news release also quotes John Russell, president of the American Fitness Association, as saying that even small doses of exercise can benefit people beyond the well-documented cardiovascular effects. Exercise, he said, can alter one's mood by releasing the brain chemical called endorphins. He speculates that endorphins, by putting the exerciser in a better mood, may indirectly improve an athlete's body image.

The idea that sports participation can help improve one's mood is well supported by other scientific research. Rosemarie Kobau, Marc A. Safran, and their colleagues at the CDC reported in "Sad, Blue, or Depressed Days: Health Behaviors and Health-Related Quality of Life, Behavioral Risk Factor Surveillance System, 1995–2000" (*Health and Quality of Life Outcomes*, 2004) that individuals who do not exercise tend to experience more days in which they feel sad. Another study, "Adolescent Women's Sports Involvement and Sexual Behavior/Health: A Process-Level Investigation," conducted by S. J. Lehman and researchers at the University of California, San Diego's Mother, Child & Adolescent HIV Program (*Journal of Youth and Adolescence*, 2004), found evidence of a link between girls' involvement in organized sports and positive sexual health and behavior. This study linked participation in organized sports with positive behavior related to sexual risk-taking, sexual/reproductive health, and sexual/reproductive health-seeking behavior. This effect was connected to self-empowerment and a positive view of one's own body.

A 2003 study published in *Archives of Pediatric & Adolescent Medicine* (K. Kulig, N. D. Brener, and T. McManus, "Sexual Activity and Substance Abuse among Adolescents by Category of Physical Activity Plus Team Sports Participation") found results consistent with those from CDC and University of California at San Diego above. More specifically, this study indicated that high school students who are both physically active outside of school and participated in team sports were less likely to use cigarettes or drugs, and less likely to engage in risky sexual behavior.

Youth Sports Participation as an Indicator of Adult Behavior

Participating in sports as a child or adolescent also increases the likelihood that a person will participate as an adult. In "Childhood and Adolescent Sports Participation as Predictors of Participation in Sports and Physical Fitness Activities during Young Adulthood," Daniel F. Perkins, Janis E. Jacobs, and their colleagues analyzed data from the *Michigan Study of Adolescent Life Transitions* longitudinal study, to examine the connection between sports participation in childhood and physical fitness into young adulthood. The researchers examined survey responses about sports participation from more than six hundred respondents when they were twelve years old, seventeen, and twenty-five and found that childhood sports participation was an excellent predictor of both fitness and participation years later.

While many of the studies cited above highlight the value of sports participation for young people, the benefits of sports are truly multigenerational. Physical activity yields a number of benefits for the elderly as well as the young. Exercise has been shown to be the key to maintaining mobility in older adults, according to the Gerontological Society of America. This activity could be as simple as regular walking.

HEALTH RISKS OF SPORTS PARTICIPATION

Injuries

TYPES OF INJURIES. The National Institute of Arthritis and Musculoskeletal and Skin Diseases (NIAMSD) has published a booklet called *Sports Injuries*, which details the kinds of injuries athletes are likely to sustain and the activities in which they sustain them. *Sports Injuries* lists muscle sprains and strains, ligament and tendon tears, dislocated joints, and bone fractures as the most common types of sports injuries. (See Table 8.2.) According to the NIAMSD booklet, the knee is the most commonly injured joint, largely because of its complexity and its role in bearing weight. Every year, knee problems send over 5.5 million people to an orthopedic surgeon. Knee injuries can result from twisting it awkwardly, a direct blow, from landing badly after a jump, or from overuse. Injuries can range in severity from a minor bruise to serious damage to one or more of the four ligaments—the anterior cruciate (ACL), posterior cruciate (PCL), medial collateral (MCL), and lateral collateral (LCL)—that stabilize the joint.

The Achilles tendon, which connects the calf muscle to the back of the heel, is another common site of sports injuries. Achilles tendon injuries are especially common

TABLE 8.2

Common types of sports injuries

- Muscle sprains and strains
- Tears of the ligaments that hold joints together
- Tears of the tendons that support joints and allow them to move
- Dislocated joints
- Fractured bones, including vertebrae.

SOURCE: "Common Types of Sports Injuries," in *Sports Injuries*, U.S. Department of Health and Human Services, National Institutes of Health, National Institute of Arthritis and Musculoskeletal and Skin Diseases, April 2004, http://www.niams.nih.gov/hi/topics/sports_injuries/HOHSportsInjuries.pdf (accessed September 22, 2005)

in people who do not exercise regularly and may not bother to stretch adequately before the game or session. This makes middle-aged "weekend warriors" particularly susceptible, according to NIAMSD.

A fracture is a break in a bone. It can come from a single event, in which case it is called an acute fracture; or it can be caused by repetitive impact, which is called a stress fracture. Stress fractures usually occur in the feet or legs, the result of the pounding these bones take from long periods of running and jumping. When the bones that come together to form a joint get separated, it is called a dislocation. According to *Sports Injuries*, the joints of the hand are the most common points of dislocation, followed by the shoulder.

Sports Injuries divides all sports injuries into two broad categories: acute and chronic. Acute injuries are those that occur suddenly during an activity. They are characterized by severe pain, swelling, and inability to use the injured body part. Chronic injuries usually occur through overuse over a long period of time. They usually result in pain when engaging in the activity, and a dull ache when at rest. There may also be swelling.

The vast majority (95%) of sports injuries are minor soft tissue traumas, according to the *Gale Encyclopedia of Medicine* (*GEM*). These include bruises (or contusions), which occur when blood collects at the point of the injury causing a discoloration of the skin. Sprains, which account for about one-third of sports injuries, are partial or complete tears of a ligament. Strains are similar to sprains. The difference is that in a strain the torn tissue is a muscle or tendon rather than a ligament. Other soft tissue sports injuries include tendonitis (inflammation of a tendon) and bursitis (inflammation of the fluid-filled sacs that allow tendons to glide over bones). These two injuries usually result from repeated stress on the tissue involved rather than from a single event. The kinds of sports injuries that result from overuse appear to be on the rise among young people. A *Business Week* article ("Young Athletes, Big League Pain," June 7, 2004) by Mark Hyman notes that in 1989, overuse injuries

accounted for 20% of patients visiting the sports medicine clinic of Children's Hospital Boston. By 2004 the percentage was 70% and on the rise. The article blames increased pressure to perform from parents and coaches, who seek to turn every promising young athlete into a scholarship recipient and, eventually, a superstar.

Skeletal injuries from sports are less common than soft tissue injuries. According to *GEM*, fractures account for 5% to 6% of sports injuries, with arms and legs being the most common sites of a break. Fractures of the skull or spine are rare in sports. Repeated foot pounding associated with such sports as long-distance running, basketball, and volleyball, and the stress fractures than can result, sometimes cause an injury called shin splints. Shin splints, according to *GEM* "are characterized by soreness and slight swelling of the front, inside, and back of the lower leg, and by sharp pain that develops while exercising and gradually intensifies." Another type of sports injury described in *GEM* is a "compartment syndrome." This condition occurs when the muscles of the lower leg outgrow the membranes that encase them, causing numbness and tingling. Untreated, this condition can lead to permanent damage.

The most dangerous class of sports injuries are those to the brain. A violent jarring of the brain from a blow to the head is called a concussion. Concussions often cause loss of consciousness, and may also affect balance, coordination, hearing, memory, and vision.

STATISTICS ON FREQUENCY AND INJURY RATES. In 2003 American Sports Data, Inc. (ASD) published the first nationwide study since the 1970s on the full range of sports injuries. ASD's *Comprehensive Study of Sports Injuries in the U.S.*, based on surveys conducted in 2002, found sports injuries to be considerably more prevalent than was reported in *GEM*, though the discrepancy is largely the result of different definitions of "injury." According to ASD, there were about twenty million sports injuries in 2002, most of them fairly minor, such as scrapes, bruises, jammed fingers, and ankle twists. More than half of these injuries (53%) were not treated by a doctor, and nearly a third (30%) did not even hinder the injured party's subsequent participation in the sport. About 3.4 million sports injuries were serious enough to require a trip to the emergency room. Sports-induced injuries represented about 10% of the thirty-five to forty-five million injury-related emergency room visits (http://www.americansportsdata.com/sports_injury1.asp).

According to ASD's data, basketball, running, and soccer accounted for the greatest number of sports injuries in 2002, attributable to the fact that so many people participate in those activities. There were 2.78 million basketball-related injuries in 2002. Running and soccer resulted in about 1.65 million and 1.63 million injuries respectively. Other sports with over one million injuries

TABLE 8.3

Top injury-causing sports, 2002

	Total	Percent	Emergency room injuries
Total	**20,145**	**100.0**	**3,358**
Basketball	2,783	13.8	521
Running/jogging	1,654	8.2	*
Soccer	1,634	8.1	259
Football (tackle)	1,084	5.4	351
Softball	1,063	5.3	122
Strength training	1,062	5.3	*
Volleyball	667	3.3	128
Football (touch)	661	3.3	*
Martial arts	610	3.0	*
Baseball	602	3.0	*
Fitness walking	529	2.6	*
Bicycling (recreational)	445	2.2	109
Tennis	415	2.1	*
Ice hockey	415	2.1	171
Skateboarding	399	2.0	103
Walking (recreational)	384	1.9	*
Cheerleading	323	1.6	*
Golf	291	1.4	*
Skiing (downhill)	289	1.4	*
Aerobics (net)	279	1.4	*
Horseback riding	265	1.3	*
Roller skating (in-line)	252	1.3	105
Snowboarding	218	1.1	*
Hunting	207	1.0	103
Mountain biking	201	1.0	*

*Less than 100,000.

SOURCE: "U.S. Sports Injuries—2002 (Top 25)," in *New National Study is First Since 1970s to Document Full Range of Sports Injuries*, American Sports Data, Inc., May 15, 2003, http://www.americansportsdata.com/pr-sportsinjuries.asp (accessed September 22, 2005)

for the year were tackle football and softball, each accounting for about 1.06 million injuries. (See Table 8.3.) On a percentage basis, tackle football caused the most injuries. Its injury rate was 18.8 per one hundred players. While that number looks alarmingly high, it translates, as ASD President Harvey Lauer pointed out in the news release announcing the report, to one injury per player every five years—hardly cause for a movement to ban the sport. Ice hockey (15.9%), boxing (12.7%), and martial arts (10.2%) were below football on the list as measured by injuries per one hundred players (http://www.americansportsdata.com/pr-sportsinjuries.asp).

Pietro Tonino, an assistant professor of orthopedic surgery at Loyola University Chicago's Stritch School of Medicine, also analyzed sports injuries, using data from the U.S. Consumer Product Safety Commission. His analysis (http://www.luhs.org/depts/media/release/reportdetail.cfm?autonumber=944), conducted in 2004, arrived at somewhat different totals from those of ASD, though many of the same sports showed up at the top of his list. Like ASD's count, Tonino's tally found that basketball accounted for the greatest number of injuries, though his total of 1.6 million was well below ASD's figure. Bicycling was second with 1.3 million, followed by football (one million), soccer (456,320), and baseball (417,479).

Another way of analyzing which sports are most likely to result in injury is to measure the number of injuries per 1,000 athlete exposures, meaning the actual number of times the individual participated in the sport over the course of the year. Based on this type of assessment, according to ASD, boxing involves the greatest injury risk, 5.2 injuries per 1,000 exposures. It is followed by tackle football (3.8), snowboarding (3.8), ice hockey (3.7), alpine skiing (3.0), soccer (2.4), softball (2.2), and basketball (1.9). Surprisingly, only one of the so-called "extreme" sports—snowboarding, ranked third—seemed to carry a particularly high injury risk. Surfing, mountain biking, skateboarding, and in-line skating were all well down the list. Paintball, which bears a reputation as a risky endeavor, was associated with only 0.2 injuries per 1,000 exposures, the lowest rate among the extreme sports. That translates to one injury every five hundred years for the average paintball enthusiast (http://www.americansportsdata.com/pr-sportsinjuries.asp).

FACTORS AFFECTING INJURY RATES. ASD's *Comprehensive Study* takes on the apparent paradox of rising sports injury numbers in the face of shrinking sports participation. ASD explains that while participation in casual "pick-up" versions of traditional team sports has indeed been falling off, many organized team sports have actually flourished in recent years. One contributing factor to the rise in injuries, according to the study, is that children are introduced to sports at younger and younger ages, leading to early specialization in a particular sport and ultra-competitiveness in that sport.

According to NIAMSD, children and adolescents, middle-aged people, and women are particularly vulnerable to sports injuries. Because they are still growing, the bones, muscles, tendons, and ligaments of children are more prone to injury than those of adults. Kids are also at higher risk of injury during sports because they vary so widely in size and physical maturity. Children ages five through fourteen sustained an estimated 2.38 million sports and recreational injuries each year between 1997 and 1999, with bicycling leading the way. (See Table 8.4.) Adults over twenty-five, a much larger group, incurred only 2.29 million sports and recreational injuries during that span according to NIAMSD. (See Table 8.5.) The *Gale Encyclopedia of Medicine* (*GEM*) also states that children are more likely than adults to suffer sports injuries, explaining that children's reflexes and coordination are not as developed as those of adults, and they are not as equipped to recognize and evaluate risks and respond appropriately. Each year, according to *GEM*, about 3.2 million children between the ages of five and fourteen are injured while participating in sports. As many as 20% of the children who participate in sports receive injuries, accounting for about 40% of all sports injuries. About one-quarter of their injuries are considered serious;

TABLE 8.4

Kids' sports injuries, 1997–99

Children aged 5 through 14 sustained an estimated 2.38 million sports and recreational injuries annually from 1997 through 1999. By sport, this number includes the following:

Pedal cycling	332,000 injuries
Basketball	261,000 injuries
Football	243,000 injuries
Playground equipment	219,000 injuries
Baseball/softball	185,000 injuries

SOURCE: "Injuries in Kids, by Sport," in *Sports Injuries*, U.S. Department of Health and Human Services, National Institutes of Health, National Institute of Arthritis and Musculoskeletal and Skin Diseases, April 2004, http://www.niams.nih.gov/hi/topics/sports_injuries/HOHSportsInjuries.pdf (accessed September 22, 2005)

TABLE 8.5

Adults' sports injuries, 1997–99

Adults age 25 and over sustained an estimated 2.29 million sports and recreational injuries annually from 1997 through 1999. By sport, this number includes the following:

Recreational sports*	370,000 injuries
Exercising	331,000 injuries
Basketball	276,000 injuries
Pedal cycling	231,000 injuries
Baseball/softball	205,000 injuries

*Includes racquet sports, golf, bowling, hiking, and other leisure sports.

SOURCE: "Injuries in Adults, by Sport," in *Sports Injuries*, U.S. Department of Health and Human Services, National Institutes of Health, National Institute of Arthritis and Musculoskeletal and Skin Diseases, April 2004, http://www.niams.nih.gov/hi/topics/sports_injuries/HOHSportsInjuries.pdf (accessed September 22, 2005)

over three-quarters of a million children under fourteen require emergency room treatment for sports injuries each year. Contact sports lead to the greatest number of injuries, but the injuries sustained in individual sports tend to be the most serious. According to *GEM*, less than half of these injuries occur during official games; between one-half and two-thirds occur either during practice or during unorganized play.

In the ASD study, children ages six to seventeen represented 38% of sports injuries, which is consistent with the figure cited in *GEM*. Since children represent only about 19% of the population over six, it appears that children incur sports injuries at about twice the rate you would expect if children and adults were equally at risk. Children's injuries were responsible for 46% of the emergency room visits for sports injuries. The highest-risk group was teenage boys. Boys ages twelve to seventeen, a mere 5% of the population, accounted for 17% of all sports injuries, and nearly a quarter (23%) of those requiring treatment in the emergency room.

Middle-aged people are susceptible to injury because they are not as agile and resilient as when they were younger. Some people expect their bodies to perform as well at fifty as they remember it performing at twenty or thirty. They put themselves at risk of injury as a result. The risk is highest when an individual tries to make too quick a transition from an inactive lifestyle to an active one.

As women's sports become faster-paced and more physical, injuries among female athletes are increasing. Women were the recipients of 40% of all sports injuries in 2002 and 37% of emergency room admissions, according to the ASD study. Women's sports injuries also tend to be more sports-specific than men's. For reasons that are unclear, women have higher injury rates than men in several sports, including basketball, soccer, alpine skiing, volleyball, and gymnastics, according to *Sports Injuries*. A female college basketball player is six times more likely than her male counterpart to tear an ACL in her knee, according to a University of Medicine and Dentistry of New Jersey study of 11,780 athletes at ninety-five high schools and colleges during the 1994–95 and 1995–96 seasons. NCAA data collected since 1982, as reported in "Knee Injury Patterns among Men and Women in Collegiate Basketball and Soccer" by Elizabeth Arendt and Randall Dick (*American Journal of Sports Medicine*, 1995) show that women soccer players also have a much higher incidence of ACL injuries than male players.

YOUTH SPORTS AND HEALTH

The Gatorade Sports Science Institute (GSSI) has called attention to the hazards of both too much and too little sports participation among young athletes. According to GSSI—a research and education facility affiliated with the sports drink brand—kids who spend too much time engaging in sports risk overuse injuries and burnout, while those who get too little activity increase their chances of developing obesity and type 2 diabetes. A fact sheet from the GSSI 2004 Conference (available online at http://www.gssiweb.com/) emphasized the value of sports participation in battling skyrocketing child obesity rates in the United States. The fact sheet also took on the issue of burnout (a phenomenon described in more detail below), urging parents to make sure school sports and after-school sports programs emphasize fun and skill development rather than winning. GSSI estimated that the sports dropout rate may be as high as 75% by age thirteen. GSSI alerted parents to the hazards of dietary supplements as well. It pointed out that use of supplements was rampant among young athletes, as they emulate their professional role models. According to GSSI, 3% to 5% of middle school athletes, 38% of high school athletes, and 76% of college athletes report using dietary supplements. Access to supplements and the pressure to use them may come from peers, trainers, or even coaches. According to GSSI, it is inappropriate to place any performance pressure on young athletes, since it is impossible to predict at young ages which children will emerge as champions. The keys to avoiding burnout, according to the fact sheet, are positive coaching and encouraging kids to engage in many different sports rather than focus too seriously on a particular one.

PSYCHOLOGICAL IMPACT OF YOUTH SPORTS PARTICIPATION. In an article in the *Journal of Physical Education, Recreation & Dance* (*JOPERD*; "Children's Organized Sports: A Developmental Perspective," February 2004), Frank Brady noted that the "positive effect of sports participation for some youths appears to be offset by the negative experiences of others." The article goes on to quote a 1993 article titled "Intensive Participation in Children's Sports," originally published in the journal *Human Kinetics*, which stated:

> Sports are like a double-edged sword. Swung in the right direction, the sword can have tremendously positive effects, but swung in the wrong direction it can be devastating. Adults who supervise children's sports hold the sword. Whether sport is constructive or destructive in the psychological development of young children greatly depends on the values, education and skills of those adults.

The biggest culprit in the negative psychological impact of youth sports participation is an overemphasis on competition, which Brady likewise attributes to misplaced priorities on the part of the adults in supervisory roles.

As a result, there is a high rate of burnout and subsequent dropout in youth sports. According to the *JOPERD* article, sports participation peaks at age eleven, followed by a steady decline through the teenage years. The article singles out a subset of the dropout group under the category of "burnout." Burnout refers to young athletes who have been very successful in their sport(s) and have participated intensively over a number of years. Concentrated training at the expense of other activities can result in diminished enjoyment, competitive anxiety, and ultimately real psychological and emotional damage.

In his *JOPERD* article, Brady also points to conflicts between heavy sports participation and cognitive development in young children. Most children are not capable of fully grasping the competitive process until about age twelve, and have trouble understanding the complex interrelationships that form a "team." Some adult coaches get angry and frustrated when, for example, young soccer players swarm to the ball rather than play their positions properly, when in fact many players at age seven or eight are physically incapable of absorbing the concept of a position.

The American Psychological Association (APA) has argued that whether youths benefit from sports participation may depend to a large degree on their environment. An APA news release describing presentations on this topic at its 2001 annual convention describes two studies

with seemingly contradictory messages (http://www.apa.org/releases/sportinvolvement.html). A Clark University study of seventh-graders from inner-city neighborhoods in central Massachusetts found that boys and girls who participated in organized sports had higher self-esteem and were perceived by their teachers as having better social skills. Boys involved in sports were less likely to have experimented with marijuana. These positive traits were not accompanied by measurable negative behavior, such as increased aggression.

However, the authors of the Clark University study explicitly cautioned against making "sweeping pronouncements about the benefits or risks of sports involvement...." A larger study of female African-American students in rural high schools told a very different story. This study by Matthew J. Taylor ("Sports Participation, Delinquency, and Substance Use among Rural African-American Girls," University of Wisconsin–LaCrosse, August 2001) found that sports participation may actually increase the likelihood of substance use and other undesirable behaviors. Participation in sports did not appear to have a deterrent effect on gang involvement or other forms of delinquency. The researchers explained that the reason for conflicting results is that there are so many other variables involved, such as peer groups and community attitudes toward sports.

PHYSICAL INJURIES AMONG YOUNG ATHLETES. While much of the attention to the hazards of youth sports focuses on the mental and emotional pitfalls, physical injuries are a major concern as well. As noted above, children suffer injuries in greater proportion than adults relative to population. A June 13, 2005, article in *People Weekly* elaborated on the theme of youth sports and their connection to increased injury risks. The article, "Wearing Out Their Bodies? As More Kids Train for Sports Like Pros, They're Suffering Grown-Up Injuries," cites numerous examples of young athletes pushed into extremely vigorous regimens at very early ages, who end up damaging their bodies. One sports surgeon is quoted as saying that ten years ago, he had never seen a baseball pitcher under nineteen years old who needed the elbow ligament replacement operation known as "Tommy John surgery," while in 2004 he performed fifty-one such operations on teenage pitchers. Another orthopedic surgeon bemoaned the increase in foot damage among young gymnasts, who are being asked to perform more and more heel-pounding feats at earlier and earlier ages. The *People* article takes parents to task for pressuring their children into trying to become the next Michael Jordan, when the odds of even the most talented young athlete ever making the big leagues, much less excelling there, are microscopic. The article notes that about nine million boys play in organized baseball leagues, but there are only about 9,700 players on Division I college teams,

7,500 minor leaguers, and 829 players in Major League Baseball. The article advises parents and coaches that children need at least three months off a year from throwing sports. It also urges them not to ignore discomfort, as pain is an indication of an injury that needs to be addressed.

According to the National Alliance for Youth Sports (NAYS), parents and coaches can play a big role in helping kids avoid injuries. NAYS pointed to three overarching strategies for minimizing the risk of sports injuries: (1) wearing appropriate, sport-specific, properly fitting protective gear, including helmets and goggles; (2) protecting the skin from damaging solar rays by wearing hats and sunglasses and applying sun block when playing sports in the sun; and (3) keeping adequately hydrated by consuming sports drinks to replace lost fluids and electrolytes lost through sweat.

SPORTS AND HEALTH: THE OUTLOOK

Are Americans heeding all of the advice coming from their doctors and their government about the importance of physical activity? In May 2003 the CDC released the report *Physical Activity among Adults: United States, 2000*, based on data from the 2000 National Health Interview Survey (NHIS) conducted by CDC's National Center for Health Statistics (NCHS). CDC's analysis found that about one in five (19%) American adults engaged in a high level of physical activity, and another quarter (23.5%) engaged in a medium-high level of physical activity overall. These activity levels were determined by combining responses to several different survey questions about various activities, such as regular leisure-time exercise and ordinary daily activities.

CDC has since released some of the data from the 2004 NHIS. Figure 8.1 shows the trend in percentage of adults engaging in regular leisure-time physical activity from 1997 to 2004. The chart shows percentages for both the whole year and for just January through September, since the percentage engaging in regular physical activity is generally so much lower during the last quarter of the year. Only the January–September figure is shown for 2004. The graphic illustrates an increase from 29.9% in 1998 to 31.9% in 2000. It then remained stable for the next two years, before increasing slightly (not a statistically significant increase) in 2003. The percentage then dropped off significantly in the first three quarters of 2004.

Figure 8.2 breaks down by age and gender the percentage of adults engaging in leisure-time physical activity in January through September of 2004. The graphic illustrates that regular leisure-time physical activity declines with age among both genders. Among those between the ages of twenty-five and sixty-four, men and women were about equally likely to engage in

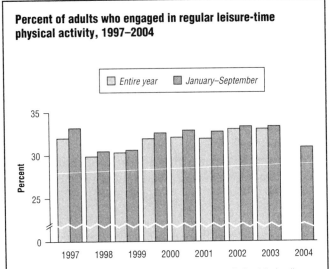

FIGURE 8.1

Percent of adults who engaged in regular leisure-time physical activity, 1997–2004

Notes: This measure reflects the definition used for the physical activity Leading Health Indicator (Healthy People 2010). Regular leisure-time physical activity is defined as engaging in light-moderate leisure-time physical activity for greater than or equal to 30 minutes at a frequency greater than or equal to five times per week or engaging in vigorous leisure-time physical activity for greater than or equal to 20 minutes at a frequency greater than or equal to three times per week. Both annual estimates and estimates for January–September are presented due to the seasonality of leisure-time physical activity. The analyses excluded persons with unknown physical activity participation (about 3% of respondents each year).

SOURCE: "Figure 7.1. Percent of Adults Aged 18 Years and Over Who Engaged in Regular Leisure-Time Physical Activity: United States, 1997–2004," in *Early Release of Selected Estimates Based on Data From the January–September 2004 National Health Interview Survey*, National Center for Health Statistics, Centers for Disease Control, U.S. Department of Health and Human Services, March 2005, http://www.cdc.gov/nchs/data/nhis/earlyrelease/200503_07.pdf (accessed September 22, 2005)

leisure-time physical activity. In all other age groups, a larger proportion of men were physically active during their free time. CDC also analyzed this data by race. White adults (33.9%) were more likely than African-American (24.2%) or Hispanic (22.7%) adults to engage in regular leisure-time physical activity in the first three quarters of 2004.

Overall, 31.8% of adults engaged in regular leisure-time physical activity. A greater percentage of men than women (21.3% to 16.9%) engaged in a high level of activity, but men and women were about equally likely to engage in a medium-high level (23.3% to 23.8%). Overall, men were more likely than women to engage in regular leisure-time physical activity, 35.4% to 28.5%; women were more likely than men to *never* engage in any physical activity, at 11.6% and 7.3% respectively. Hispanic adults and African-American adults were less likely to engage in these levels of activity. Physical activity was found to decline with age and increase with education and income. Those living in the South were less active than adults living in other regions of the country. The CDC report includes a summary of the health benefits of physical activity, specifically mentioning

FIGURE 8.2

FIGURE 8.3

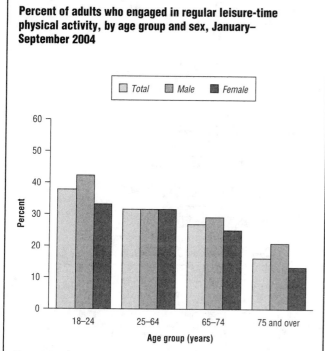

Percent of adults who engaged in regular leisure-time physical activity, by age group and sex, January–September 2004

Notes: This measure reflects the definition used for the physical activity Leading Health Indicator (Healthy People 2010). Regular leisure-time physical activity is defined as engaging in light-moderate leisure-time physical activity for greater than or equal to 30 minutes at a frequency greater than or equal to five times per week or engaging in vigorous leisure-time physical activity for greater than or equal to 20 minutes at a frequency greater than or equal to three times per week. The analyses excluded 681 persons (3.0%) with unknown physical activity participation.

SOURCE: "Figure 7.2. Percent of Adults Aged 18 Years and Over Who Engaged in Regular Leisure-Time Physical Activity, by Age Group and Sex: United States, January–September 2004," in *Early Release of Selected Estimates Based on Data From the January–September 2004 National Health Interview Survey*, National Center for Health Statistics, Centers for Disease Control, U.S. Department of Health and Human Services, March 2005, http://www.cdc.gov/nchs/data/nhis/earlyrelease/200503_07.pdf (accessed September 22, 2005)

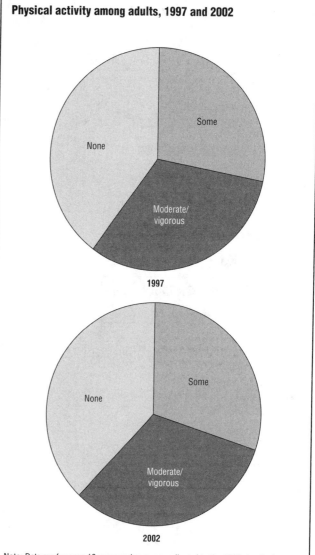

Physical activity among adults, 1997 and 2002

Note: Data are for ages 18 years and over, age adjusted to the 2000 standard population. Moderate physical activity is regular leisure-time physical activity (moderate activity 30+ minutes/5+ times a week or vigorous activity 20+ minutes/3+ times a week).

SOURCE: "Physical Activity among Adults," in *Focus Area 22: Physical Activity and Fitness Progress Review*, Centers for Disease Control and Prevention, U.S. Department of Health and Human Services, April 14, 2004, http://www.cdc.gov/nchs/ppt/hpdata2010/focusareas/fa22_progress_review.ppt (accessed September 22, 2005)

decreased risk of coronary heart disease, obesity, diabetes, osteoporosis, and post-menopausal endometrial cancer. The report also notes that research has linked physical activity with increased lifespan and lower rates of disability.

Figure 8.3 compares physical activity among adults in 1997 and 2002, using data from the National Health Interview Survey as reported in the *Focus Area 22* presentation. While the change is not great, the graphic shows a decrease between those years in the percentage of adults who engaged in no physical activity whatsoever. The presentation goes on to focus on *Healthy People 2010* goals for reducing this percentage, breaking it down by gender, age, and race/ethnicity. Figure 8.4 shows decreases between 1997 and 2002 in the percentage of inactive adults among both genders; however, as of 2002 both genders were still well above the 2010 target of 20%. Each age group except the eighteen to twenty-four bracket likewise demonstrated a decrease in the percentage that did not engage in any physical activity, though again each

group was well above the 20% target. Among the racial/ ethnic categories, only Asians experienced an increase between 1999 and 2002 in the percentage of adults engaging in no physical activity. Whites, African-Americans, and Hispanics all showed improvement in that span, though as with age and gender categories, no group even came close to the 2010 target of 20%. (See Figure 8.5.)

Figure 8.6 spotlights *vigorous* physical activity, defined in the question as "at least ten minutes that cause heavy sweating or large increases in breathing or heart rate." According to the *Focus Area 22* presentation, both genders and all age groups except those aged forty-five to

FIGURE 8.4

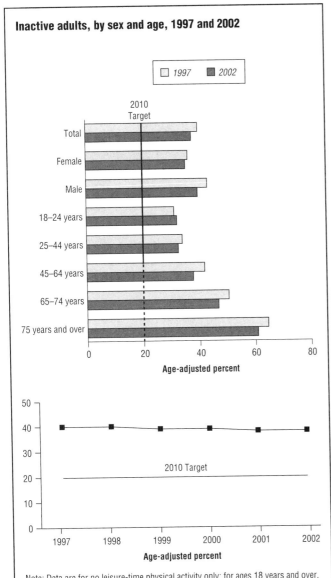

Inactive adults, by sex and age, 1997 and 2002

☐ *1997* ■ *2002*

Note: Data are for no leisure-time physical activity only; for ages 18 years and over, age adjusted to the 2000 standard population.

SOURCE: "No Physical Activity for Adults by Sex and Age," in *Focus Area 22: Physical Activity and Fitness Progress Review*, Centers for Disease Control and Prevention, U.S. Department of Health and Human Services, April 14, 2004, http://www.cdc.gov/nchs/ppt/hpdata2010/ focusareas/fa22_progress_review.ppt (accessed September 22, 2005)

FIGURE 8.5

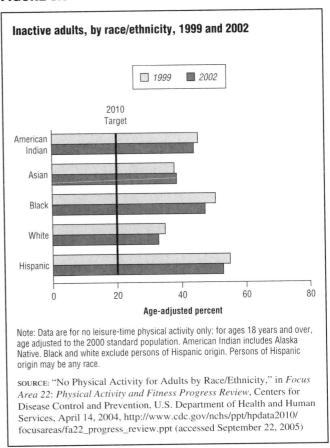

Inactive adults, by race/ethnicity, 1999 and 2002

☐ *1999* ■ *2002*

Note: Data are for no leisure-time physical activity only; for ages 18 years and over, age adjusted to the 2000 standard population. American Indian includes Alaska Native. Black and white exclude persons of Hispanic origin. Persons of Hispanic origin may be any race.

SOURCE: "No Physical Activity for Adults by Race/Ethnicity," in *Focus Area 22: Physical Activity and Fitness Progress Review*, Centers for Disease Control and Prevention, U.S. Department of Health and Human Services, April 14, 2004, http://www.cdc.gov/nchs/ppt/hpdata2010/ focusareas/fa22_progress_review.ppt (accessed September 22, 2005)

sixty-four saw increases in the percentage engaging in vigorous physical activity. One age category, eighteen–twenty-four, exceeded the *Healthy People 2010* target of 30%. The other groups all fell short. Figure 8.7 illustrates vigorous physical activity among adolescents, assessed by race and gender. "Vigorous physical activity" in this instance has a different definition from the one above. Here it is defined as "physical activity for at least twenty minutes that made you sweat and breathe hard, such as basketball, soccer, running, swimming laps, fast bicycling, fast dancing, or similar aerobic activities." None of the groups approaches the 85% target for 2010. Male adolescents came the closest. White adolescents engaged

in vigorous physical activity at a much higher rate than minority adolescents. Only among African-American adolescents was there significant improvement between 1999 and 2001. Figure 8.8 illustrates the decrease in vigorous physical activity that takes place during the high school years. In 2001, ninth-graders participated in vigorous physical activity a little more than tenth-graders, who in turn participated at a higher rate than eleventh-graders, who out-participated twelfth-graders.

In the face of an epidemic of obesity in the United States, the federal government has in recent years taken an active role in promoting fitness among Americans. In 1996 the CDC's National Center for Chronic Disease Prevention and Health Promotion published *Physical Activity and Health: A Report of the Surgeon General* (http://www.cdc.gov/nccdphp/sgr/pdf/sgrfull.pdf), a blueprint for improving the physical condition of the American population. Among the report's major conclusions were that people of all ages and genders benefit from regular physical activity, and that significant health benefits can be obtained by engaging in a moderate amount of physical activity, examples of which include thirty minutes of brisk walking, fifteen minutes of running, or forty-five minutes of volleyball. The report notes that additional benefits can be gained through more vigorous activity and greater amounts.

FIGURE 8.6

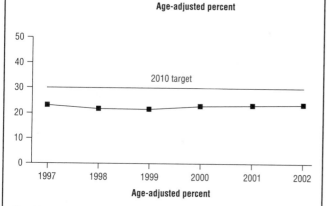

Vigorous physical activity for adults, by sex and age, 1997 and 2002

Note: Data are for ages 18 years and over, age adjusted to the 2000 standard population. Vigorous physical activity is leisure-time vigorous physical activity 20+ minutes/3+ times a week.

SOURCE: "Vigorous Physical Activity for Adults by Sex and Age," in *Focus Area 22: Physical Activity and Fitness Progress Review*, Centers for Disease Control and Prevention, U.S. Department of Health and Human Services, April 14, 2004, http://www.cdc.gov/nchs/ppt/hpdata2010/focusareas/fa22_progress_review.ppt (accessed September 22, 2005)

FIGURE 8.7

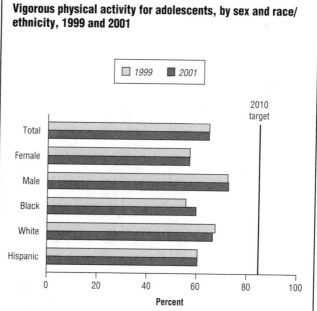

Vigorous physical activity for adolescents, by sex and race/ethnicity, 1999 and 2001

Note: Black and white exclude persons of Hispanic origin. Hispanic can be any race. Vigorous physical activity is activity that made students in grades 9–12 sweat or breathe hard for 20+ minutes on 3+ of the past 7 days.

SOURCE: "Vigorous Physical Activity for Adolescents by Sex and Race/Ethnicity," in *Focus Area 22: Physical Activity and Fitness Progress Review*, Centers for Disease Control and Prevention, U.S. Department of Health and Human Services, April 14, 2004, http://www.cdc.gov/nchs/ppt/hpdata2010/focusareas/fa22_progress_review.ppt (accessed September 22, 2005)

FIGURE 8.8

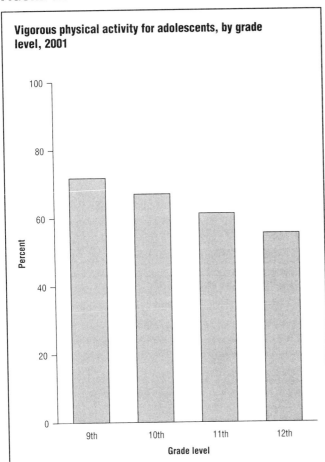

Vigorous physical activity for adolescents, by grade level, 2001

Note: Vigorous physical activity is activity that made students in grades 9–12 sweat or breathe hard for 20+ minutes on 3+ of the past 7 days.

SOURCE: "Vigorous Physical Activity for Adolescents by Grade Level: 2001," in *Focus Area 22: Physical Activity and Fitness Progress Review*, Centers for Disease Control and Prevention, U.S. Department of Health and Human Services, April 14, 2004, http://www.cdc.gov/nchs/ppt/hpdata2010/focusareas/fa22_progress_review.ppt (accessed September 22, 2005)

CHAPTER 9
PERFORMANCE-ENHANCING DRUGS

The spirit of sport is the celebration of the human spirit, the body and the mind. Doping is contrary to the spirit of sport, erodes public confidence and jeopardizes the health and well-being of athletes.

—from the World Anti-Doping Agency's Athlete's Guide

The word "doping" is often used to refer to any practice involving prohibited substances or other methods to give an athlete an unfair advantage over other competitors. An article called "Doping in Sports: Steroids and Supplements" in the 2005 *World Almanac and Book of Facts* notes that the word "dope" probably comes from the Dutch word "dop," an alcoholic beverage made from grape skins that traditional Zulu warriors believed enhanced their fighting ability.

A BRIEF HISTORY OF DOPING

For as long as people have been engaging in athletic competition, they have been seeking ways to gain an edge on their opponents. There is evidence that doping took place in the ancient Olympics, which lasted from 776 BC until 393 AD. It is known, for example, that Spartan "coaches" fed their athletes special herbs and mushroom concoctions—during a period in which they were supposed to be consuming nothing but cheese and water—believed to render them oblivious to pain (Will Carroll, *The Juice: The Real Story of Baseball's Drug Problems* (Chicago: Ivan R. Dee, 2005).

The first known case of an athlete dying as a result of doping occurred in 1896, when Welsh cyclist Andrew Linton died during a race from Paris to Bordeaux. The substance he ingested was thought to be trimethyl, an alcohol-based product used by distance racers to ease pain and increase stamina.

The modern era of doping, according to Will Carroll, began with the development of injectable testosterone in 1935. Testosterone is a male hormone produced naturally by the body. Injecting additional testosterone into the system increases muscle mass and strength. Originally introduced by Nazi doctors to make soldiers more aggressive, it did not take long for laboratory-produced testosterone to make its way from the battlefield to the athletic field. German athletes dominated the medals in the 1936 Olympics, very probably with the assistance of these newly developed synthetic drugs.

The father of anabolic steroids—chemical variants of testosterone—in the United States was Dr. John Ziegler, a physician for the U.S. weightlifting team in the mid-twentieth century. Ziegler learned from his Russian counterparts that the Soviet Union's weightlifting success was in part attributable to their use of performance-enhancing drugs, the formulas for which had been brought east by German scientists defecting to Russia after the war. Deciding that U.S. athletes needed chemical assistance to remain competitive, Ziegler worked with the Ciba Pharmaceutical Company to develop an oral anabolic steroid. These efforts resulted in the creation of Dianabol, the trade name given by Ciba to the steroid methandrostenolone. Dianabol appeared on the market in 1960. During the Olympics that year, Danish cyclist Knut Enemark Jensen collapsed and died while competing in the 100-kilometer race. An autopsy revealed the presence of amphetamines and a drug called nicotinyl tartrade in his system.

Drug testing was introduced at the Olympics in 1968. By this time, the International Olympic Committee (IOC) had developed a list of officially banned substances; however, because no test had yet been invented that could distinguish between anabolic steroids and naturally occurring testosterone in the body, the testing was largely ineffective. Only one athlete was found to be in violation of the new drug policy in 1968: Swedish pentathlete Hans-Gunnar Liljenwall, who was found to have too much alcohol in his blood after drinking a few beers before the shooting portion of his event.

Steroids found their way into professional football in the late 1960s, as teams began hiring strength and conditioning coaches, who were charged with the task of growing a new breed of bigger, bulkier players. Taking their cue from the weightlifting world, these coaches turned to steroids as the fastest way of accomplishing that goal. In the 1970s the dopers were still way ahead of the dope detectors in the scientific arena. The East Germans showed up at the 1976 Olympics in Montreal with a team of women swimmers sporting man-sized muscles and deep voices. They won most of the medals. However, while there was much talk about the likelihood that they were using banned substances, not a single one of these athletes tested positive. It later became clear that the athletes themselves were the victims of a mandatory doping program overseen by East German Olympic officials, who injected the swimmers with steroids without their informed consent. Several East German swimmers of that era have suffered serious long-term health consequences as a result of doping.

Doping in sports has increased dramatically since then. As the practice has grown, so have methods for detecting it and for keeping it from being detected. By the 1970s use of performance-enhancing drugs had reached epidemic proportions among elite athletes. It was widely known that there were whole national sports programs whose success was based largely on sophisticated doping techniques, but scientists lacked the tools to prove what was going on. A breakthrough took place in 1983, when newly developed technology for analyzing blood for the presence of banned substances was deployed at the Pan Am Games in Caracas, Venezuela. Eleven athletes from nine countries were caught with performance-enhancing drugs in their systems. Many other athletes, including thirteen members of the U.S. track and field squad, withdrew from the event rather than risk the embarrassment of being caught cheating.

The first big-time Olympic disqualification due to steroids occurred in 1988, when Canadian sprinter Ben Johnson was stripped of both his gold medal and his world record in the 100-meter dash after testing positive for the banned steroid stanozolol. Years later, it was revealed that a number of American track competitors had tested positive for illicit drugs prior to that year's Seoul Olympics.

THE BALCO SCANDAL

The cat-and-mouse game of doping and detection methods went on for two more decades. Another major turning point came in June 2003, when a disgruntled track and field coach named Trevor Graham turned over to authorities a syringe containing what turned out to be tetrahydrogestrinone, or THG, a previously unknown anabolic steroid. THG is what is known as a "designer steroid," manufactured specifically to be undetectable by the existing methods. Lab testing methods were quickly adjusted to detect THG. Government investigators soon turned their attention to the Bay Area Laboratory Co-Operative (BALCO), the California-based distributor of the drug.

On September 3, 2003, agents of the Internal Revenue Service, the U.S. Food and Drug Administration, the San Mateo County Narcotics Task Force, and the U.S. Anti-Doping Agency raided BALCO facilities and seized containers of steroids, human growth hormone, and testosterone. Two days later officials searched the home of baseball star Barry Bonds's personal weight trainer, Greg Anderson, and seized more steroids, as well as documents thought to implicate a number of high-profile athletes. Over the next few months, urine samples from the U.S. Track and Field Championships were retested for THG, and several came up positive. One of those athletes was Kelli White, who had captured both the 100-meter and 200-meter world championships in 2003. White was stripped of her titles and banned from competition for two years. Evidence was collected from computers and documents connecting a number of other athletes to BALCO.

BALCO founder and owner Victor Conte, Jr.; BALCO executive James Valente; trainer Greg Anderson; and track coach Remi Korchemny were indicted in February 2004 for distributing steroids. Later that year, Conte described on the December 3, 2004, broadcast of ABC's *20/20* how he provided performance-enhancing drugs to numerous elite athletes, including sprinters Tim Montgomery and Marion Jones, though neither of those individuals had ever tested positive for drugs. Jones later sued Conte for defamation of character. As of October 2005, twelve top-level track and field athletes had been banned from competition for at least two years, and other cases were still pending or remained under investigation. The BALCO scandal also brought fines and suspensions for a handful of professional football players: Chris Cooper, Barrett Robbins, and Dana Stubblefield. Another player, Bill Romanowski, was reported by the *San Jose Mercury News* to have been implicated by Conte, but Romanowski retired before the NFL could take any formal action against him. Romanowski later admitted to having used steroids during his playing career (Elliot Almond and Peter Carey, "Bonds, Marion Jones Alleged to Have Received Steroids," April 25, 2004).

In March 2005 a congressional committee held hearings on the issue of steroids in baseball. A number of legislators mocked Major League officials for the sport's weak policy and feeble efforts to deal with the problem. Many of those who testified came out looking bad, including former homerun champion Mark McGwire, who time and again was evasive when asked whether his power-hitting abilities were chemically aided. Other current and former baseball players who testified included Jose Canseco, Curt Schilling, Sammy Sosa, Rafael Palmeiro, and Frank Thomas. Later in the spring, Barry Bonds was widely criticized for working out under the supervision of the indicted trainer Anderson as he attempted to come back from the serious knee injury that had sidelined him for months (Mark Fainaru-Wada and Lance Williams, "Bonds Working with Anderson," *San Francisco Chronicle*, April 9, 2005).

On October 18, 2005, Conte was sentenced to four months in prison and another four months of house arrest. Anderson received three months each of prison time and home confinement. Valente walked away with just probation, and Korchemny's sentence was still pending as of October 2005.

WHAT ARE PERFORMANCE-ENHANCING DRUGS?

Anabolic Steroids

When people speak of performance-enhancing drugs, more often than not they are referring to anabolic steroids. *Steroid Abuse in Today's Society*, a March 2004 publication of the U.S. Drug Enforcement Administration's (DEA) Office of Diversion Control, defines anabolic steroids as "synthetically produced variants of the naturally occurring male hormone testosterone." The full name of this class of drugs is "androgenic anabolic steroids." *Androgenic* means that the drugs promote masculine physical characteristics. *Anabolic* means tissue-building. According to the DEA publication, the list of commonly abused steroids commercially available in the United States includes: fluoxymesterone (trade name Halotestin), methyltestosterone, nandrolone (Deca-Durabolin, Durabolin), exandrolone (Oxandrin), oxymetholone (Anadrol), stanozolol (Winstrol), and boldenone (Equipoise). Others that are not approved for use in the United States include ethylestrenol, methandriol, methenolone, and methandrostenolone.

The main users of anabolic steroids are athletes seeking to add bulk and strength to their bodies. In addition to building lean body mass, another way steroids are purported to help athletes get stronger is by reducing the amount of recovery time needed between workouts, allowing them to train harder. Anabolic steroids are currently banned by most sports organizations, including the International Olympic Committee, the National Football League, the National Basketball Association, the National Collegiate Athletic Association, the National Hockey League, and Major League Baseball.

The only way to get steroids legally is through a doctor's prescription, and there are many legitimate medical uses for which a doctor might recommend them, including growth deficiencies, muscle-wasting diseases, loss of testicular function, breast cancer, low red blood cell count, or debilitated states resulting from surgery or illness. Steroids are also widely used in veterinary medicine, to promote weight gain, to treat anemia, or to counteract tissue breakdown from illness or trauma.

Most illicit steroids come from one of two sources. Some are diverted from the legitimate market, often through stolen or fraudulent prescriptions. The largest share, however, is smuggled into the United States from Mexico or some European country where a prescription is not required to obtain steroids. According to an article in the May 2005 issue of the *IDEA Fitness Journal*, black market sales of steroids exceed $100 million a year (http://www.ideafit.com/pub_source.asp). The article also cites a 2001 survey indicating that 1.1% of NCAA student athletes used steroids, and 40% of those users got the drug from a physician. Apparently it is pretty easy for a college athlete to get his or her hands on steroids. Only 0.7% of survey respondents said they did not use steroids because they were "hard to get."

Steroids are available in several different forms, including tablets, liquids, gels, and creams. Typically, users ingest the drugs orally, inject them into muscle, or rub them on their skin. The doses taken by people who abuse steroids can be ten to one hundred times stronger than those recommended for medical conditions. Many steroid abusers engage in what is called "stacking," which means mixing oral steroids with injectable ones, often taking multiple forms of the drug. Another common practice among steroid abusers is "pyramiding," which means administering doses in cycles of six to twelve weeks where the dose is slowly increased to a peak midway through the cycle, then tapered back down toward the end. There is a widespread belief among steroid users that stacking and pyramiding maximize the benefits of the drugs while reducing their harmful effects, though to date there is no scientific evidence to support those contentions.

Other Substances and Supplements

There are a number of performance-enhancing substances besides anabolic steroids, some of which have until recently escaped the scrutiny of those in the business of regulating sports. As a result, these substances, often billed as "dietary supplements," have been readily available, to youths as well as adults, usually as nearby as the nutrition and vitamin store in a local mall.

ERYTHROPOIETIN. Erythropoietin, or EPO, is a hormone produced naturally by the kidneys. It plays a role in regulating the number of red blood cells in the blood stream. A synthetic version of EPO was developed in the 1980s, and it quickly became popular as a performance-enhancing drug, particularly among athletes involved in endurance sports such as cycling. When used excessively, EPO can increase the number of red blood cells to such a degree that the blood becomes too thick to flow properly, potentially leading to heart attacks and strokes. In the late 1980s, shortly after the appearance of synthetic EPO, thirty top endurance athletes, mainly cyclists, in Belgium, the Netherlands, Denmark, and Sweden died; the likely cause of their deaths was EPO, according to the 2005 *World Almanac and Book of Facts*.

CREATINE. One of the most popular supplements used by athletes at all levels is creatine. Creatine is available over the counter and is reputed to help improve performance in sports that involve short bursts of power, like weightlifting, wrestling, and sprinting. While reliable research has not yet established a connection between creatine and serious health problems, there is some evidence that heavy use may cause kidney, liver, and heart problems. Known side effects of creatine include muscle cramps and digestive problems like stomach pain, diarrhea, and nausea. According to the Mayo Clinic Web site, what actually happens when a person takes creatine is that their muscles draw water away from the rest of the body, creating the illusion of added muscle mass. The increased bulk is really just extra water stored in the muscles (http://www.mayoclinic.com/health/performance-enhancing-drugs/HQ01105).

ANDROSTENEDIONE (ANDRO). Androstenedione (or andro) enjoyed a huge burst of popularity in the late 1990s, as baseball slugger Mark McGwire chased, and eventually shattered, the old record for homeruns in a season. McGwire admittedly used andro, which was perfectly legal and within the rules of Major League Baseball at the time. Countless young aspiring power hitters followed his lead. Whether andro really helped McGwire hit seventy homeruns in 1998 is not known.

Andro is a direct precursor to testosterone—meaning it turns into testosterone in the body—and is found naturally in humans. It is also found naturally in Scotch pine trees, which is why manufacturers were allowed to sell it as a dietary supplement. Andro was discovered in the 1930s, but it was not until the 1950s that scientists became aware that it turned into testosterone in the body. Andro is widely believed to boost testosterone production, which in turn increases muscle mass, energy, and strength. The Mayo Clinic disputes these claims, though proponents of andro—including companies that make money selling it—cite research (not necessarily rigorous research that would pass muster with scholars) supporting andro's effectiveness as a performance enhancer.

Andro is now classified as a controlled substance. The Anabolic Steroid Control Act of 2004 essentially reclassified andro as an anabolic steroid, making it illegal for use as a performance enhancer (http://www.dea.gov/pubs/cngrtest/ct031604.html).

Heavy use of andro can produce side effects similar to those associated with other anabolic steroids. Andro can actually *decrease* testosterone production in men and increase production of the female hormone estrogen. It can also cause acne, shrinking of the testicles, and reduced sperm count. In women side effects of andro can include acne as well as the onset of masculine characteristics like deepening of the voice and male pattern baldness.

EPHEDRA. Ephedra is an herb that has been used in Chinese medicine—where it is known as Ma Huang—for thousands of years. An American version widely used by early settlers in the Southwest was called Mormon tea, or Squaw tea. The main chemical constituent in ephedra is ephedrine, which is a powerful stimulant, similar to amphetamines. It also contains another chemical called pseudoephedrine, which has long been used as a nasal decongestant but has recently come under tighter regulation because of its role in manufacturing illegal methamphetamine. In addition to its use by athletes as an energy booster, ephedra has been used as an ingredient in popular over-the-counter weight loss pills. It has also long been used by people seeking to stay alert for late-night studying or socializing activities; until recently, it was an ingredient in many popular energy drinks.

Ephedra has been linked to very serious side effects, such as strokes, seizures, and heart attacks, and many people have died as a direct result of its use. Ephedra can also cause elevated blood sugar levels and irregular heartbeats. It may be addictive when used over time. In December 2003 the U.S. Food and Drug Administration banned ephedra from being sold over the counter as a dietary supplement. However, in April 2005 a federal judge overturned the FDA's ban on procedural grounds. As of late 2005 ephedra was legal, though manufacturers were hesitant to reintroduce ephedra-based products into the market due to its uncertain status.

HEALTH RISKS OF STEROID USE

Steroid abuse has been linked with a wide range of health hazards, both physical and mental. Among the physical problems are liver and kidney tumors, high blood pressure, elevated cholesterol levels, fluid retention, and severe acne. Some studies, according to the *IDEA Fitness Journal* article cited above (http://www.ideafit.com/pub_source.asp), have associated steroid use with serious cardiovascular problems, including cardiomyopathies (inflammation of the heart muscle), irregular heart rhythm, development of embolisms, and heart failure. One 2000 study found a dramatic increase in premature deaths among power lifters who used anabolic steroids (M. Parssinen et al., "Increased Premature Mortality of Competitive

Powerlifters Suspected to Have Used Anabolic Agents," *International Journal of Sport Medicine*, 2000). Men sometimes experience such sexual/reproductive system symptoms as shrunken testicles, reduced sperm count, baldness, breast development, and increased risk of prostate cancer. Among women, growth of facial hair, male-pattern baldness, menstrual cycle disruptions, and deepening of the voice have all been reported. Adolescents who use steroids run the risk of halting their growth prematurely, as their bones fuse ahead of schedule. Another problem for teens is that steroids cause muscles to grow but do not strengthen the tendons that connect these muscles to bones. This can increase the risk of injury.

People who inject steroids with needles take on additional health risks. Many cases of HIV and hepatitis (both B and C) have been reported among steroid users who share injection needles.

Emotional/psychological problems stemming from abuse of steroids include extreme mood swings, depression, paranoid jealousy, irritability, delusions, and impaired judgment. Sometimes these steroid-induced mood swings lead to violent behavior, a condition popularly referred to as "'roid rage."

STEROID USE AND YOUTH

Each year the National Drug Intelligence Center produces a report called the *National Drug Threat Assessment*. The 2005 edition of the *National Drug Threat Assessment*, published in February 2005, found increased rates of past-year steroid use among eighth-, tenth-, and twelfth-graders since the 1990s. It noted, however, that steroid use rates appear to have peaked, and may even have begun to recede. Citing data from *Monitoring the Future* (*MTF*), an ongoing study of behavior among secondary school students, college students, and young adults conducted by researchers at the University of Michigan, the report shows that steroid abuse among high school students has risen overall since the early 1990s. Twelfth-graders had the highest rate of past year use in 2004, at 2.5%. The rate among tenth-graders was 1.5%, and eighth-graders 1.1%. The good news was that the rate declined significantly among eighth- and tenth-graders between 2002 and 2004; there was no significant change during that period for twelfth graders. (See Figure 1.1 in Chapter 1.)

MTF data suggest substantial variation in steroid use by gender. Abuse is more common among males than females in every age category covered by the survey, ranging from eighth grade through adults age thirty. Males in twelfth grade had the highest rate of all, 3.2%; their female classmates were only about one-third as likely to use steroids (1.1%). Ethnicity did not appear to make much of a difference in steroid abuse rates according to *MTF*. White tenth- and twelfth-graders had slightly higher rates than their African-American and Hispanic peers; among eighth-graders, the differences were negligible.

Perhaps the most disturbing *MTF* findings described in the *2005 Drug Threat Assessment* were related to attitudes. The perceived harmfulness of steroid use among twelfth-graders—the only grade for which this data exists—has declined significantly since the early 1990s. Since peaking at 70.7% in 1992, the percentage of seniors who believe steroid use is harmful declined to 55.7% in 2004. The percentage of seniors who disapprove of people using steroids has fallen to 87.9% in 2004 from its 1992–93 peak of 92.1%.

The *Newsweek* cover story "Steroids and Kids" (December 2004) included an analysis of *MTF* data and pointed out that a growing percentage of the nation's 300,000 plus high-school-age steroid users were kids who idolize not homerun-pounding baseball players but sculpted models like those who grace the cover of Abercrombie & Fitch catalogs. This phenomenon led to the creation of a new psychological diagnosis: muscle dysmorphia, sometimes referred to as "reverse anorexia." The *Newsweek* story recounts the biggest high-school level steroid scandal to date, which resulted in the suspension of no less than ten varsity football players in Buckeye, Arizona, rounded up in a single September 2003 sweep that saw local police descend on the team's practice field.

PERFORMANCE-ENHANCING DRUGS IN COLLEGE SPORTS

According to the NCAA's most recent *Study of Substance Use Habits of College Student-Athletes*, conducted in 2004, steroid use has dropped consistently every year since 1990, when football players in Divisions I and II were first subject to year-round testing (http://www2.ncaa.org/media_and_events/association_news/ncaa_news_online/2005/08_29_05/front_page_news/4218n02.html). The NCAA now has year-round drug testing in all Division I and II sports. The NCAA survey, which is administered every four years during the fall semester, found that overall steroid use declined from 1.4% in 2001 to 1.2% in 2005. This figure has remained relatively stable since 1997. The biggest drop occurred between 1989 and 1993, suggesting a major impact from the implementation of testing on football players. According to the survey, men were more likely than women to use steroids. Steroid use among whites decreased in 2005, while use among African-Americans and other races increased. Of those who used steroids, 43% said the reason was to improve their athletic performance, while 19% cited injury rehabilitation as the purpose of their steroid use. (See Table 9.1.)

The NCAA survey found a substantial decrease in the use of ephedrine; it dropped from 3.9% in 2001 to 2.3% in

TABLE 9.1

Drug use among college athletes, selected years, 1997–2005

	Division 1			Division 2			Division 3		
Drug	1997 population= 6,123	2001 population= 8,776	2005 population= 8,805	1997 population= 3,234	2001 population= 4,867	2005 population= 4,482	1997 population= 4,537	2001 population= 7,520	2005 population= 6,658
Amphetamines	2.5%	3.1%	3.7%	3.3%	3.3%	3.5%	3.7%	3.6%	4.3%
Anabolic steroids	1.2%	1.6%	1.2%	1.1%	1.3%	1.2%	1.3%	1.4%	1.1%
Ephedrine	3.0%	3.6%	2.3%	4.2%	4.1%	2.4%	3.8%	4.2%	2.6%

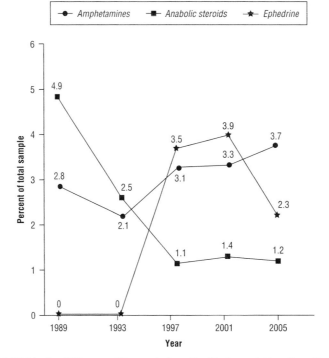

SOURCE: "Ergogenic Drug Use by NCAA Division" and "Patterns of Ergogenic Drug Use," in *Latest Athlete Drug-Use Data Continue Downward Pattern*, National Collegiate Athletic Association, August 29, 2005, http://www2.ncaa.org/media_and_events/association_news/ncaa_news_online/2005/08_29_05/front_page_news/4218n02.html (accessed September 22, 2005)

2005. The number one reason cited by college athletes for using ephedrine is weight loss. Most use of performance-enhancing drugs, according to the survey, starts in high school, though a small number of athletes start even earlier. The number of students who report already using ephedrine by the time they arrive at college has been increasing since 1997.

STEROIDS IN PROFESSIONAL SPORTS

Every sport has its own way of testing for performance-enhancing drugs and its own policy for dealing with players who use them. The NFL has the strictest policy among the major sports. Professional football players are subject to year-round drug tests. The penalty for those caught using banned substances for the first time is a suspension that lasts four games, which amounts to a quarter of a season. In the NBA first-time offenders are suspended for five games. The NHL implemented

random drug testing for the first time at the beginning of the 2005–06 season. Major League Baseball's first-time penalty is a ten-day suspension; given the length of the baseball season (162 games), it could be argued that this is a fairly lenient sentence. Rep. Christopher Shays (R-Connecticut) was quoted in a September 2005 issue of *Current Events* as saying, "It's a joke. A ten-day suspension in baseball is basically a vacation. It has no deterrent impact." (http://www.looksmartsoccer.com/p/articles/mi_m0EPF/is_1_105/ai_n15337800).

Football

The NFL's drug testing policy is generally regarded as the best among professional sports leagues in the United States. About seven players per year fail the NFL steroid test, but there is reason to believe that many more steroid users are getting away with it. In 2005 Onterrio Smith of the Minnesota Vikings was suspended for a year after being caught with a device called a

Whizzinator, designed to undermine the accuracy of a urine test. Three other players were placed under scrutiny after *CBS News* uncovered information that they had each filled prescriptions for steroids written by a single doctor in South Carolina. The doctor has since been indicted on federal charges. None of those three players failed a drug test, but the league has indicated that they will be monitored closely.

Since the NFL started testing for steroids in 1989, fifty-seven players had been suspended for steroid use as of October of 2005. In addition, there had been another sixty positive tests recorded by players who either retired or were released from team rosters before their suspensions were announced.

Baseball

Major League Baseball was hit with scandal when Rafael Palmeiro, one of the all-time leading homerun hitters and only the fourth player in history to surpass both the 3,000 hit and 500 homerun landmarks, tested positive for steroids in July 2005. Just four months earlier, Palmeiro had testified under oath at a Congressional hearing on steroids in sports that, "I have never used steroids. Period. I don't know how to say it any more clearly than that." Palmeiro was on the stand largely because he had been identified as a steroid user by former pro baseball player Jose Canseco, whose book *Juiced* (New York: Regan Books, 2005) painted a lurid picture of rampant steroid use throughout the sport. In the book Canseco alleged that he had personally tutored Palmeiro in the finer points of steroid use in the early 1990s. Palmeiro later added the word "knowingly" to his denial of using steroids, but by then his credibility had been seriously damaged. As writer Brad Stone pointed out in an August 2005 *Newsweek* article, the drug Palmeiro tested positive for was one used by veterinarians to promote weight gain in sick animals; it is not one that would be easy to ingest accidentally in an energy drink or health bar. Palmeiro is paid well enough that the $164,000 fine and ten-day suspension he was assessed probably did not hurt him badly. Of greater concern is the potential criminal charges he may face for lying to Congress.

Palmeiro was not the first high-profile baseball player to get caught using steroids. Barry Bonds, another record-breaking player, admitted during grand jury testimony in 2004 to having used steroids, though he claimed that he had done so unknowingly via an arthritis cream he thought was steroid-free. Bonds has never failed an official drug test. While baseball players test positive on a regular basis—Palmeiro was the seventh to do so in 2005—most of them are lesser known, and the stories do not make the headlines. The only prominent baseball player to admit in public to using steroids is Jason Giambi, who confessed that he had used

performance-enhancing drugs during his stellar 2003 season, in which he hit forty-one homeruns.

Baseball had no official steroid policy before 2002. That year, as part of the collective bargaining agreement between players and owners, a plan was put in place to hold survey testing in 2003; if more than 5% of players came up positive in anonymous tests, a formal testing policy, with accompanying penalties, would be implemented the following year. When the results of the survey showed a positive rate of between 5% and 7%, the policy development process was triggered. Beginning in 2004 every player was to be tested once a year during the season. The first time a player tested positive, he was to be placed in treatment; a second positive test would result in a fifteen-day suspension. A fifth positive test could result in a suspension lasting up to a year (http://sportsillustrated.cnn.com/2003/baseball/mlb/11/13/mlb.steroids.ap/).

Under the policy, not a single player was suspended. However, it was clear that performance-enhancing drugs were still being used on a large scale, and pressure mounted to toughen the policy. The 2005 season brought a new policy in which steroids, steroid precursors (such as andro), designer steroids, masking agents, and diuretics were all banned. All players would be subject to unannounced mandatory testing during the season. In addition, there would be testing of randomly selected players, with no maximum number, and random testing during the off-season. The penalties for a positive result were a ten-day suspension for the first offense, thirty days for a second, sixty days for the third, and one year for the fourth. All of these suspensions were without pay (http://www.usatoday.com/sports/baseball/2005-01-12-steroid-policy_x.htm).

Lenient as this policy seemed in comparison to those of other sports, baseball's new drug policy appeared to have an immediate impact. A May 2005 article in *Sport Illustrated* noted that the first part of the 2005 season seemed to be marked by a noticeable decline in power hitting, a new dominance by pitchers, and greater emphasis than in recent years on aspects of the game that are based on finesse—bunting, stolen bases, fielding—rather than raw strength (Tom Verducci, "When Bigger Gets Smaller, Small Gets Big," May 30, 2005). Homeruns were down, complete games by pitchers were up, and bodies were smaller.

Basketball

In the NBA rookies are tested up to four times per season, and veterans are subject to one random test during training camp. Prohibited substances include amphetamines, cocaine, LSD, opiates, PCP, marijuana, and steroids. Penalties range from suspensions for a number of games to lifetime bans. To date, basketball has largely avoided the kind of scandals involving performance-enhancing drugs that have plagued the baseball world.

Hockey

Until 2005 the National Hockey League had no formal anti-doping policy. However, in the wake of scandals that have dogged other major sports in recent years, the league unveiled its first such policy in September 2005 at a congressional hearing on drug use in professional sports. Under the new policy, NHL players are subject to a maximum of two random tests with no advance notice during the NHL season for the performance-enhancing drugs designated on the World Anti-Doping Agency out-of-competition list (http://www.wada-ama.org/en/prohibitedlist.ch2). A first-time positive test will result in a twenty-game suspension. The suspension increases to sixty games for a second offense, and a third positive test can result in permanent suspension from the league.

Cycling

Perhaps no other sport has been tainted by doping scandals more than professional bicycle racing, particularly the sport's most illustrious event, the Tour de France. During the 1967 Tour, British cyclist Tom Simpson died on one of the climbs in the race after using large amounts of amphetamines. The biggest drug scandal in cycling history took place in 1998, when the Festina cycling team was thrown out of the competition after team masseur Willy Voet was caught in possession of various narcotics and other banned substances, including erythropoietin (EPO), growth hormones, testosterone, and amphetamines. In 2004 time trial world champion David Millar was banned from the Tour following the discovery of banned drugs at the offices of his cycling team, Cofidis. Doping allegations have plagued the career of American cyclist Lance Armstrong, who won his seventh consecutive Tour de France in 2005 before announcing his retirement. In 2002 Armstrong was linked to sports physician Dr. Michele Ferrari, who was reputed to have developed a system for taking EPO without detection. In 2005 EPO was found in Armstrong's old laboratory samples from the 1999 Tour de France. Armstrong has vehemently denied ever using banned drugs and has questioned the validity of such old samples that have passed through so many hands over the years.

STEROIDS AND THE LAW

On October 22, 2004, the federal Anabolic Steroids Act of 2004 was signed into law (http://www.deadiversion.usdoj.gov/fed_regs/rules/2005/fr1216.htm). The Act updated the Anabolic Steroid Control Act of 1990 in a number of ways. It amended the definition of anabolic steroids, adding tetrahydrogestrinone (THG), androstenedione, and certain related chemicals to the list of substances the law covered. The Act also directed the U.S. Sentencing Commission to review federal sentencing guidelines for offenses related to steroids, and provided for increased penalties for committing these offenses. It authorizes the Attorney General to exempt from regulation steroid-containing drugs that do not pose a drug abuse threat. Finally, the law directs the Secretary of Health and Human Services to provide grants for the development of science-based educational programs for elementary and secondary schools on the hazards of anabolic steroid use.

Anti-Doping Agencies

By the end of the twentieth century, the global sports community recognized that it would take a coordinated international effort to bring the problem of performance-enhancing drugs under control. In 1999 the World Anti-Doping Agency (WADA; http://www.wada-ama.org/en/) was created as a collaborative initiative between sports agencies and governments across the globe. WADA's role is to lead international efforts against doping in sports through public education, advocacy, research, and drug testing, and to provide leadership for the efforts of agencies working against doping in individual countries. In October of the following year, the United States Anti-Doping Agency (USADA; http://www.usantidoping.org/default.aspx) was launched to lead this work at the national level. USADA, an independent nonprofit organization, oversees testing, education, research, and adjudication on drug issues for U.S. athletes competing in the Olympics, the Pan Am Games, and the Paralympic Games. USADA has also taken the lead in the aspects of the BALCO investigations pertaining to sports.

Legislative Proposals

As the BALCO scandal continued to unfold, members of Congress began to assume a more active role in addressing the issue of performance-enhancing drugs. The most prominent piece of legislation was the Clean Sports Act of 2005, introduced in May of 2005 by Sen. John McCain (R-Arizona). The Clean Sports Act would create drug policy standards for the four major professional sports leagues and require that each of them implement rules that would suspend players for at least two years the first time they are caught using banned substances. The sports leagues would have to administer these policies under the supervision of the federal government. The bill was referred to the Senate Commerce, Science, and Transportation Committee, and hearings were held in late September; no further action on the bill had taken place as of late October 2005. A similar bill, the Drug-Free Sports Act of 2005, was introduced around the same time in the House of Representatives by Rep. Cliff Stearns (R-Florida); that bill too was making its way through the committee approval process.

CHAPTER 10
SPORTS AND GAMBLING

The drive in humans to gamble on sports seems to be almost as strong as the drive to participate in them. People have been betting on the outcome of sporting events since ancient times, in every corner of the world. In ancient Rome the wealthy class wagered on chariot races, animal fights, and gladiator battles. The Romans spread their penchant for gambling across the breadth of their empire, including Britain. In the sixteenth and seventeenth centuries people throughout Europe enjoyed betting on cockfights, wrestling, and footraces. In the eighteenth century horse racing and boxing rose to prominence as spectator sports on which the public enjoyed gambling. The nineteenth and twentieth centuries brought a new emphasis on team sports, and Europeans began risking their wages on rugby, soccer, and cricket games.

Colonists brought their yen for gambling on sports with them to America. Horse racing was a particularly popular sport among those inclined toward gambling. Most forms of gambling, including sports gambling, became illegal in America during the nineteenth century, as laws changed to conform to the morals of the time. Nevertheless, it remained legal to bet on horse racing, and other sports gambling continued to flourish underground. The state of Nevada legalized gambling in 1931, but after a couple of decades it was so tainted by organized crime and other scandals that it was the subject of government crackdowns in the 1950s. A new, highly regulated version of sports betting returned to Nevada in 1975; centered in Las Vegas, this segment of the gambling industry continues to thrive today.

Modern sports gambling in the United States can be roughly divided into three categories: (1) pari-mutuel gambling on horse racing, dog racing, and jai alai games; (2) legal sports betting through a licensed bookmaker; and (3) illegal sports gambling. The third category makes up the biggest portion of sports gambling in the nation by far.

PARI-MUTUEL GAMBLING

Pari-mutuel betting was invented in late nineteenth-century France by Pierre Oller. "Pari-mutuel" is a French term that means "mutual stake." In this kind of betting all the money bet on an event is combined into a single pool, which is then split among the winning bettors, with management first taking some share off the top before distribution. The share management receives is called the "takeout"; the takeout rate, set by state law, is usually about 20% of the total betting pool. Unlike placing a bet with a bookmaker, an individual betting on a pari-mutuel event is betting against other gamblers rather than against the house. The house keeps the same percentage of the total bets regardless of the outcome of the event. Another source of revenue from pari-mutuel gambling is what is known as "breakage." Winning bettors are not usually paid out to the exact penny total; payouts are rounded down. The leftover money, or breakage, is usually only a few cents per bet, but it adds up to a substantial sum over the course of thousands of transactions. Breakage may be split in various ways. Breakage generated by California horse tracks, for example, is split among the state, the track operators, and the horse owners.

In pari-mutuel betting the total "pool" in a race depends on how much is bet on that race. Every bet that is placed on a particular horse or player affects the odds; so the more people who bet on a particular outcome, the lower the payout is for those who bet on that outcome. Betting on a "longshot" offers a potentially better payout, but a lower likelihood of winning anything.

The pari-mutuel system has been used in horse racing since about 1875, but it did not become widespread until the 1920s and 1930s, with the introduction of the "totalizor," a special calculator that could automatically calculate the odds for each horse in a race based on the bets that had been placed. Before the 1930s most betting on horse races was done through bookmakers.

TABLE 10.1

Pari-mutuel gambling, 2004

	Horse racing	Greyhound racing	Jai Alai	Additional features
Alabama		X		
Arizona	X	X		
Arkansas	X	X		
California	X			
Colorado	X	X		
Connecticut		X	X	
Delaware	X			Slot machines
Florida	X	X	X	Card rooms
Idaho	X			
Illinois	X			
Indiana	X			
Iowa	X	X		Slot machines
Kansas	X	X		
Kentucky	X			
Louisiana	X			Slot machines
Maine	X			
Maryland	X			
Massachusetts	X	X		
Michigan	X			
Minnesota	X			Card rooms
Missouri	X			
Montana	X			
Nebraska	X			
Nevada	X			
New Mexico	X			Slot machines
New Hampshire	X	X		
New Jersey	X			
New York	X			Slot machines
North Dakota	X			
Ohio	X			
Oklahoma	X			
Oregon	X	X		
Pennsylvania	X			
Rhode Island		X	X	Slot machines & video lottery terminals
South Dakota	X			
Tennessee	X			
Texas	X	X		
Vermont	X			
Virginia	X			
Washington		X		
West Virginia	X	X		Slot machines
Wisconsin		X		
Wyoming		X		

SOURCE: Created by Kim Masters Evans for Thomson Gale, 2004

Corruption was widespread. In 1933 California, Michigan, Ohio, and New Hampshire legalized pari-mutuel gambling on horse racing mainly as a way to regulate the industry, decrease corruption, and generate revenue for the state. Many other states followed their lead over the next several years. Table 10.1 lists the states that allowed pari-mutuel gambling as of 2004. Some states allow pari-mutuel betting by law, but do not have any facilities actually offering it.

Historically, most pari-mutuel betting has taken place in person at the location where the event is happening. In recent years most bets are placed at off-track betting (OTB) facilities, which were first approved by the New York legislature in 1970. Wagering via telephone or Internet is also available in some states. Many races are simulcast to in-state and out-of-state locations, including OTB sites. This allows bettors to engage in intertrack

wagering (ITW), which means you can bet on a race at one track while being physically present at a completely different track.

The American Gaming Association estimates that total gross revenue from pari-mutuel gambling in the United States was $3.8 billion in 2003. The vast majority of that total, $3.4 billion, came from horse racing. Greyhound racing generated $398 million, and jai alai $25 million (http://www.americangaming.org/).

Thoroughbred Horse Racing

People have been betting on horse races for thousands of years. Horse racing was a popular spectator sport among wealthy Greeks and Romans. Later, knights returning to Western Europe from the Crusades brought with them speedy Arabian stallions, which were bred with English mares to create the line now called Thoroughbreds. Thoroughbreds are fast, graceful runners, identified by their height and long, slim legs. Thoroughbred racing quickly caught on among the British aristocracy, and it was soon dubbed the "Sport of Kings." The sport came to America with the colonists; there are records of horse racing taking place in the New York area as early as 1665.

Thoroughbred racing remained popular in the United States throughout the eighteenth and nineteenth centuries. The sport was scaled back significantly during World War II, and after the war remained in steep decline. Reasons for horse racing's loss of popularity in the postwar years include competition from the rise of amusement parks and malls; the failure of the racing industry to embrace television; and the rise of other gambling opportunities, such as casinos and lotteries. However, while attendance at horse races has declined substantially, the money continues to flow, and has actually increased since the 1990s. In 1990 the total amount bet on thoroughbred races, or the "handle," in the United States was $9.4 billion. By 2003 the handle had grown to $15.2 billion, before tailing off slightly to $15.1 billion in 2004, the first year in which it declined in more than a decade.

As of 2005 there were about ninety Thoroughbred racetracks in the United States; those in warm parts of the country are open throughout the year, while others are active only during the warm months. Some are government-owned, while others are privately held. The Thoroughbred gambling business is dominated by a handful of companies, the largest being two publicly traded firms: Churchill Downs and Magna Entertainment.

The three most prestigious Thoroughbred races together make up the "Triple Crown" of horse racing. Those races, which take place over a five-week period in May and June each year, are the Kentucky Derby at Churchill Downs in Louisville, Kentucky; the Preakness Stakes at Pimlico in Baltimore, Maryland; and the Belmont Stakes at Belmont Park in Elmont, New York.

The 2005 Kentucky Derby attracted $103.3 million in betting, the first time in history more than $100 million had been bet on a single race. Most of that total—$93.3 million—was bet off-track; $58 million was wagered on the Preakness in 2005, while the Belmont Stakes drew a handle of $48 million (http://www.kentuckyderby.com/2005/).

Non-Thoroughbred Horse Racing

While Thoroughbreds dominate the horse racing scene in the United States, pari-mutuel gambling is available on other types of horses as well. Harness racing, in which horses trot or pace rather than gallop and pull the jockey in a two-wheeled cart called a sulky, uses a horse called a standardbred, which is typically shorter and more muscular than a Thoroughbred. There are about thirty licensed harness racing tracks around the country. Another type of horse commonly raced is the quarter horse, which gets its name from the fact that it excels at sprinting short distances, under a quarter of a mile. And finally, about fifteen tracks around the United States feature Arabian horses, the only true purebred horses on the circuit.

Greyhound Racing

Like horses, greyhounds have been raced for amusement and gambling purposes for centuries. Greyhound racing has been called the "Sport of Queens," probably because it was Queen Elizabeth I of England who first standardized the rules for greyhound "coursing" (a sport in which greyhounds are used to hunt rabbits) in the sixteenth century. Greyhound racing came to America in the late nineteenth century, and the first circular greyhound track was opened in 1919 in California.

Greyhound racing is not nearly as popular as horse racing, and its popularity is declining quickly. The sport reached its peak of popularity in 1992, when, according to the Greyhound Racing Association of America (GRA-America), nearly 3.5 million people attended the 16,827 races that took place at more than fifty tracks. Nearly $3.5 billion was bet on greyhound races that year (http://www.gra-america.org/tracks.html). Revenue has dropped by nearly half since then. As of 2005 there were about forty greyhound tracks operating in fifteen states, though it remains legal in forty-two states. More than a third of the tracks currently in operation are located in Florida. The tracks in a few states, according to GRA-America, subsist primarily on revenue from slot machines rather than from gambling on the races themselves. The decline in the popularity of greyhound racing is in part due to allegations, many of them well documented, of mistreatment of the dogs. The Greyhound Protection League collects data on cruelty and deaths related to greyhound racing, and lobbies for the sport to be banned altogether (http://www.greyhounds.org/gpl/contents/entry.html).

Jai Alai

Jai alai is a sport similar to handball. Like handball, it is played on a court and involves bouncing a ball against a wall. In jai alai the ball is caught using a long, curved basket called a cesta. The first permanent jai alai arena, or fronton, was built in Florida in 1924 (http://www.fla-gaming.com/history.htm). Jai alai is an endangered sport in the United States. At its peak of popularity in the 1980s, more than $600 million was bet on jai alai in the United States. By 1996 the total jai alai handle had shrunk to $240 million. By 2002–03 the figure was a mere $102 million. In the United States jai alai is confined almost entirely to Florida, where the sport retains a sizeable following. Most of the frontons in Florida, however, rely on revenue from other forms of gambling, such as poker, to help keep them in business.

LEGAL SPORTS GAMBLING

As of 2005 gambling on sports was legal in only one state: Nevada. Nowhere else in the United States is betting allowed on big-time sports like professional football, basketball, or baseball. This state of affairs was essentially locked into place by the 1992 passage of the Professional and Amateur Sports Protection Act, which banned sports betting everywhere except those states where it was already allowed in some form—Nevada, Oregon, Delaware, Montana, Washington, and New Mexico (http://www.gambling-law-us.com/Federal-Laws/sports-protection.htm). However, aside from Nevada, the action is very limited; it may be part of a lottery game, or fantasy leagues and office pools may be legal.

In Nevada legal sports gambling takes place through licensed "books," or establishments that accept and pay out bets on sporting events. Sports books are legal only in Nevada. One must be at least twenty-one years old to place bets with licensed bookmakers. There were 173 locations licensed to operate sports and/or race books as of February 2005, according to the Nevada Gaming Control Board (http://gaming.nv.gov/). More than half of them are in Las Vegas, and most are in casinos.

Bookmaking

Bookmaking is the term for determining gambling odds and handling bets and payouts. The person doing the bookmaking is called a bookmaker or bookie. Bookmakers make their money by charging a commission on each bet; the commission, called "juice" in gambling slang, is usually between 4% and 5%.

Most sports bets are based on the "line" set by the bookmaker. In most sports the line is also called a point spread. A point spread is how much a favored team must win a game by in order for those betting on that team to collect. For example, if Team A is a ten-point favorite to defeat Team B, the bettor is actually betting on whether Team A will beat Team B by at least that margin. If Team A wins by nine points, then those betting on Team B are winners and those picking team A are losers. In this example, Team B has lost the game, but has "beat the spread." The point spread concept was introduced in the 1940s by bookmaker Charles McNeil as a way of encouraging people to bet on underdogs. Prior to the point spread system, bookmakers risked losing large sums on lopsided games in which everybody bet on the favorite to win.

Nevada: America's Gambling Capital

The State of Nevada legalized gambling in the 1930s as a way of generating revenue during the Depression. The state's legislature made off-track betting on horses legal in the 1940s. Sports and race betting was popular in Nevada's casinos throughout that decade. At the beginning of the 1950s, however, the Nevada gambling world came under the scrutiny of Congress for its ties to organized crime. Senator Estes Kefauver (D-TN) initiated hearings to investigate the matter. These hearings, televised nationally, drew attention to a culture of corruption and gangland activity that had settled in Las Vegas. The hearings resulted in the imposition of a 10% federal excise tax on sports betting. This tax effectively shot down casino-based sports bookmaking in Nevada.

The sports books mounted a comeback in the 1970s, after the excise tax was reduced to 2% in 1974, and by the 1980s sports and race bookmaking was a booming industry, helped along by another reduction in the excise tax, to .25% in 1983. Bookmakers like Jimmy "The Greek" Snyder became national celebrities, appearing regularly on television. Between 1982 and 1987 Nevada sports book betting increased by 230%. Betting volume began to taper off in the mid-1990s, in part due to the rise of online wagering, but has been rebounding in the mid-2000s. Licensed books took in $2.1 billion in bets in 2004 according to *USA Today* (Michael McCarthy, "Viva Pro Sports? Vegas Makes Play for Team," November 30, 2005), an improvement over the $1.86 billion wagered a year earlier, but still well below the 1996 handle of $2.5 billion (http://www.usatoday.com/sports/football/nfl/2005-09-07-betting_x.htm). Figure 10.1 shows the historical trend in Nevada's sports book handle from 1996 through 2003.

Football is the biggest betting draw among the major sports. According to the Nevada Gaming Commission and Gaming Control Board, football typically accounts for about 40% of sports book wagering, basketball about 27%, and baseball 20%. Figure 10.2 shows the precise percentages for 2002; they have remained fairly stable since then. Parlays, one of the categories in the graphic, refer to bets placed on a sequential series of events; each component bet must succeed in order to win the

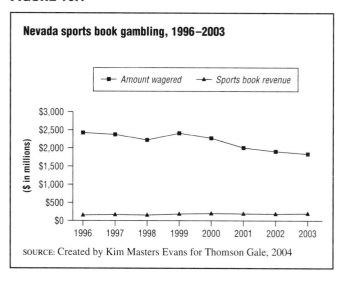

FIGURE 10.1

Nevada sports book gambling, 1996–2003

SOURCE: Created by Kim Masters Evans for Thomson Gale, 2004

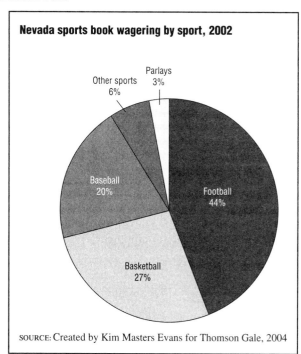

FIGURE 10.2

Nevada sports book wagering by sport, 2002

SOURCE: Created by Kim Masters Evans for Thomson Gale, 2004

parlay. The Super Bowl alone is a gigantic gambling event. According to the Nevada Gaming Commission, $90.76 million was bet on the 2005 Super Bowl, by far the most in Super Bowl history, and the second record year in a row. Table 10.2 shows total Super Bowl betting with Nevada sports books for the last several years. The NCAA Basketball Tournament brings in a similar sum, though it involves sixty-four teams and six rounds of games. In 2004 legal betting volume for the tournament surpassed $85 million. Industrywide, about one-third of the bets placed legally in Nevada sports books are on college sports. It is currently illegal to gamble on high school sports and on the Olympics.

TABLE 10.2

Nevada sports book wagering on Super Bowls, 1996–2005

Year	Wagers	Win/loss	Win %	Game results
2005	$90,759,236	$15,430,138	17.0%	New England 24, Philadelphia 21
2004	$81,242,191	$12,440,698	15.3%	New England 32, Carolina 29
2003	$71,693,032	$5,264,963	7.3%	Tampa Bay 48, Oakland 21
2002	$71,513,304	$2,331,607	3.3%	New England 20, St. Louis 17
2001	$67,661,425	$11,002,636	16.3%	Baltimore 34, N.Y. Giants 7
2000	$71,046,751	$4,237,978	6.0%	St. Louis 23, Tennessee 16
1999	$75,986,520	$2,906,601	3.8%	Denver 34, Atlanta 19
1998	$77,253,246	$ 472,033	0.6%	Denver 31, Green Bay 24
1997	$70,853,211	$2,265,701	3.2%	Green Bay 35, New England 21
1996	$70,907,801	$7,126,145	10.1%	Dallas 27, Pittsburgh 17

SOURCE: "Summary of Nevada Sports Book Performance for the Last Ten Super Bowls," Nevada Gambling Control Board, February 8, 2005, http://gaming.nv.gov/documents/pdf/pr_05superbowl.pdf (accessed September 22, 2005)

ATTITUDES TOWARD SPORTS GAMBLING

In spite of gambling's reputation as a "vice," Americans are overwhelmingly comfortable with sports gambling, though a relatively small percentage actually participate. Data from the Gallup Organization's December 2003 lifestyle poll found that about two-thirds of Americans had engaged in some form of gambling over the past year, but only about 10% of those surveyed said they had bet on a professional sporting event in the past year, and 6% had bet on college sports. (See Table 10.3.) Another 4% had bet on horse racing, and 2% had wagered on boxing. Those figures were historical lows in each category. Fifteen percent said they had participated in an office betting pool related to some type of sporting event, like the Super Bowl or NCAA Basketball Tournament.

While not many people actually participate, the majority of Americans approve of gambling in general, and sports gambling in particular, though they express concern about how gambling may taint their favorite game. In Gallup's most recent polling on attitudes toward gambling, conducted in April and May of 1999, 1,523 adults and 501 teenagers were asked a series of questions about their participation in and approval of sports gambling. At that time, 64% of adults and 52% of teens approved of legalized gambling in general. Fifty-three percent of adults and 55% of teenagers said they thought off-track betting on horse races should be legal as a means of raising state revenue; 41% of adults and 60% of teenagers endorsed legalizing gambling on professional sports for that purpose. However, about two-thirds of each group said they believed "legalized betting on sporting events leads to cheating or fixing games."

Indeed, the vast government revenue potential of legal sports gambling is the strongest argument for proponents of legalizing betting on pro and college sports in states where it is currently banned. A 2003 *Forbes* article (Art Wienberg, "The Case for Legal Sports Gambling,"

TABLE 10.3

Participation in sports gambling, previous 12 months

Bet on a professional sports event such as baseball, basketball, or football

	Yes %	No %	No opinion %
2003 Dec 11–14	10	90	*
1999 Apr 30–May 23	13	87	—
1996 Jun 27–30	10	90	—
1992 Nov 20–22	12	88	—
1990 Feb 15–18	21	79	—
1989 Apr 4–9	22	78	—

Bet on a college sports event such as basketball or football

	Yes %	No %	No opinion %
2003 Dec 11–14	6	94	*
1999 Apr 30–May 23	9	91	—
1996 Jun 27–30	7	93	—
1992 Nov 20–22	6	94	—
1990 Feb 15–18	11	89	—
1989 Apr 4–9	14	86	—

Bet on a boxing match

	Yes %	No %	No opinion %
2003 Dec 11–14	2	98	*
1996 Jun 27–30	3	97	*
1992 Nov 20–22	6	94	—
1990 Feb 15–18	5	95	—
1989 Apr 4–9	8	92	—

Participated in an office pool on the World Series, Superbowl, or other game

	Yes %	No %	No opinion %
2003 Dec 11–14	15	85	*
1999 Apr 30–May 23	25	75	—
1996 Jun 27–30	23	77	—
1992 Nov 20–22	22	78	—

*Less than 0.5%

SOURCE: Jeffrey M. Jones, "Gambling Activity in the United States," in *Gambling a Common Activity for Americans*, The Gallup Organization, March 24, 2004, http://poll.gallup.com/content/default.aspx?CI=11098 (accessed September 22, 2005). Copyright © 2004 by The Gallup Organization. Reproduced by permission of The Gallup Organization.

January 27, 2003) estimated that the 1992 law that locks all states except Nevada out of the sports gambling market deprives states of taxes on perhaps hundreds of billions of dollars in illegal sports bets each year (http://www.forbes.com/2003/01/27/cx_aw_0127gambling.html).

ILLEGAL SPORTS GAMBLING

While gambling is legal in one form or another—whether casinos, racetracks, or lotteries—in every state except Utah and Hawaii, illegal gambling nevertheless flourishes as well. The American Gaming Association estimates that the Nevada sports books account for only 1% to 3% of all sports gambling in the United States. So prevalent is illicit sports gambling that it is almost impossible to calculate the dollar amounts involved. The 1999 report of President Bill Clinton's Gambling Impact Study Commission estimated that illegal sports gambling in the United States amounted to between $80 billion and $380 billion a year (http://govinfo.library.unt.edu/ngisc/). The FBI put the figure at $100 billion a year earlier.

A lot of different activities fall into the category of illegal gambling, ranging from betting on sports outside of the legitimate, licensed bookmaking system to benign office pools. Sports gambling has a long history of association with organized crime, which ran illegal bookmaking operations across the country as early as the 1920s. After Nevada legalized casino gambling in 1931, organized crime quickly took control of the industry. When the federal government made progress in driving organized crime out of the casino business in the 1950s, the mobsters focused their efforts on bookmaking, which was not yet available in the casinos. To this day, a large portion of sports gambling is controlled by organized crime figures.

FIXING, SHAVING, AND TAMPERING: SPORTS GAMBLING SCANDALS

Shady characters, including prominent organized crime figures, have always gravitated toward sports, sometimes as a means for laundering money obtained illicitly in other industries. The history of sports is rife with tales of gamblers paying off athletes to "take a dive" or miss the crucial shot. Major professional sports leagues and the NCAA have taken measures to distance themselves from sports gambling, but their efforts have not prevented a long list of sports gambling scandals from taking place over the years.

Perhaps the most notorious sports gambling scandal in history was the so-called Black Sox Scandal of 1919, in which gamblers bribed several members of the Chicago White Sox to intentionally throw the World Series (http://www.chicagohs.org/history/blacksox.html). A huge point-shaving scandal encompassing seven schools and thirty-two players rocked college basketball in 1951. Point shaving is a type of game fixing in which players, usually bribed by gamblers, conspire to avoid beating a published point spread. College basketball has continued to prove tempting to gamblers since then. In 1978 associates of the Lucchese organized crime family orchestrated a point-shaving scheme with key members of the Boston College basketball team. Another point-shaving scheme involving college basketball was uncovered at Arizona State University in 1994. Lesser-known scandals have taken place in the intervening years.

Many high-profile professional athletes have gotten in trouble over the years for gambling on the sport in which they participate, which inevitably creates suspicion about game fixing. In 1963 NFL stars Alex Karras of the Detroit Lions and Paul Hornung of the Green Bay Packers were suspended for betting on their own teams' games. Denny McLain of the Detroit Tigers, the last pitcher (as of 2005) to win thirty games in a season, was suspended for most of the 1970 season for associating with gamblers. In 1989 baseball player Pete Rose, who holds the record for most career hits, was kicked out of baseball for gambling on Major League Baseball games. He denied doing so at the time but has since admitted to betting on baseball games while serving as manager of the Cincinnati Reds. Rose's lifetime suspension has kept him out of the Baseball Hall of Fame, into which he would certainly have been inducted had his gambling activities not come to light. In 1999 former San Francisco 49ers owner Eddie DeBartolo was fined $1 million and suspended by the NFL for paying a $400,000 bribe to obtain a license to operate a casino in Louisiana.

College sports have been at the center of the most visible sports gambling scandals since the 1990s. In 1994–95 two Northwestern University basketball players were caught shaving points. Two years later, thirteen football players at Boston College were suspended for gambling on college football games. Other cases have involved: University of Washington football coach Rich Neuheisel; University of Michigan basketball player Chris Webber; Florida State University quarterback Adrian McPherson; and University of Florida basketball player Teddy Dupay.

After decades of taking measures to avoid even the appearance of impropriety by distancing themselves from gambling entirely, there are some signs that the major sports leagues are ready to establish a cozier relationship with the gambling industry, simply because the money in sports gambling is too good to resist. A prime example is the Maloof brothers, Joe, Gavin, and George, Jr., who together own both the NBA's Sacramento Kings and the Palms Casino in Las Vegas. Joe and Gavin run the Kings, while George oversees the Palms. When the Maloofs sought to buy the Kings in 1998, the NBA was willing to give its blessing provided the Maloofs quit accepting bets on NBA games in their casino's legal bookmaking operation. Before the Maloofs, there was ITT Corp., a conglomerate that owned three Las Vegas casinos at the time, which was allowed to purchase half interest in two New York teams, the Knicks and the Rangers. In Pittsburgh the National Hockey League's Penguins were, as of October 2005, attempting to obtain a license for a slot machine casino in order to raise funds to build a new stadium. Meanwhile, Pittsburgh Steelers running back Jerome Bettis went public with the news of his limited partnership in a proposed horse track/casino/hotel complex, raising a few eyebrows around the NFL (but not as many as would have been raised a few years earlier). Of course, Bettis had a good role model; his employers the Rooney family, owners of the Steelers, also own two horse-racing facilities.

GAMBLING IN COLLEGE SPORTS

The college sports gambling cases noted above are probably just the tip of the iceberg. Gambling on sports, which is technically legal only in Nevada and only by adults, is extremely common among college athletes themselves. The *2003 NCAA National Study on Collegiate Sports Wagering and Associated Behaviors* found that more than two-thirds (69%) of male student athletes and nearly half (47%) of female student athletes participated in some form of gambling in the past year; more than a third of male athletes (35%) and about 10% of female athletes reported having bet on sporting events in the past year, in direct violation of NCAA rules regarding sports wagering (http://www.ncaa.org/library/research/sports_wagering/2003/2003_sports_wagering_study.pdf). The report included the startling finding that 20% of male student athletes and 5% of female student athletes had gambled on *collegiate* sporting events in the past year. About 1% of football players and 0.5% of men's basketball players reported having accepted money to play poorly in a game. About 2% of men's football and basketball players said they had been asked to affect the outcome of a game.

The NCAA has long supported a complete ban on college sports gambling. Naturally, Nevada-based gambling interests strongly oppose such a measure. The gaming industry points out that the problems associated with gambling on college sports are mostly related to illegal gambling, not legitimate wagering that takes place through licensed bookmakers. They point out, for example, that the $90 million or so that is bet legally on the NCAA basketball tournament represents a minute fraction of the total sum—a March 2005 *St. Petersburg Times* article (Brady Dennis, "March on Vegas is Bettors' Ritual," March 31, 2005) cites estimates of $3.5 billion, roughly the gross national product of Mozambique—wagered when Internet bets and informal office pools are factored in.

Since 2000, members of Congress have advocated banning college sports betting, but they have met with little success. The biggest proponent in the Capitol of banning all gambling on college sports has been Senator John McCain (R-AZ), who first introduced the Amateur Sports Integrity Act in 2000 (http://www.govtrack.us/congress/bill.xpd?bill=s107-718). Initially, the bill had Nevada gambling businesses worried, but in the end it made little progress in the face of heavy lobbying on the part of the gaming industry and a lack of significant public support. McCain reintroduced the bill over the

next couple of congressional sessions, but it met the same fate. Representative Tom Osborne (R-NE), the House sponsor of the bill, reintroduced a version in March 2005 (though McCain opted not to do so in the Senate at the time), just as the NCAA basketball tournament was in high gear. As of November 2005, the bill was still languishing in the House Subcommittee on Commercial and Administrative Law, with dim prospects for success. Gaming industry representatives working against the bill claimed that it would have a devastating effect on their business, noting that college sports gambling accounts for a sizeable share of total bets placed with licensed Nevada bookmakers. In a March 2005 *Las Vegas Review-Journal* article (Tony Batt, "College Betting Ban Resurfaces," March 19, 2005), Bob Scucci, sports book director at the Stardust Casino, said, "It would be tough to put an exact dollar amount on it, but college football and basketball combine for maybe one-third of our handle" (http://www.reviewjournal.com/lvrj_home/2005/Mar-19-Sat-2005/news/26111563.html).

ONLINE GAMBLING

The new frontier of sports gambling is the Internet. Nobody knows exactly how much money is bet online, and nobody seems to really know whether it is legal, either. The U.S. Government Accountability Office has estimated that there are 1,800 online gambling operations, nearly all of them outside of the United States (http://www.gao.gov/new.items/d0389.pdf). Christiansen Capital Advisors, LLC, estimated that about $1 billion worth of sports bets were placed online from the United States in 2003 (http://www.cca-i.com/). Of that total, $248 million was bet on pro football. Another $207 million was bet on college football. Professional and college basketball were close behind, with $196 million and $165 million in bets, respectively. Each of these figures is roughly ten times what was bet on these sports with licensed Nevada sports books, based on Christiansen estimates.

Internet gambling first became available in the late 1990s, and the Nevada sports books quickly sensed that it presented a serious challenge. Many authorities argue that online sports gambling is technically illegal in the United States based on the federal Wire Act of 1961, which was originally enacted to get organized crime out of sports betting; however, not everybody agrees with that analysis. Moreover, most Internet gambling operations are based offshore, which is murky legal territory. The Internet knows no geographic boundaries—an online gambling operation based in Antigua can be accessed as easily from Dubai, Saudi Arabia, as from Dubuque, Iowa. The U.S. government has attempted to take measures to curb online gambling, both sports betting and other types, but since these businesses are not based in the United States, enforcement is problematic. How do you get an enterprise to stop a business practice that is perfectly legal in its home country? The World Trade Organization has urged the United States to give up its attempts to ban Internet betting. That has not stopped some members of Congress from introducing legislation to ban online gambling. Some of the proposed legislation approaches the issue from the financial angle, creating barriers to electronic transfers of money to online gambling operations. The most active proponent of banning Internet gambling has been Senator Jon Kyl (R-AZ), who first introduced the Internet Gambling Prohibition Act in 1997 (http://thomas.loc.gov/cgi-bin/query/z?c105:S.474.RS:). Others in Congress argue that rather than trying to prohibit online gambling, which may be next to impossible, it should instead be regulated and taxed, generating substantial revenue for state and federal governments. As of November 2005, Congress had not passed significant legislation to ban online sports gambling.

IMPORTANT NAMES AND ADDRESSES

Amateur Athletic Union (AAU)
P.O. Box 22409
Lake Buena Vista, FL 32830
(407) 934-7200
FAX: (407) 934-7242
URL: http://www.aausports.org/

American Gaming Association (AGA)
555 13th St. NW, Suite 1010 E
Washington, DC 20004
(202) 637-6500
URL: http://www.americangaming.org/

ATP Tour (Association of Tennis Professionals)
201 ATP Blvd.
Ponte Vedra Beach, FL 32082
(904) 285-8000
FAX: (904) 285-5966
URL: http://www.atptennis.com/

Bowling Proprietors' Association of America (BPAA)
615 Six Flags Dr.
Arlington, TX 76011
1-800-343-1329
URL: http://www.bpaa.com/

Champ Car World Series
5350 Lakeview Pkwy South Dr.
Indianapolis, IN 46268
(317) 715-4100
FAX: (317) 715-4110
URL: http://www.champcarworldseries.com/

ESPN
ESPN Plaza
Bristol, CT 06010
(860) 766-2000
URL: http://www.espn.go.com/

Indy Racing League (IRL)
4565 West 16th St.
Indianapolis, IN 46222
(317) 484-6526
URL: http://www.indyracing.com/

International Boxing Federation (IBF)
516 Main St., 2nd Floor
East Orange, NJ 07018
(973) 414-0300
URL: http://www.ibf-usba-boxing.com/

International Olympic Committee (IOC)
Chateau de Vidy
CH-1007 Lausanne, Switzerland
011-41-21-621-6111
URL: http://www.olympic.org/

LPGA Tour (Ladies' Professional Golf Association)
100 International Golf Dr.
Daytona Beach, FL 32124
(386) 274-6200
FAX: (386) 274-1099
URL: http://www.lpga.com/

Major League Baseball (MLB)
Office of the Commissioner
245 Park Ave., 31st Floor
New York, NY 10167
(212) 931-7800
URL: http://www.mlb.com/

Major League Baseball Players Association
12 East 49th St., 24th Floor
New York, NY 10017
(212) 826-0808
URL: http://www.mlbplayers.com/

Major League Soccer (MLS)
110 East 42nd St., 10th Floor
New York, NY 10017
(212) 450-1200
URL: http://www.mlsnet.com/

NASCAR
P.O. Box 2875
Daytona Beach, FL 32120
(386) 253-0611
URL: http://www.nascar.com/

National Alliance for Youth Sports (NAYS)
2050 Vista Parkway
West Palm Beach, FL 33411
(561) 684-1141
1-800-729-2057
FAX: (561) 684-2546
E-mail: nays@nays.org
URL: http://www.nays.org/

National Basketball Association (NBA)
Olympic Tower
645 Fifth Ave.
New York, NY 10022
(212) 407-8000
URL: http://www.nba.com/

National Collegiate Athletic Association (NCAA)
700 West Washington St.
P.O. Box 6222
Indianapolis, IN 46206
(317) 917-6222
FAX: (317) 917-6888
URL: http://www.ncaa.org/

National Football League (NFL)
280 Park Ave.
New York, NY 10017
(212) 450-2000
URL: http://www.nfl.com/

National Hockey League (NHL)
1251 Avenue of the Americas, 47th Floor
New York, NY 10020
(212) 789-2000
URL: http://www.nhl.com/

National Sporting Goods Association (NSGA)
1601 Feehanville Dr., Suite 300
Mt. Prospect, IL 60056
(847) 296-6742
E-mail: info@nsga.org
URL: http://www.nsga.org/

National Thoroughbred Racing Association (NTRA)
2525 Harrodsburg Rd.
Lexington KY 40504
(859) 223-5444
FAX: (859)223-3945
E-mail: ntra@ntra.com
URL: http://www.ntra.com/

NBA Players Association
Two Penn Plaza, Suite 2430
New York, NY 10121
(212) 655-0880
URL: http://www.nbpa.com/

Nevada Gaming Commission and State Gaming Control Board
1919 East College Pkwy.
P.O. Box 8003
Carson City, NV 89702-8003
(775) 684-7750
FAX: (775) 687-5817
URL: http://gaming.nv.gov/

NFL Players Association
2021 L St. NW, Suite 600
Washington, DC 20036
(202) 463-2200
1-800-372-2000
URL: http://www.nflpa.org/main/main.asp

NHL Players' Association
777 Bay St., Suite 2400
P.O. Box 121
Toronto, ON M5G 2C8 Canada
(416) 408-4040
URL: http://www.nhlpa.com/

PGA of America
100 Avenue of the Champions
Palm Beach Gardens, FL 33410
(561) 624-8400
URL: http://www.pga.com/

PGA Tour
112 PGA Tour Blvd.
Ponta Vedra, FL 32082
(904) 285-3700
URL: http://www.pgatour.com/

Professional Bowlers Association (PBA)
719 Second Ave., Suite 701
Seattle, WA 98104
(206) 332-9688
FAX: (206) 654-6030
URL: http://www.pba.com/

SGMA International
1150 17th St. NW, #850
Washington, DC 20036
(202) 775-1762

FAX: (202) 296-7462
E-mail: info@sgma.com
URL: http://www.sgma.com/

Sony Ericsson Women's Tennis Association Tour
One Progress Plaza, Suite 1500
St. Petersburg, FL 33701
(727) 895-5000
FAX: (727) 894-1982
URL: http://www.wtatour.com/

Special Olympics
1133 19th St., NW
Washington, DC 20036
(202) 628-3630
FAX: (202) 824-0200
URL: http://www.specialolympics.org/

The Sporting News
10176 Corporate Square Dr., Suite 200
St. Louis, MO 63132
(314) 997-7111
URL: http://www.sportingnews.com/

Sports Business Daily
120 West Morehead St., Suite 220
Charlotte, NC 28202
(704) 973-1500
FAX: (704) 973-1501
E-mail: thedaily@sportsbusinessdaily.com
URL: http://www.sportsbizdaily.com/

Sports Illustrated
1271 Avenue of the Americas,
32nd Floor
New York, NY 10020-1339
(212) 522-1212
Fax: (212) 522-0475
URL: http://www.si.com/

United States Anti-Doping Agency
1330 Quail Lake Loop, Suite 260
Colorado Springs, CO 80906
(719) 785-2000
1-866-601-2632
FAX: (719) 785-2001
E-mail: webmaster@usantidoping.org
URL: http://www.usantidoping.org/

United States Bowling Congress
5301 South 76th St.
Greendale, WI 53129
1-800-514-2695
E-mail: bowlinfo@bowl.com
URL: http://www.bowl.com/

United States Golf Association (USGA)
P.O. Box 708, Liberty Corner Rd.
Far Hills, NH 07931
(908) 234-2300

FAX: (908) 234-9687
URL: http://www.usga.org/

United States Olympic Committee (USOC)
One Olympic Plaza
Colorado Springs, CO 80909
(719) 632-5551
E-mail: media@usoc.org
URL: http://www.usoc.org/

United States Tennis Association (USTA)
70 West Red Oak Lane
White Plains, NY 10604
(914) 696-7000
URL: http://www.usta.com/

Women's National Basketball Association (WNBA)
Olympic Tower
645 5th Ave.
New York, NY 10022
(212) 688-9622
FAX: (212) 750-9622
URL: http://www.wnba.com/

Women's Sports Foundation
Eisenhower Park
East Meadow, NY 11554
(516) 542-4700
FAX: (516) 542-4716
E-mail: info@womenssportsfoundation.org
URL: http://www.
womenssportsfoundation.org/

World Boxing Association (WBA)
P.O. Box 377
Maracay 2101-A Estado Aragua Venezuela
011-58-244-663-1584
FAX: 011-58-244-663-3177
E-mail: wbaven@wbaonline.com
URL: http://www.wbaonline.com/

World Boxing Council (WBC)
Cuzco 872, Col. Lindavista
Mexico City, C.P. 07300,
D.F. Mexico
011-52-55-5119-52-74
E-mail: info@wbcboxing.com
URL: http://www.wbcboxing.com/

World Boxing Organization (WBO)
1st Federal Bldg.
1056 Ave Muñoz Rivera, Suite 711
San Juan, PR 00927
(787) 765-4444
FAX: (787) 758-9053
E-mail: boxing@wbo-int.com
URL: http://www.wbo-int.com/

RESOURCES

Much of the information in *Sports in America* pertaining to sports participation originated in the *Superstudy of Sports Participation* conducted annually by the independent research company American Sports Data, Inc. (ASD). *Superstudy* data were interpreted and reported by industry organizations such as SGMA International, the trade association for sporting goods manufacturers; and the National Sporting Goods Association (NSGA), the trade group for sporting goods retailers. SGMA International releases an annual *Topline Report* based on *Superstudy* data, as well as other reports on specific aspects of sports participation. NSGA also conducts its own survey research on participation, as well as industry research on nationwide sales of sporting goods. Another source of data on sports participation was the U.S. Census Bureau's *Statistical Abstract of the United States*. ASD has also published *Comprehensive Study of Sports Injuries in the U.S.* (2003), which provided some of the information on that topic presented in Chapter 8.

The *Statistical Abstract* also includes information on attendance at sporting events. Most of the attendance figures for the major sports were obtained from ESPN.com. This was supplemented by information from a variety of print media, including *USA Today*, *Sports Illustrated*, the 2005 *ESPN Sports Almanac*, and United Press International.

Polling data provided by The Gallup Organization was key in assembling information on the preferences of sports fans, including trends related to race, gender, age, and geography.

The Museum of Broadcast Communications provided information on the history of sports on television. Nielsen Media Research was also a rich source of information on sports and the media, specifically television viewership data. Another key source on this topic, as well as other aspects of sports media, was the book *The Business of Sports*, edited by Scott R. Rosner and Kenneth L. Shropshire (Sudbury, MA: Jones and Bartlett, 2004). *The*

Business of Sports provides comprehensive coverage of all economic aspects of the sports industry. In addition to sports media, the book provided essential information on the financial structure of professional team sports, college sports, and the Olympics. ESPN and Street & Smith's *SportsBusiness Journal* provided additional information on the broadcast contracts of major sports, as did the *ESPN Sports Almanac* cited above.

Nonprofit advocacy and public education groups provided substantial information for various chapters of *Sports in America*. The Center on Alcohol Marketing and Youth (CAMY) provided data on alcohol advertising during sports programming. Children Now, in its report *Boys to Men: Sports Media*, provided information on violence and race and gender portrayals in sports programming. The Women's Sports Foundation, which was founded by tennis champion Billie Jean King, has conducted research on gender equity in sports. Another key source of information on gender equity was "Women in Intercollegiate Sport: A Longitudinal, National Study," sponsored by Brooklyn College and Smith College's Project on Women and Social Change.

The National Collegiate Athletic Association provided a wealth of data on many aspects of college sports. Key NCAA publications that contributed information include: the *1981–82—2003–04 Sports Sponsorship and Participation Report*; the *2002–03 NCAA Gender-Equity Report*; the *1999–00—2003–04 NCAA Student-Athlete Ethnicity Report*; and the *2002–03 NCAA Revenues and Expenses of Divisions I and II Intercollegiate Athletics Programs Report*. Information on eligibility rules for college athletes was found in the NCAA's *Guide for the College-Bound Student-Athlete*.

Another independent research company, Plunkett Research, Ltd., was the source of information on revenues of the major professional sports. Team-by-team revenue and valuation figures were provided by *Forbes* magazine on its Web site, while *SportsBusiness Journal* provided data on sales of licensed merchandise. Most of the information about the structure and workings of the major sports leagues came from the leagues themselves. Likewise, information about the PGA Tour (golf), ATP Tour (tennis), NASCAR (auto racing), the various boxing organizations, and other non-team sports was obtained from the Web sites of those organizations. Revenues from Sports Venues, a company specializing in directories and other publications about the sports venue industry, also provided helpful information.

The Web site of the International Olympic Committee provided a wealth of information about the structure and workings of the Olympic Movement. One particular document available via the site, the *2005 Olympic Marketing Fact File*, contained detailed information on Olympic financial matters, including sources of revenue and how it is distributed.

Steroid Abuse in Today's Society, a 2004 publication of the U.S. Drug Enforcement Administration's Office of Diversion Control, provided valuable information about steroids. Also useful was the National Drug Intelligence Center's *National Drug Threat Assessment*. Data on steroid use in college sports came from the NCAA's *Study of Substance Use Habits of College Student-Athletes*.

The American Gaming Society and the Nevada Gaming Commission and Gaming Control Board were useful sources of information on legal sports gambling. Data on the magnitude of illegal sports gambling was obtained from the 1999 report of President Bill Clinton's Gambling Impact Study Commission. The NCAA provided information about college sports betting in its *2003 NCAA National Study on Collegiate Sports Wagering and Associated Behaviors*. Christiansen Capital Advisors, LLC provided research on Internet sports gambling.

INDEX

Page references in italics refer to photographs. References with the letter t *following them indicate the presence of a table. The letter* f *indicates a figure. If more than one table or figure appears on a particular page, the exact item number for the table or figure being referenced is provided.*

A

Aaron, Hank, 48
Academic eligibility, 71, 83
Advertising. *See* Alcohol advertising; Corporate sponsorship
Aerobic exercise, 103
African-Americans
    fans, 22–24
    favorite sports to watch on television, 38, 39 (*f*3.2)
    integration of baseball, 48
Alcohol advertising, 41–42, 42*t*, 43*t*, 44*t*
Allen, Mel, 34
Amateur sports
    Olympics as, 100
    overview, 5–7
Amateur Sports Integrity Act (proposed), 129
American Football League, 51–52
American Professional Football Association, 51
Anabolic Steroid Control Act, 118, 122
Anabolic steroids. *See* Doping
Anabolic Steroids Act, 122
Anderson, Greg, 116, 117
Androstenedione, 118
Anti-doping agencies, 122
Armstrong, Lance, 122
Association of Tennis Professionals, 63
Attendance
    auto racing, 28–29, 29 (*t*2.19)
    overview, 2–3
    professional baseball, 25, 26*t*
    professional basketball, 25–26, 27*t*
    professional football, 28*t*

professional hockey, 27–28, 29 (*t*2.18)
professional soccer, 28
by sport, 31*t*–32*t*
by sport and frequency, 30*t*
Auto racing
    attendance, 28–29, 29 (*t*2.19)
    overview, 64–66
    television contracts, 40

B

BALCO scandal, 8, 116–117
Baseball, professional
    attendance, 25, 26*t*
    doping, 49–50, 121
    fans, 24*f*
    history, 48–49
    labor issues, 49
    structure, 47–48
    team values and revenues, 48 (*t*4.2)
    teams and division, 48 (*t*4.1)
    television contracts, 34–35
Basketball
    fans, 24*f*
    participation, 11, 12
Basketball, professional
    age, 55
    attendance, 25–26, 27*t*
    doping, 121–122
    history, 53
    labor issues, 54–55
    race/ethnicity, 55–56
    salary caps, 55*t*
    structure, 53–54, 54 (*t*4.5)
    team values and revenue, 54 (*t*4.6)
    television contracts, 38–39, 39*t*
    women's, 56
Basketball Association of America, 53
Bell, Bert, 51–52
Bettis, Jerome, 128–129
Bird, Larry, 53
Black Sox scandal, 48, 128
Bonds, Barry, 49, 116, 117, 121

Bookmaking, 125–126, 126*f*, 127 (*t*10.2)
Boston Marathon, 29–30
Bowling, 12
Boxing, professional, 66–67
Brown, Larry, 53
Bryant, Kobe, 45
Budge, Don, 63
Burnout, 109
Byers, Walter, 71

C

Cable television, 34, 35, 38
Calories burned, by physical activity, 104*t*
Camacho, Héctor "Macho," 67
Canseco, Jose, 117, 121
Carlesimo, P. J., 45
Carnegie Foundation for the Advancement of Education, 70
Carpentier, Georges, 67
CART, 65–66
Carter, David, 38
Champ Car racing, 66
Champions Tour (golf), 62
Chastain, Brandi, 59
Clean Sports Act (proposed), 122
Coaches, 81*t*
Cobb, Ty, 48
Cognitive functioning, 104, 109
Collective bargaining
    National Basketball Association, 54
    Women's National Basketball Association, 56
College sports
    academic eligibility, 83
    alcohol advertising, 42, 44*t*
    athletes per college, 78 (*t*6.11)
    doping, 119–120, 120*t*
    football and basketball spending and revenue, 87*f*
    gambling, 128, 129
    men athletes, 76 (*t*6.8)

most popular women's sports, 80*t*

National Collegiate Athletic Association history, 69–72

NCAA championship sports teams, 77*t*

NCAA sports participation, 72–75, 73*t*, 74*t*

overview, 5–6

participation, by race/ethnicity, 84*t*

participation by gender, 79 (*f*6.1)

race/ethnicity, 82*t*, 83*f*

recruitment practices, 87–88, 89*t*

revenue sources, 88*t*

spending, by gender, 79 (*f*6.2), 80*f*

spending and revenue, 79–81, 85*f*, 86*t*

teams per college, 78 (*t*6.10)

television contracts, 38

Title IX, 72–73, 76–77

women, 73*t*, 75–77, 76 (*t*6.7)

See also Specific sports

College Sports Television, 38

Congressional hearings on doping, 116–117, 121

Constitutional Compliance Committee, 70–71

Conte, Victor, Jr., 116, 117

Cooper, Chris, 116

Corporate sponsorship

Olympics, 99

stadiums, 60

Costs. *See* Economic issues

Coubertin, Pierre de, 6, 96

Creatine, 118

Cycling, 122

D

Daly, John, 62

Deaflympics, 101

Dean, Dizzy, 34

DeBartolo, Eddie, 128

Dempsey, Jack, 67

Dietary supplements, 108

Disability, 100–101

Diversity, 59

Doping

anabolic steroids, 117

BALCO scandal, 116–117

college sports, 119–120, 120*t*

erythropoietin, 117–118

health issues, 118–119

history, 115–116

legal issues, 122

Olympics, 100, 115–116

overview, 8, 117

professional baseball, 49–50, 50

professional sports, 120–122

youth and, 8*f*

Dress codes, 55–56

Drug testing. *See* Doping

Duncan, Tim, 56

Duval, David, 62

E

Economic issues

advertising revenue, 41–42

alcohol advertising, 42*t*

auto racing television contracts, 40

baseball television contracts, 33–34

college football and basketball spending and revenue, 87*f*

college football television contracts, 36–38

college sports revenue sources, 88*t*

college sports spending and revenue, 79–81, 79 (*f*6.2), 80*f*, 85*f*, 86*t*

extreme sports television contracts, 40–41

luxury box prices, 60*t*

Olympics, 98–99

professional baseball revenues and team values, 47, 48 (*t*4.2)

professional baseball television contracts, 35

professional basketball revenue, 54, 54 (*t*4.6)

professional basketball television contracts, 38–39

professional football team values and revenue, 50–51, 50*t*

professional football television contracts, 35–36

professional hockey revenue, 56

professional hockey team values and revenue, 57 (*t*4.8)

professional hockey television contracts, 39–40

sporting goods sales, 3*t*, 20–21, 22 (*t*2.10)

stadium financing, 59–60

Education

academic eligibility, 71, 83

achievement and high school sports participation, 87

high school sports participation by parents' level of, 94*f*

Elderly persons, 104, 105

Els, Ernie, 62

Employment, 87

Ephedra, 118

Equipment sales. *See* Sporting goods sales

Erythropoietin, 117–118

ESPN, 35

Exercise

inactive adults, by race/ethnicity, 112 (*f*8.5)

inactive adults by age and sex, 112 (*f*8.4)

mental health benefits, 104–105

physical activity survey, 110–112, 110*f*, 111 (*f*8.2), 111 (*f*8.3)

physical benefits, 103–104

Extreme sports

participation, 19, 22 (*t*2.8)

television contracts, 40–41

F

Fans, 21–25

by age, 24*t*

baseball, 24 (*f*2.2)

basketball, 24 (*f*2.3)

gender, 23*t*

geography, 25, 25 (*t*2.14)

professional football, 51*f*

race/ethnicity, 25 (*t*2.13)

by sport, 2 (*t*1.1)

survey, 23*f*

Ferrari, Michele, 122

Football, college, 36–37

Football, professional

advertising revenue, 41

attendance, 26–27, 28*t*

doping, 120–121

fans, 51*f*

history, 51–52

labor issues, 52

stadiums, 59–60

structure and administration, 50–51

team values and revenue, 50*t*

teams and divisions, 51*t*

television contracts, 35–36

video games, 44

Foudy, Julie, 59

France, William, 65

Free agency, 49

Friedman, Benny, 51–52

Furyk, Jim, 62

G

Gambling

college sports, 129

illegal, 127–128

Internet, 129–130

legal, 125–127

Nevada bookmaking, 126*f*, 127 (*t*10.2)

overview, 8–9

pari-mutuel, 123–125, 124*t*

participation in, 127 (*t*10.3)

public opinion, 127

scandals, 128–129

Gaming. *See* Video games

Gehrig, Lou, 48

Gender

college athletics expenses, 79 (*f*6.2), 80*f*

college sports participation, 79 (*f*6.1)

high school sports participation, 92*t*, 93*f*

participation, 17–18
television viewing, 42–43
Gender equity, 75–77
Geography, fans by, 25, 25 (*t*2.14)
Giambi, Jason, 121
Girls
high school sports participation, 86–87
most popular high school sports, 91*t*
Golf, professional, 61–63, 62*t*
Graham, Trevor, 8, 116
Grand Slam events (golf), 62*t*
Grand Slam events (tennis), 63
Grange, Red, 51
Gravity Games, 40–41
Greyhound racing, 125

H

Hagler, Marvin, 67
Hamm, Mia, 59
Health issues
calories burned, by physical activity, 104*t*
high school sports participation, benefits of, 87
overview, 7–8
physical activity, benefits of, 103–104, 111–112
steroid use, 118–119
High school sports
college recruitment practices, 87–88, 89*t*
most popular sports, 90 (*t*6.21), 91*t*
overview, 6, 83, 85–88
participation, 70*t*, 90 (*t*6.20), 90 (*t*6.22), 92*t*, 93*f*, 94*f*
Hippocrates, 103
History
gambling, 123
National Football League, 52
Olympics, 95–96
professional baseball, 48–49
Professional Golfers' Association of America, 61–62
television sports, 4–5, 33–34
tennis, 64
Hockey, professional
attendance, 27–28, 29 (*t*2.18)
doping, 122
history, 57–58
labor issues, 58
structure, 56–57
team values and revenue, 57 (*t*4.8)
teams and divisions, 57 (*t*4.9)
television contracts, 39–40
Holmes, Larry, 67
Hornung, Paul, 52, 128
Horse racing, 123–125
Hunter, Billy, 55

I

IBF, 66, 67
Illegal gambling, 9
Illegal sports gambling, 127–128
Individual sports
participation, 12, 16
professional, 4
See also Specific sports
Indy Racing League, 65–66
Injuries
adult, 108 (*t*8.5)
college sports, 70
frequency and rates of, 106–108
overview, 7–8
sports causing, 107*t*
types, 105–106, 106*t*
youth, 108 (*t*8.4), 109–110
Integration of baseball, 48
Intercollegiate Athletic Association, 70
International Boxing Federation, 66, 67
International Federation of PGA Tours, 62–63
International Federations, 97
International Olympic Committee, 7, 96–101, 115
International Tennis Federation, 64
Internet gambling, 129–130
Internet Gambling Prohibition Act (proposed), 130

J

Jackson, Janet, 41
Jackson, Stephen, 56
Jai alai, 125
Jamieson, Lynn, 45
Jensen, Knut Enemark, 115
Johnson, Ben, 116
Johnson, Magic, 53
Jones, Marion, 116
Jordan, Michael, 53

K

Karl, George, 53
Karras, Alex, 128
Kefauver, Estes, 126
Kennedy Foundation, 100
King, Billie Jean, 64
Korchemny, Remi, 116, 117
Kyl, Jon, 130

L

Labor issues
Major League Baseball, 49
National Basketball Association, 53, 54–55, 55*t*
National Football League, 52
Lacrosse, 19–20, 22 (*t*2.9)
Ladies Professional Golf Association, 63

Las Vegas, Nevada, 123
Laver, Rod, 63
Layden, Elmer, 51–52
Layne, Bobby, 52
Lee, Bob, 67
Legislation
Amateur Sports Integrity Act (proposed), 129
Anabolic Steroid Control Act, 118, 122
Anabolic Steroids Act, 122
Clean Sports Act (proposed), 122
Internet Gambling Prohibition Act (proposed), 130
Liljenwall, Hans-Gunnar, 115
Linton, Andrew, 115
Lombardi, Vince, 35
Louis, Joe, 67
LPGA, 63
Luxury boxes, 59, 60*t*

M

Madden NFL, 44
Major League Baseball
doping, 49–50, 121
history, 48–49
labor issues, 49
structure, 47–48
teams and divisions, 48 (*t*4.1)
television contracts, 35
Major League Baseball Player's Association, 49
Major League Soccer, 58–59, 59*t*
Maloof brothers, 128
Mancini, Ray "Boom Boom," 67
Martin, Ed, 72
Mascots, 45
Mays, Willie, 48
McCain, John, 122, 129
McDermott, John, 62
McGwire, Mark, 8, 18, 49, 116
McLain, Denny, 128
Mental health
high school sports participation, benefits of, 87
physical activity, benefits of, 104, 105
steroid use, 119
television sports, 44–45
youth sports, 109
Millar, David, 122
MLB. *See* Major League Baseball
MLS. *See* Major League Soccer
Morris, Darrin, 67

N

Nader, Ralph, 59
Naismith, James, 53
NASCAR, 65

National Association for Stock Car Auto Racing. *See* NASCAR

National Basketball Association
doping, 121–122
history, 53
labor issues, 54–55
professional basketball television contracts, 39*t*
race/ethnicity, 55–56
salary caps, 54–55, 55*t*, 56*t*
structure, 53–54
team values and revenue, 54 (*t*4.6)
teams and divisions, 54 (*t*4.5)
television contracts, 38–39

National Collegiate Athletic Association (NCAA)
athletes per college, 78 (*t*6.11)
championship sports teams, 77
college football and basketball spending and revenue, 87*f*
college football television contracts, 36–37
college sports by race/ethnicity, 82*t*, 83*f*
college sports participation by race/ethnicity, 84*t*
divisions, 71*t*
gambling, 129
history, 69–72
men college athletes, 76 (*t*6.8)
overview, 5–6
participation by gender, 79 (*f*6.1)
recruitment practices, 87–88, 89*t*
revenue sources, 88*t*
spending and revenue, 79–81, 85*f*, 86*t*
spending by gender, 79 (*f*6.2), 80*f*
sports participation, 72–75, 73*t*, 74*t*
sports sponsorship, by sport and division, 72*t*
teams per college, 78 (*t*6.10)
women college athletes, 76 (*t*6.7)

National Football League
doping, 120–121
history, 51–52
labor issues, 52
professional football team values and revenue, 50*t*
stadiums, 59–60
structure, 50–51, 51*t*
television contracts, 35–36
video games, 44

National Hockey League
doping, 122
history, 57–58
labor issues, 58
structure, 56–57
team values and revenue, 57 (*t*4.8)
teams and divisions, 57 (*t*4.9)

National Sporting Goods Association Survey, 16–17

Nationwide Tour (golf), 62
Native Americans, 45
NCAA. *See* National Collegiate Athletic Association
Nevada, 123, 125, 126, 126*f*, 127 (*t*10.2)
NFL. *See* National Football League
NFL Players Association, 52
NFL Players Union, 52
Non-thoroughbred horse racing, 125

O

Obesity
child, 108
physical activity, 104, 112
Off-track betting, 124
Oller, Pierre, 123
Olympic Games Organizing Committees, 99–100
Olympic Partners program, 99
Olympics
Deaflympics, 101
doping, 100, 115–116
history, 95–96
overview, 6–7
Paralympics, 101
politics and, 96
revenue, 98–99
site selection, 96, 98, 99–100
Special Olympics, 100–101
sports, 7*t*
structure, 96–98
O'Neal, Jermaine, 55
Online gambling, 129–130
Open-wheeled car racing, 65–66
Osborne, Tom, 129
Otto, Ed, 65
Outdoor Life Network, 40

P

Palmeiro, Rafael, 117, 121
Paralympics, 101
Pari-mutuel gambling, 123–125, 124*t*
Participation
adults engaged in regular physical activity, 110*f*, 111 (*f*8.3)
adults engaged in regular physical activity, by age and sex, 111 (*f*8.2)
college sports, by race/ethnicity, 84*t*
extreme sports, 19, 22 (*t*2.8)
gambling, 127 (*t*10.3)
high school sports, 83, 85–87, 90 (*t*6.20), 90 (*t*6.22), 92*t*, 93*f*, 94*f*
inactive adults, by race/ethnicity, 112 (*f*8.5)
inactive adults by age and sex, 112 (*f*8.4)
lacrosse, 19–20, 22 (*t*2.9)
men college athletes, 76 (*t*6.8)

NCAA sports participation, 72–75, 73*t*, 74*t*
overview, 1–2
physical activity, 110–112
post high school, 70*t*
soccer, 20
by sport, 2 (*t*1.2), 17*t*
team sports, 11–12, 16*t*
ten-year history, 18*t*
trends, 13*t*–15*t*
vigorous physical activity, by sex and age, 113 (*f*8.6)
vigorous physical activity for adolescents, by grade, 114*f*
vigorous physical activity for adolescents, by sex and race/ethnicity, 113 (*f*8.7)
women, 20*t*, 21*t*
women college athletes, 76 (*t*6.7)
youth, 19*t*
Patrick, Danica, 65
PGA, 61–63
Point shaving, 128
Prize money, 64
Professional Golfers' Association of America, 61–63
Professional sports
attendance, 2–3
doping, 116–117, 120–122
gambling scandals, 128
Olympics as, 100
overview, 3–4
See also Specific sports
Proposition 48, 71
Psychological issues. *See* Mental health
Public opinion
favorite sports to watch, 36*f*, 37*t*
favorite sports to watch, by race, 39*f*
gambling, 127, 127 (*t*10.3)
women's sports, 80*t*

R

Race/ethnicity
college sports, 77, 79, 82*t*, 83*f*, 84*t*
diversity in major sports, 59
fans, 22–23, 25 (*t*2.13)
favorite sports to watch on television, 39*f*
high school sports participation, 92*t*
integration of baseball, 48
physical activity and inactivity, 111, 112, 112 (*f*8.5)
television sports, 45
vigorous physical activity for adolescents, 113 (*f*8.7)
Racism, 45, 56
Recruitment practices, 87–88, 89*t*
Reese, Albert, 71
Revenue
college sports, 79–81, 85*f*, 86*t*

National Basketball Association, 54
Olympics, 98–99
professional baseball, 47, 48 (t4.2)
professional basketball, 54 (t4.6)
professional football, 50–51, 50t
professional hockey, 56, 57 (t4.8)
stadium naming rights, 60
Richardson, Jason, 56
Ripken, Cal, Jr., 49
Robbins, Barrett, 116
Robinson, Jackie, 48, 59
Romanowski, Bill, 116
Roosevelt, Theodore, 70
Rose, Pete, 128
Rozelle, Pete, 51
Rozelle Rule, 52
Rudolph, Eric Robert, 96
Ruth, Babe, 48

S

Salaries and salary caps
Major League Baseball, 49
National Basketball Association, 53,
54–55
National Football League, 52
National Hockey League, 56, 58
Women's National Basketball
Association, 56
"Sanity Code," 70–71
Schilling, Curt, 117
Scucci, Bob, 129
Selig, Bud, 48
Sentencing, 122
Shays, Christopher, 120
Shriver, Eunice Kennedy, 100
Simpson, Tom, 122
Site selection, Olympic, 96, 98, 99–100
Skeletal injuries, 106
Smith, Onterrio, 120
Snyder, Jimmy "The Greek," 126
Soccer
participation, 11, 12, 20
professional, 58–59, 59t
Soft tissue traumas, 106
Sosa, Sammy, 49, 117
Southern Methodist University, 71
Special Olympics, 100–101
Spending. See Economic issues
Sporting goods sales, 3t, 20–21, 22 (t2.10)
Sprewell, Latrell, 45
Stadiums, 59–60
Stanley, David, 71
Stanley Cup, 57
Statistical Abstract of the United States
(U.S. Census Bureau), 18
Statistical information
adults engaged in regular physical
activity, 110f, 111 (f8.3)
adults engaged in regular physical
activity, by age and sex, 111 (f8.2)

alcohol advertising, 42t, 43t, 44t
attendance, by sport and frequency,
30t
attendance by sport, 31t–32t
auto racing attendance, 29 (t2.19)
baseball fans, 24 (f2.2)
basketball fans, 24 (f2.3)
college athletes per college, 78 (t6.11)
college football and basketball
spending and revenue, 87f
college sports, by race/ethnicity, 82t,
83f
college sports participation by gender,
79 (f6.1)
college sports participation by race/
ethnicity, 84t
college sports revenue sources, 88t
college sports spending and revenue,
85f, 86t
college sports spending by gender,
79 (f6.2), 80f
doping, 120t
extreme sports participation, 22 (t2.8)
fans, 23f
fans, by age, 24t
fans, by gender, 23t
fans, by race, 25 (t2.13)
fans, by region, 25 (t2.14)
fans, by sport, 2 (t1.1)
gambling, participation in, 127 (t10.3)
high school sports, 90 (t6.21), 91t
high school sports participation, 90
(t6.20), 90 (t6.22), 92t, 93f, 94f
inactive adults, by race/ethnicity, 112
(f8.5)
inactive adults by age and sex, 112
(f8.4)
injuries, 106t, 107t, 108t
lacrosse participation, 22 (t2.9)
luxury box prices, 60t
men college athletes, 76 (t6.8)
men's NCAA sports participation, 73t
National Basketball Association salary
caps, 55t
NCAA championship sports teams,
77t
NCAA sports sponsorship, by sport
and division, 72t
Nevada bookmaking,
126f, 127 (t10.2)
pari-mutuel gambling, 124t
participation, by sport, 2 (t1.2), 17t
participation history, by sport, 18t
participation trends, 13t–15t
post–high school participation, 70t
professional baseball
attendance, 26t
professional baseball team values and
revenues, 47, 48 (t4.2)
professional basketball attendance,
27t

professional basketball team values
and revenue, 54 (t4.6)
professional basketball television
contracts, 39t
professional football attendance, 28t
professional football fans, 51f
professional football team values and
revenue, 50t
professional hockey attendance, 29
(t2.18)
public opinion on favorite sports to
watch, 36f, 37t, 39f
sporting goods sales, 3t, 22 (t2.10)
steroid use by youth, 8f
team sports participation, 16t
team values and revenue, 57 (t4.8)
teams per college, 78 (t6.10)
vigorous physical activity, by sex and
age, 113 (f8.6)
vigorous physical activity for
adolescents, by grade, 114f
vigorous physical activity for
adolescents, by sex and race/
ethnicity, 113 (f8.7)
women college athletes, 76 (t6.7)
women college sports coaches, 81t
women's collegiate sports, 80t
women's NCAA sports participation,
73t
women's participation, by sport, 20t,
21t
youth sports participation, 19t
Stearns, Cliff, 122
Stern, David, 55
Steroids. See Doping
Stock car racing, 65
Strikes
National Basketball
Association, 53
professional baseball, 49
professional football, 52
Structure
Major League Baseball, 47–48
National Collegiate Athletic
Association, 71t
National Football League, 50–51, 51t
Olympics, 97
professional baseball, 48 (t4.1)
Stubblefield, Dana, 116
Studies, reports, and surveys
National Sporting Goods Association
Survey, 16–17
Superstudy of Sports Participation
(SGMA International),
11–12, 16, 19
Super Bowl
advertising, 41, 42
gambling, 127 (t10.2)
television contracts, 36
Superstudy of Sports Participation (SGMA
International), 11–12, 16, 19

T

Tagliabue, Paul, 51
Team sports
  participation, 16*t*
  professional, 3–4
  See also Specific sports
Television
  alcohol advertising, 41–42, 42*t*, 43*t*, 44*t*
  auto racing coverage, 40
  baseball coverage, 34–35
  extreme sports coverage, 40–41
  favorite sports to watch on television, by race, 39*f*
  football coverage, 35–37
  gender and viewing, 42–43
  history of sports on, 4–5, 33–34
  hockey coverage, 39–40
  National Collegiate Athletic Association, 71
  Olympics coverage, 98
  professional basketball coverage, 38–39, 39*t*
  public opinion on favorite sports to watch, 36*f*, 37*t*
Tennis, professional, 63–64, 64*t*
Terrorism, 96
Texas Tech, 72
Thomas, Frank, 117
Thoroughbred horse racing, 124–125
Tilden, Bill, 64
Title IX, 72–73, 76–77
Toms, David, 62
Tour de France, 122
Tully, Matthew, 59

U

Unitas, Johnny, 52
United States Anti-Doping Agency, 122
United States Olympic Committee, 97–98, 101
University High School, 88
University of Minnesota, 72

V

Valente, James, 116, 117
Video games, 43–44
Vigorous physical activity, 111–112, 113*f*, 114*f*
Violence, 45
Voet, Willy, 122

W

Wanamaker, Rodman, 61
WBA, 66, 67
WBC, 66, 67
WBO, 66, 67
Webber, Chris, 72
WHA, 57
White, Kelli, 116
Williams, Willie, 88
Wingfield, Walter C., 64
Winter Olympics, 96
WNBA, 56
Women
  college sports, 75–77, 76 (*t*6.7)
  college sports by race/ethnicity, 83 (*f*6.5)
  college sports coaches, 81*t*
  major sports, 59
  most popular college sports, 80*t*
  NCAA sports participation, 73*t*
  participation, by sport, 20*t*, 21*t*

professional basketball, 56
professional golf, 63
professional soccer players, 58–59
professional tennis, 63–64
sports injuries, 108
television sports viewing, 42–43
Women's National Basketball Association, 56
Women's Tennis Association, 63–64
Women's United Soccer Association, 58–59
World Anti-Doping Agency, 122
World Boxing Association, 66, 67
World Boxing Council, 66, 67
World Boxing Organization, 66, 67
World Hockey Association, 57
World Series
  advertising, 41
  television coverage, 35
World Trade Organization, 130

X

X Games, 40–41

Y

Youth
  benefits of sports, 105
  injuries, 7–8, 107, 108 (*t*8.4), 109–110
  participation, 2, 17, 19*t*
  steroid use, 8, 8*f*, 119
  vigorous physical activity, 113 (*f*8.7), 114*f*

Z

Ziegler, John, 8, 115